T0302972

Clarence Dillon

CLARENCE DILLON

This biography tells the story of a first-generation American who dazzled Wall Street in the 1920s with his spectacular deals. After liquidating his investments prior to the Crash, Dillon devoted the rest of his life to developing his cultural life while preserving his wealth and influencing international events. This portrait by Fülöp E. Lázló was given to Harvard by Douglas Dillon in 1977 and hangs in the Dillon Field House. (*Photo courtesy of Harvard University Portrait Collection*)

CLARENCE DILLON

A Wall Street Enigma

Robert C. Perez
and
Edward F. Willett

MADISON BOOKS
Lanham • New York • London

Published by Madison Books
4720 Boston Way
Lanham, Maryland 20706

3 Henrietta Street
London WC2E 8LU, England

Distributed by National Book Network

Library of Congress Cataloging-in-Publication Data

Perez, Robert C.
Clarence Dillon : a Wall Street Enigma / by Robert C. Perez and
Edward F. Willett.
p. cm.
Includes bibliographical references and index.
1. Dillon, Clarence, 1882–1979. 2. Capitalists and financiers—United
States—Biography. 3. Businessmen—United States—Biography.
I. Willett, Edward F. II. Title..
HG172.D49P47 1995 332'.092—dc20 [B] 94–48138 CIP

ISBN 1–56833–048–0 (cloth : alk. paper)

℗™ *The paper used in this publication meets the minimum requirements of*
American National Standard for Information Sciences—Permanence of
Paper for Printed Library Materials, ANSI Z39.48–1964.
Manufactured in the United States of America.

Contents

Chronology of Clarence Dillon's Life

1882   Born in San Antonio, Texas, on September 27, son of Samuel
        Lapowski and Bertha (Stenbock) Lapowski.

1901   Graduates from Worcester Academy, Worcester, Massachusetts;
        formally adopts his paternal grandmother's maiden name, Dillon.

1905   Graduates from Harvard College.

1907   Nearly killed in freak railroad accident.

1908   Marries Anne Douglass on February 4 and leaves on two year
        health-honeymoon tour of Europe.

1909   Birth of son, C. (Clarence) Douglas, in Geneva, Switzerland, on
        August 21.

1912   Death of father, Samuel Lapowski, of brain tumor in San Francisco
        on June 23.

1912   Organizes Milwaukee Machine Tool Company with brother-in-
        law, George Douglass.

1912   Birth of daughter, Dorothy Anne, in Milwaukee on October 9.

1913   Joins William A. Read & Co. in its Chicago branch office.

1914   Makes first fortune with organization of Phenol business with

Schlesinger interests in Milwaukee to capitalize on wartime need for explosives. Promoted and transferred to New York office.

1916   Becomes a partner in William A. Read & Co.; William A. Read dies suddenly and Dillon becomes head of firm.

1917   Becomes Baruch's deputy in charge of expediting shipments of war *matériel* during the first world war.

1919   Commences three-year $100 million financing program to create Youngstown Sheet & Tube, the fifth largest steel producer in the country.

1921   Firm renamed Dillon, Read & Co., Inc.

1921 $90.5 million Goodyear rescue completed.

1923   Purchases land at Dark Harbor on the Maine island of Islesboro for a Bar Harbor-style summer cottage.

1924   United States & Foreign Securities investment trust launched with $30 million offering followed by $60 million offering of companion trust in 1928.

1924   Purchases several large farms in Far Hills, New Jersey, fox hunting estate area and begins construction of Dunwalke mansion.

1925   Dillon buys out Dodge Motors with $146 million cash offer, outbidding J. P. Morgan.

1926 $55 million initial public offering of National Cash Register, largest such stock offering up to that time.

1926   Arranges financing for the $100 million amalgamation of six German steel companies into a giant cartel, second in size only to U.S. Steel.

1927   Goodyear litigation settled out-of-court.

1927   Dillon buys apartment at 22 rue Barbet-de-Jouy in Paris.

1928   Orchestrates $236 million buyout of Dodge by Chrysler.

1928   Builds Georgian-style townhouse on East 80th Street in New York City.

1929   Rebuilds Harvard field house destroyed by fire, renamed Dillon Field House.

1930   Dillon closes down retail branch office system and withdraws from firm, retaining control but giving over day-to-day management to Forrestal and Phillips. Dillon spends more time in Europe pursuing his new life style.

1935   Purchases Chateau Haut-Brion and its famed vineyards in the Bordeaux wine district for $250,000.

1938   Selects Forrestal as president of firm.

1939   Offers the use of Chateau Haut-Brion to the French as a hospital and rest center for French officers wounded in action.

1942   Heads up wartime National Citizens Committee drive to raise $10 million in funds for the Navy Relief Society to provide aid to the widows and families of Navy servicemen killed or incapacitated from service-related injuries. For his efforts, Dillon receives the Certificate of Merit.

1949   First of two cataract operations reduces his activity.

1951   Death of mother, Bertha, in New York City on January 1.

1954   Buys site on Caribbean island of Jamaica for construction of winter home, "High Rock."

1961   Anne Douglass Dillon dies on June 21.

1961   Dillon listed in *Fortune* magazine as one of the fifty richest men in America with $100 to $200 million in assets.

1968   Sells his landmark Georgian-style East Side townhouse.

1979   Dillon dies on April 9 after illness following fall; his estate gives the Dunwalke mansion to Princeton as a retreat and conference center.

Acknowledgments

This biography involved a considerable number of interviews with members of Clarence Dillon's family and close associates from Wall Street and government. I supplemented these personal interviews with field trips to various Dillon properties including Dunwalke in Far Hills, New Jersey, and Dark Harbor on Islesboro, Maine. With the aid of Clarence Dillon's daughter, Mrs. Dorothy Dillon Eweson, I was able to review both Clarence Dillon's private papers and his unpublished personal memoir, *Anne's Story*, all of which give valuable insights into his personality. In addition, I visited and interviewed the members of the staff of Chateau Haut-Brion, Dillon's celebrated wine estate in the Bordeaux district of France. With the help of Douglas Dillon, I also visited and interviewed owners and managers of ten other noted vineyards in the Bordeaux area on their recollections of Dillon.

I wish to acknowledge and thank Iona College for its financial aid and support in this endeavor. I also wish to thank C. Douglas Dillon and Mrs. Dorothy Dillon Eweson for their support and assistance as well as their willingness to make available access to the private papers and homes of Clarence Dillon. The author owes special thanks to Suzanne Campbell, a specialist in the history of the Jewish community of the Southwest, for her valuable research on the Lapowski family in Texas. Paul Nitze also contributed valuable information and insights into Clarence Dillon's personality and career, based on his more than thirty-year close association with him on and off Wall Street. Special thanks to Dr. Willett's daughter, Lynne Robbins Knox, who took time from her English teaching duties to help edit the manuscript.

Robert C. Perez, Ph.D.
New York City, January 1995

Introduction

Clarence Dillon thrived in the rough and tumble competitive financial world that characterized the 1920s. He rose from obscure beginnings to revitalize a small firm into the Wall Street juggernaut, Dillon, Read & Co., Inc. Robert Lovett of Brown Brothers remarked: "Dillon . . . was ranked as aggressive, opportunistic, and flamboyant . . . something of a pirate ship roaming the market for booty. . . ."[1] As such, Dillon successfully challenged the leadership of the dominant banking houses such as J. P. Morgan and Kuhn Loeb, especially in the foreign financing field.

Daring, secretive, cunning, cautious and not given to familiarity with his partners or business associates, Dillon was characterized as "very cold and aloof" by one top aide; "I don't think I had ten words with Clarence Dillon in the four years that I was with the firm in the 1920s."[2] At Harvard, Dillon established lasting fame as a legendary poker player and in his financing operations he operated as the low-profile player concealing his intentions until he was ready to strike with lightning force. Even his close associates had no idea of his motives; he covered his tracks carefully and he was a master of deception. Despite his Machiavellian personality, Dillon had a keen sense of humor which helped his partners cope with his frequent tantalizing and provoking moods.[3] Shrewd, smart and blessed with a superb sense of timing, Clarence Dillon, or "Baron" as his Harvard classmates came to call him, was an authentic Wall Street genius.

While his style and deals dazzled Wall Street in the 1920s and established Dillon Read as a major force, Dillon himself was regarded as an upstart by the Wall Street Establishment. Although bold and resourceful, brash and young, Dillon had virtually no social contacts with the Street's blue bloods; he was not part of Wall Street's elite. Dillon resented this exclusion by banking's top echelon, and in later life made a major effort to develop a network of influential friends and contacts. His social ambition was aided by his ability to discuss a wide range of subjects in a brilliant and witty way.[4]

Dillon had a flair for the dramatic and his moods were unpredictable; after building Dillon Read into a powerhouse, he surprised the financial world by withdrawing from active participation in the 1930s with a personal fortune of more than $100 million. Before his withdrawal, however, Dillon had rocked Wall Street with one mega-deal after the other. In the process of engineering these coups, Dillon pioneered a number of important financing techniques, many of which have become standard tactics in the investment banker's quiver.

In his first major coup, Dillon brought off a brilliant three-tiered $90.5 million rescue of the floundering Goodyear Tire Company in 1921. Probably Dillon's most spectacular deal, however, was the $146 million cash buyout of Dodge Brothers in 1925, snatching this coveted prize away from the Morgan interests. Following up this coup, Dillon then launched an initial public offering raising $55 million for National Cash Register Company, the largest common stock offering on record up to that time, in a deal carefully structured to preserve the founder's control. Two years later, he brought about the $236 million buyout of Dodge by Chrysler, after several tortuous months of non-stop bargaining aided by a complicated stock arbitrage scheme dreamed up by his star financing partners, Ferdinand Eberstadt and James V. Forrestal.

Dillon did not limit himself to conventional financings. Impressed with the record of the British-style trusts, Dillon adopted the technique to the American market and launched the first postwar closed-end investment trust, United States and Foreign Securities Corp., raising $30 million initially in 1924 (followed by an additional $60 million offering of a companion trust in 1928). Spreading his wings further, Dillon expanded his foreign financings with a $100 million amalgamation of six major German steel producers to forge a giant cartel in 1926 that can be compared to Morgan's earlier creation of U.S. Steel in 1901. Dillon's foreign financings in the 1920s were diverse, raising $498 million for European corporations and governments (including $340 million for Germany), $433 million for Canadian businesses and governments and $244 million for Latin American countries and businesses (including $177 million for Brazil).[5]

Dillon intuitively anticipated the Great Depression by liquidating his firm's securities inventory before the Crash.[6] In the 1920s, he had led his partners into ventures which despite their limited risks dazzled admiring onlookers. During the next decade, however, with the gloom of depression descending on the economy, he transformed Dillon Read into a house targeting its financing on high-quality, conservative businesses such as utilities and energy companies; he deliberately avoided innovative investments in the chemical, drug and electrical industries. His stubborn reluctance to innovate and finance new growth industries stifled the firm, further aggravating the country's economic decline.

In the 1920s, however, Dillon Read was an exciting place for young men seeking fame and fortune. Hugh Bullock, the colorful, outspoken investment fund pioneer, recalls looking for a job in the early twenties and asking everyone he knew, "which is the coming firm in Wall Street?" They all mentioned Dillon Read, and he succeeded in getting a job with the firm, ultimately rising to manage the sales operations in the Western district. From the start, Bullock was struck by Dillon's "chain-lightning" intellectual brilliance.[7] Dillon mined more pay dirt than any of his rivals. In 1928, a partnership in his firm was probably worth more, financially if not in prestige, than a comparable position in either Morgan or Kuhn Loeb.[8]

Clarence Dillon was perhaps the most celebrated investment banker of the roaring twenties, with reporters bestowing upon him the reputation of a fearless, high-flying, and resourceful financier. However, he succeeded mainly because his caution and brilliance in calculating risk-reward ratios virtually assured the success of his ventures. Ferdinand Eberstadt, a foreign financing and legal specialist who became a Dillon partner in the 1920s, utilized the same cautious approach with his own firm's financings of his so-called little blue chips during the 1930s.

Eliot Janeway, the economist and author, emphasized another characteristic of Dillon: "Dillon was well known at Harvard as a gambler; he made a lot of money at cards, later adapting his winning touch to a string of financial successes." However, Janeway also stressed that Dillon was a cheapskate and cheated his partners, adding: "Dillon was a mean miserable bastard; there was not a generous bone in [his] body. . . ." Janeway further noted: "Dillon's attitude . . . was all in the price; he was nothing but a money guy. Dillon wouldn't have bought God with a whore house attached if it wasn't a bargain." Janeway concluded: "After Dillon relinquished active management of the firm in the mid-1930s, the firm drifted. . . ."[9]

Janeway notes that Dillon was secretive and maintained a very low profile with the press. Forrestal was Dillon's shield against the world.[10] Paul Nitze, who became one of Dillon's closest aides, tends to agree, adding: "Janeway was a good friend of Forrestal in the 1930s and my recollection is that Forrestal had good relations with the press, so he may well have become the informal spokesman for the firm."[11]

Clarence Dillon's personality evokes much of the strengths and weaknesses of leaders of the past such as Napoleon and Churchill. When analyzed in tests widely used by professional psychologists to help classify patterns of human behavior, Dillon's personality clearly fits that of the Field Marshal, with strong secondary attributes related to inventors, scientists and architects. According to Ernest Auerbach, a business entrepreneur with extensive experience in these studies, the Field Marshal type needs:

> to lead and has a strong urge to [create] a structure . . . and assign people to long-range goals. [Field Marshals tend to focus] more on policy and goals than . . . procedures, [rejecting] inefficiency; repetitive errors [make them] impatient.[12]

So it was with the Baron!

But there was a warmer, kinder side to Dillon. When the Crash came, he personally bailed out a number of his partners and associates who were forced into personal bankruptcy by injudicious purchases of stock on margin. Anticipating the Crash, Dillon had laid off most of his sales staff by late 1929. Many of them had margin accounts of as much as $100,000 and couldn't settle them. Dillon forgave those debts.[13] Both his son and daughter describe their father as kind and caring. Dorothy, his daughter, adored him, recollecting, "he was my great hero; I don't think I have ever met a more attractive man. . . ."[14] His grandson, Philip Allen, who pursued a career in finance for a time at Dillon Read, recollected:

> My grandfather had a flair for doing things his way—[which was] usually the right way. If he had a visitor coming over from Germany, he would have German wine for lunch. . . . He went out of his way to make the other person comfortable.[15]

Dillon was a financial genius to his fingertips, and his unusual ability drove Dillon Read to the forefront of the financial world in the 1920s. The renowned speculator, Bernard Baruch, thought him "one of the keenest minds on Wall Street."[16] The mystery that surrounds Dillon is why he abruptly withdrew from the "wars" of Wall Street after the Crash. Surely a man who could calculate profitably the present value of the most risky venture and succeed on Wall Street ought to have deduced that the deflated values caused by the Depression created enormous opportunities. Much of this book will focus on why he withdrew, and into what new fields he channeled his "chain-lightning" intellectual brilliance.

Notes

1. From an interview with former *Fortune* editor, Charles J. V. Murphy, (no date).
2. An anonymous associate.
3. Mathey, Dean, *Fifty Years of Wall Street with Anecdotiana*, Princeton, 1966, pp. 9-10, hereinafter referred to as Mathey, Dean, *Fifty Years of Wall Street.*

4. Paul H. Nitze interview, November 11, 1991.

5. Based on *U.S. Senate, Committee on Banking and Currency*, 73rd Congress, 2d Session, "Stock Exchanges Practices: Report" (Washington, 1934), pp. 2175-93, 2260-65; *Investment Dealers' Digest*, "Corporate Financing Directory," various issues; *National Statistical Service*, "American Underwriting Houses and Their Issues," (vols. I & II, 1925-29); Dillon, Read & Co., Inc., Securities Offerings by Dillon, Read & Co., 1921-27, (New York, March 1, 1928). *Ibid*, Annual Issues, 1925-28, hereinafter referred to as Author's survey of Dillon Read financings.

6. Clarence Dillon, *Anne's Story*, an unfinished and unpaginated memoir in typescript written after the death of his wife in 1961 and contained in Dillon's private papers in the possession of Mrs. Dorothy Dillon Eweson at her home in Far Hills, New Jersey; hereinafter referred to as *Anne's Story*.

7. Hugh Bullock telephone interview, April 11, 1991.

8. Winkler, John, "Profiles: A Billion Dollar Banker," *The New Yorker*, October 20, 1928, p. 29, hereinafter referred to as Winkler, *The New Yorker*.

9. Eliot Janeway interview, April 4, 1991.

10. Eliot Janeway interview, April 4, 1991.

11. Paul H. Nitze interview, November 11, 1991.

12. "Manager's Journal: Not Your Type, but Right for the Job," *Wall Street Journal*, Ernest Auerbach, January 6, 1992.

13. Joseph Haywood interview, October 28, 1991.

14. Mrs. Dorothy Dillon Eweson interview, October 1 and 4, 1991.

15. Philip D. Allen interview, April 9, 1992.

16. Hoopes, Townsend and Douglas Brinkley, *Driven Patriot: The Life and Times of James V. Forrestal*, pp. 52-3, hereinafter referred to as Hoopes/Brinkley, *Driven Patriot*.

1

The Goodyear Rescue:
An Insight into the Dillon Financing
Technique

Perhaps Dillon's three greatest banking innovations of the 1920s were the rescue of Goodyear, the buyout of Dodge Brothers and its later merger into Chrysler, and the launching of the closed-end investment trust movement in 1924.

The first of these coups—the Goodyear Rescue—occurred early in 1920, in the midst of the short but severe postwar depression. During the first world war, American business had enjoyed unparalleled prosperity with little attention paid by corporate executives to financial controls. In the first two decades of the twentieth century, the growth of the automotive industry and its allied field, tire manufacture, had far outstripped that of any comparable industry in the previous century.

The automobile tire producers' rapid sales and earnings growth generated enormous stock market profits for their backers. Leadership in the industry was aggressive and daring; entrepreneurs developed more efficient production facilities and launched creative advertising and selling programs that brought the automobile within the reach of the vast majority of American homes. In the immediate postwar market, sales of both automobiles and tires soared to new records reflecting the pent-up demand brought on by the wartime ban on civilian automobile production.

Under the dynamic leadership of Frank Seiberling, the founder, Goodyear had become the largest producer of tires, accounting for 50 percent of all original tire equipment for automobiles.[1] Goldman Sachs had earlier provided $113 million of financing for Goodyear in which William A. Read & Co. participated as a member of the underwriting syndicate.[2]

Goodyear benefitted substantially from the huge pent-up demand for automobiles; its tire sales soared to $200 million in 1919 and its order backlog

1

indicated $300 million was not an unreasonable goal for 1920.[3] The huge backlog caused shortages of goods with the price of crude rubber leaping seven-fold in a matter of months. Economists and marketing specialists forecast a substantial boom in new-car sales. To meet the increased demand, Goodyear, along with other tire companies, made huge forward purchase contracts for crude rubber and cotton at inflated prices as producers scrambled to build up inventory to sustain high production levels.[4]

Then, suddenly, the markets collapsed during the short but deep depression of 1921-1922. The price of rubber fell by over 90 percent to 15 cents a pound, causing tremendous losses on forward purchase contracts. Consumers cut back on tire purchases, tire prices fell sharply, and Goodyear was forced to sell tires below cost. By Christmas, Goodyear's situation was desperate. To make matters worse, Goodyear had not developed solid sources of financing on Wall Street, other than Goldman Sachs, reflecting the founders' distrust of Eastern financiers.[5] Accordingly, Goodyear had no strong banking affiliations and not even Goldman Sachs was willing to come forward to rescue the company; it had no "financial godfathers."[6]

The company was strapped for cash and could not pay its obligations; credit was tight and banks around the country were calling loans. Goodyear's stock plummeted from $400 to $10 a share in 1922. With its swollen inventory of crude rubber and cotton, Goodyear faced bankruptcy, and a distress liquidation seemed inevitable. Fear spread through Wall Street that a Goodyear bankruptcy could trigger a panic.

The bankers' lack of confidence in the integrity of the Seiberling management was further aggravated by the disclosure of Seiberling's large secret personal indebtedness to the company. At one meeting in late 1920 in New York City, lasting until the early hours of the next morning, the bankers were adamant and refused to provide either temporary or permanent financing for Goodyear.[7] However, Goodyear's investment banker, Goldman Sachs, finally provided a temporary revolving credit of $25 million on November 3 to help tide the company over its short-term problems but Goodyear had to pledge its accounts receivables to guarantee repayment of the loan. This proved inadequate and Goldman refused to provide permanent financing when Seiberling's misuse of company funds was revealed.

At that juncture, a New York lawyer, Paul D. Cravath, acting for Goodyear, called a conference of creditors and bank representatives to survey the situation. Several bankers offered to help if someone would take the lead, but by then the total financing needed had risen to $90 million.[8] There was no Chapter 11 in those days to enable a company to keep operating while restructuring its debt with its creditors. However, the

Cravath law firm in New York had pioneered a plan to avoid receivership which later became the framework for Chapter 11 restructurings. Instead of placing a temporarily distressed business in the "hands of receivers," the Cravath plan called for a voluntary procedure to work out financial difficulties with bankruptcy court proceedings to be initiated only as a last resort.[9]

With receivership looming in early January 1921, Cravath called another crisis meeting of the heads of the principal banks of New York, Boston, Cleveland and Chicago. Again, the bankers refused to take the lead in a rescue attempt[10] but Joseph Cotton, a New York lawyer representing some of the creditors, suggested that Clarence Dillon of Dillon Read was the type of leader who had the financial ingenuity and resources to arrange the restructuring. Insiders also noted that Forrestal had met Seiberling's son as an undergraduate at Princeton and he may have sought out Forrestal's help to save Goodyear from failure.[11] Dillon was then invited and immediately came to the emergency meeting and agreed to look into the problem. Asking for a few days to study the situation, Dillon sent Cravath a short memorandum on January 14 giving the fundamentals of the plan by which Goodyear was eventually saved.[12]

The methods by which Dillon conducted all operations are illustrated by his 1921 rescue of the nearly bankrupt Goodyear Tire and Rubber Company. Dillon began the Goodyear rescue by sending Edward G. Wilmer, a former business associate and lawyer from Milwaukee, to Akron on a fact-finding mission. Controversy reigned over the diverse interests, with bankers demanding settlement of their claims without delay and suppliers anxious to safeguard their advances to Goodyear. Wilmer found chaotic conditions prevailing at the Goodyear factory in Akron. Conditions had deteriorated to the point where lines of workers stood outside the Goodyear offices waiting to be paid daily instead of weekly because of the shortage of cash in the company's tills.[13] However, Wilmer believed the situation could be turned around if adequate financing could be found.[14] At the outset, Dillon insisted that Goodyear "must stand up to all its obligations including the accrued dividends on the preferred stock."[15]

Clarence Dillon's solution to Goodyear's problems was a three-tiered package of high-yield bonds, debentures and preferred stock that would look familiar to a reader of latter-day junk bond prospectuses. The bonds carried an 8 percent coupon, at a time when high-grade corporates were yielding only 5 percent. But since the bonds were issued at 90 and would mature at 120 serially over the next twenty years, Goodyear's effective interest rate was closer to 14 percent. As part of the deal, Goodyear agreed to issue $33 million in 8 percent "prior preferred" stock to pay off the merchandise creditors so that each creditor received 125 percent of his claim.[16]

Dillon Read agreed to syndicate the most senior piece, $30 million of first mortgage bonds, but only if the trade creditors agreed to underwrite the $27.5 million of debentures. Dillon, in short, forced the creditors to help him finance the rescue. The debentures—which the trade creditors had to buy—were also high-yielding. Issued at 90 to mature serially at 110 over the next ten years, the effective yield to maturity came to over 15 percent even though the nominal coupon on the debentures was set at 8 percent. On top of that, Dillon sweetened the deal by giving the purchasers of the debentures an equity kicker; each debenture purchaser received ten shares of common stock for each $1,000 of debentures purchased.[17]

Before Dillon could begin the refinancing, the company had to obtain near-unanimous approval of the plan from Goodyear's shareowners and creditors. Goodyear's salesmen were pressed into service as proxy solicitors carefully coached by the company's legal counsel, the Cravath law firm. Several creditors sought to block the reorganization by filing suits but Cravath persuaded the Ohio legislature to enact a law asserting corporate rights to act despite the suits.[18] As it was, it took three months of hard work to persuade the various interests to accept Dillon's plan to restructure the company's debt and equity.

With the creditor rebellion rebuffed and with over 90 percent of stockholders approving, the Seiberling management stepped down and Dillon moved ahead with the refinancing. The entire package raised $90.5 million for Goodyear, a sum equivalent to about $700 million in today's dollars, making it one of the largest reorganizations of its day. To safeguard his clients' money, Dillon insisted on a major role in management. He created a special class of 10,000 shares of "management stock," owned by himself and two other trustees, which gave him and the two trustees complete control of the company until the first mortgage bonds were paid off.[19]

Actually, Dillon's rescue plan nearly unravelled when some of the creditors backed out on their commitments at the last minute. Frantic efforts were made by the Seiberlings to get Dillon to make up this shortfall but Dillon snapped: "That is no part of my job. I never said that I would do anything more than head a syndicate to underwrite the first mortgage bonds."[20] Thereafter, it took all of Dillon's persuasive powers to restore the commitments of the creditors. Finally, with the creditors' commitments restored, the plan was in place.[21]

Soon after the Goodyear rescue was finalized, a five-year contract was entered into with Leonard Kennedy & Co., a management talent business, under which it agreed to supply Goodyear with executive talent for a fee of $250,000 a year plus a 5 percent bonus on Goodyear's earnings above a certain level.[22] The management contract was lucrative; in the first year alone, the Kennedy company received $560,000 for providing management services.[23] Dillon selected Edward G. Wilmer as president and P. S. Hart as treasurer, both men recruited from a management consulting firm run by Armin A. Schlesinger, Dillon's old Harvard crony. Dillon had earlier met and worked with Wilmer when Wilmer was corporate counsel for one of Schlesinger's Milwaukee companies.

It was revealed that 45 percent of the Kennedy company was owned by Dillon interests (later transferred to Anne Dillon) with the balance owned by Schlesinger, Wilmer and two other men affiliated with Schlesinger.[24] Since Wilmer and Hart's compensation combined came to only $60,000 a year, Dillon and Schlesinger and the other interests received a windfall profit of $500,000 a year. The lucrative Kennedy management contract subsequently became a major contention in the increasingly rancorous litigation that followed.

After completing the refinancing, Dillon's team soon produced a major turnaround and Goodyear recovered quickly from its near-insolvency. By 1925, sales were back to $200 million and profits approached $20 million.[25] Dillon profited handsomely from his financing efforts. In addition to his underwriting fees and other commissions and trading profits totalling $815,000, Dillon received an option from Goodyear permitting him to buy 170,000 shares of Goodyear common stock at $1 a share for his role in arranging the rescue. Depending on when Dillon exercised these options, he made at least $2 million and as much as $5 million on these options as Goodyear's common stock became a market leader in the bull market of the late 1920s.[26]

"The company had been saved, but at quite a price," Paul Litchfield, who became president of Goodyear in 1926, would later state. After five years, although Goodyear had earned $49 million, they had to pay out nearly $60 million for interest and debt repayments. The refinancing had saddled Goodyear with a heavy load of securities ahead of the old common and preferred stock, and the book value of Goodyear common actually stood at a negative $44 per share.[27] The shareholders, who had received no dividends on their cumulative preferred stock for over five years, revolted and sued the company for agreeing to the onerous terms of the reorganization.[28]

Thereafter, Goodyear's recovery was dogged by an almost continuous series of lawsuits seeking to cancel the management stock, void the Kennedy contract and recover $15 million from Dillon interests alleged to be excessive profits from the 1921 rescue of Goodyear. Before the suits were settled in 1927 it was said that every major law firm in Cleveland, Akron and New York was involved in the litigation in one way or another.[29] All told, four former Cabinet officers were retained as attorneys, primarily for Dillon interests.

Dillon's legal effort necessitated leasing an entire floor at 120 Broadway to house the staffs of the several law firms involved.[30] The firm's complex legal defense was coordinated by Ferdinand Eberstadt, a brilliant young attorney who had been working on the firm's foreign financing business and who had become a Dillon partner in 1926. All of the suits were settled in May 1927. The Goodyear board was reorganized, with eight nominees of Dillon Read, four of Seiberling, and five others mutually agreed upon.[31]

The settlement of the Goodyear suits, however, was not without heavy costs to Dillon's firm. Under the terms of the agreement, Dillon Read paid all legal fees, which came to $2,225,000, by agreeing to forego its commission on the public offering of $60 million of new bonds to refund the higher-yielding bonds and preferred stock issued in 1921.[32] The refunding reduced Goodyear's net interest expense by about 30 percent.

The Goodyear restructuring was the largest and perhaps the most complicated corporate rescue ever undertaken in Wall Street history up to that point.[33] Despite the bitter litigation that followed, the daring financing catapulted Clarence Dillon in one fell swoop into the first echelon of Wall Street's investment banking community and was reminiscent of Morgan's rescue efforts in the money panic of 1907.[34] After Goodyear, all the hardest nuts were brought to Dillon to crack. Through all the Goodyear turmoil, Dillon kept his head; he was daring but thorough.[35] The deal established Dillon Read as a banking house of the first rank and Dillon, who was not quite 40 years of age, as the new wizard of Wall Street.[36]

Notes

1. Hoopes/Brinkley, *Driven Patriot*, p. 55; see also Allen, Hugh, *The House of Goodyear*, Akron, 1936, p. 43 and O'Reilly, Maurice, *The Goodyear Story*, Elmsford, N.Y., 1983, p. 44.
2. Sobel, Robert, *The Life and Times of Dillon Read*, p. 59.
3. Hoopes/Brinkley, *Driven Patriot*, p. 55.
4. Allen, Hugh, *The House of Goodyear*, p. 45.
5. Hoopes/Brinkley, *Driven Patriot*, p. 55.
6. Allen, Hugh, *The House of Goodyear*, p. 47.
7. "Testifies Big Banks Refused Goodyear," *New York Times*, April 12, 1927.
8. Hoopes/Brinkley, *Driven Patriot*, p. 55.
9. Swaine, Robert T., *The Cravath Firm and Its Predecessors, 1819-1947*, vol. 2, pp. 269-70, hereinafter referred to as Swaine, *The Cravath Firm*.
10. Swaine, *The Cravath Firm*, pp. 272-3.
11. Sobel, Robert, *The Life and Times of Dillon Read*, note 50, p. 366.
12. Swaine, *The Cravath Firm*, pp. 272-3.
13. "Goodyear's Straits in 1920 Described," *New York Times*, March 12, 1927.

14. "Head of Dodge Bros. Witness for Dillon," *New York Times*, March 18, 1927.

15. Winkler, *The New Yorker*, p. 32.

16. Hoopes/Brinkley, *Driven Patriot*, pp. 55-6 and Jereski, Laura, "Clarence Dillon: Using Other People's Money," *Forbes*, July 13, 1987, pp. 270, 274.

17. Jereski, Laura, "Clarence Dillon: Using Other People's Money," *Forbes*, pp. 270, 274; also Swaine, *The Cravath Firm*, p. 276.

18. Sobel, Robert, *The Life and Times of Dillon Read*, p. 67.

19. Jereski, Laura, "Clarence Dillon: Using Other People's Money," *Forbes*, pp. 270, 274.

20. "Swears Seiberling Urged Dillon Plan," *New York Times*, April 2, 1927.

21. Allen, Hugh, *The House of Goodyear*, pp. 49-51 and Swaine, *The Cravath Firm*, p. 279.

22. Hoopes/Brinkley, *Driven Patriot*, p. 56.

23. Swaine, *The Cravath Firm*, p. 280.

24. Sobel, Robert, *The Life and Times of Dillon Read*, p. 70.

25. Hoopes/Brinkley, *Driven Patriot*, p. 56.

26. Sobel, Robert, *The Life and Times of Dillon Read*, p. 68.

27. Allen, Hugh, *The House of Goodyear*, p. 51-2.

28. Jereski, Laura, "Clarence Dillon: Using Other People's Money," *Forbes*, p. 274.

29. Perez, Robert C. and Edward F. Willett, *The Will to Win: A Biography of Ferdinand Eberstadt*, Westport, Conn., 1989, p. 34, hereinafter referred to as Perez/Willett, *The Will to Win*.

30. Perez/Willett, *The Will to Win*, p. 34.

31. Swaine, *The Cravath Firm*, p. 281; "Goodyear Fight is Ended," *Akron Times-Press*, May 12, 1927 and "Goodyear Suit Ends Outside of Court; Charges Dropped," *New York Times*, May 16, 1927.

32. Sobel, Robert, *The Life and Times of Dillon Read*, p. 71.

33. Hoopes/Brinkley, *Driven Patriot*, p. 57.

34. Mathey, Dean, *Fifty Years of Wall Street*, p. 11.

35. Winkler, *The New Yorker*, p. 32.

36. Hoopes/Brinkley, *Driven Patriot*, p. 56.

2

Dillon's Heritage and Early Life

The magnitude and brilliance of Dillon's financial dealings startled the Wall Street establishment and soon resulted in his becoming one of the most prominent and successful investment bankers of the roaring twenties. However, Dillon's humble heritage provides a striking contrast to his spectacular deals. Dillon began his life as an immigrant son in the undeveloped pioneer country of western Texas.

Clarence Dillon's father, Samuel Lapowski, a Polish Jew, emigrated to the United States in 1868 a few years after the end of the Civil War along with two of his four brothers, Jacob and Ludwig. Although the record is not clear, the Lapowskis probably came from Lomza, a small agricultural town about 100 miles northeast of Warsaw and not far from the Russian border, in the section of Poland controlled by Russia under the terms of the Treaty of Vienna following Napoleon's defeat.[1] They later migrated to Warsaw. The family's livelihood was based on extensive land holdings and they were engaged in agriculture as well as raising horses. The Lapowskis were fairly prosperous and were able to send their children to the university in Warsaw and then on to the United States.[2]

After arriving in the United States, the Lapowski brothers immediately set out for San Antonio, Texas, where they became involved in peddling clothes and other dry goods. As to why Texas, Douglas Dillon, Clarence Dillon's son, reflected: "I guess [for them] it was sort of `Go West, young man.´ It could just as well have been Colorado or California."[3]

While in San Antonio, Samuel Lapowski and his brother, Jacob, met the Stenbock sisters, Bertha and Henrietta, daughters of Gustav Stenbock, a Swedish immigrant who was a miner prospecting for lead and silver in western Colorado. The brothers married the two Stenbock sisters the

9

following year in a double wedding.[4] Both Lapowski families settled down in San Antonio where Samuel and Bertha's first child, Clarence, was born on September 27, 1882; the family moved to Abilene, 250 miles northwest of San Antonio, two years later. Two daughters, Jeanie and Evelyn, followed in 1884 and 1887; all were raised as Protestants.[5]

In the beginning, the Lapowski brothers were no more than travelling peddlers struggling to survive. Katharyn Duff, in her account of early Abilene days, describes Sam Lapowski as just "a young . . . Jewish peddler with a pack on his back who . . . built . . . a major [retail dry goods] business."[6] After accumulating profits from their earlier peddling, the Lapowski brothers established their first store, a large clothing and dry goods outlet in San Angelo, Texas, which flourished for over twenty years, grossing in sales volume over $125,000 annually until the early 1900s when the family sold out.[7] As the first store prospered, the Lapowskis opened an even larger store in Abilene as well as several other stores in nearby towns in western Texas, all managed by members of the Lapowski family.[8] Sam Lapowski soon acquired the trappings of his success. The Lapowskis had a large home with well-kept gardens; they employed an English coachman and a Chinese cook.[9]

Following up his retailing successes, Samuel Lapowski branched out into banking as a sideline, becoming what was known as a "merchant banker." Most of the merchants in that pioneering country carried their customers, usually ranchers and farmers, on credit from year to year. By the time they sold their crops or cattle, they were apt to have incurred such formidable bills that they were never out of debt. Lapowski would advance money to these people. In that way, they were able to shop around and buy things more cheaply.[10] Lapowski also became a speculator in land. His financing sideline and land investments eventually produced more profits than the store operations.[11]

Periodically, there would be agricultural crises which would cause the ranchers and other farmers to fall behind, but Lapowski was nimble enough to avoid the full impact of these economic setbacks. Then a particularly severe drought occurred in Texas which caused crop failures and the death of thousands of head of cattle, and forced Lapowski to curtail his operations. In fact, Lapowski published a closing notice in the *Abilene Reporter-News* on October 19, 1894 but this setback apparently was temporary because he was soon back in the mercantile business in Abilene.[12]

Part of Lapowski's investment speculations included purchases of extensive land holdings in Paris, Texas, 400 miles east of Abilene. Nitze recalls that Dillon once told him that he sold this land when his father died, and he used the proceeds to finance the purchase of a machine tool business with his brother-in-law, George Douglass. It later turned out that the lands

Dillon sold were in the center of what became the fabled East Texas oil fields. Nitze adds: "If Dillon had kept his father's lands, he [might] have made much more money than he ever made in the investment banking business."[13] For years thereafter, Dillon was haunted by the thought of the vast potential wealth that had slipped through his hands.[14]

Aware of the ethnic and religious bigotry that existed in the United States, Samuel Lapowski determined to assimilate into the American mainstream as rapidly as possible. Accordingly, he was naturalized on September 25, 1891 in Abilene district court, having initiated the process earlier in San Antonio in April 1878.[15] Later, to facilitate the entry of his son into business and society, he permitted Clarence to legally adopt his grandmother's maiden name, Dillon. Thus, Clarence became Clarence Lapowski Dillon on September 17, 1901.[16]

Samuel Lapowski's heritage is complex and contains many bizarre twists and turns. Although his father, Joshua, was Polish, his wife was descended from the Dillon family which was equally French and Irish. The Dillon family were Irish Catholics, part of the ragtag Irish-French army formed by James II that was defeated at the Battle of the Boyne on July 12, 1690 near Dublin, and chased out of Ireland. Many of them fled to France and scattered over different parts of the country. The Dillon family had been in France for almost a century; they were prolific and in time the Dillon French clan became large. One of the Dillon clan, Arthur Richard Dillon, became Archbishop of the Catholic diocese of Narbonne in southwestern France in 1763.[17]

There was a Dillon regiment in the French Royal armies before the Revolution, and that regiment was continued in the Republican army. The Dillon Regiment had been raised in Ireland by Archbishop Dillon's great grandfather, Theobald, as part of the army to defend James II. Theobald brought the Dillon Regiment intact to France debarking with his troops at Brest. Subsequently, the regiment was absorbed intact into the French Royal Army under royal decree from Louis XIV, with its name altered to *Regiment Royal Dillon*. The French military authorities urged members of the Dillon clan to serve in the regiment named for them. Four of Theobald's five sons served in and commanded the Dillon regiment.[18]

Almost a century later, during the French Revolution, the mob beat up and killed one of Archbishop Dillon's nephews, the father of two boys aged twelve and fourteen, and Archbishop Dillon took the boys under his care. After Napoleon's overthrow of the revolutionary government, the French government acknowledged the crime and tragic killing by sending the two young men to St. Cyr, the French military academy, at government expense. After graduation, they became officers in Napoleon's *Grand Armée* serving in the Dillon regiment in Napoleon's unsuccessful campaign to conquer Russia. One of the brothers, Michel Dillon (Dylion), was a survivor of

Napoleon's defeat in Russia. However, Michel never returned to France, remaining in Poland where he married a Polish girl; one of his daughters, Paulina Dillon (Dylion), married Joshua Lapowski who fathered Samuel Lapowski.[19]

The Lapowskis, despite their Jewish heritage, may have nobility in their history. Paul Nitze, one of Dillon's closest partners in the 1930s, believes that there is a strong possibility that the Lapowskis were descended from Polish or Russian nobility. Nitze reflected:

> The Rothschilds bought their titles; so many nobles were created afterwards that it would have been possible to gain a title. I guess I am influenced by the fact that all of his Harvard classmates . . . called him "Baron." I had the impression that somehow or other there must have been a distant claim that the family had to nobility. . . . I also recall seeing a portrait out at Dunwalke of an earlier Lapowski . . . attired in the ceremonial dress of a nobleman or a high governmental official.[20]

The Irish side of the Dillon family definitely includes nobility dating from the fifteenth century in a direct line from Robert Comte Dillon, Seigneur Lord of Terrefort in Guyenne of the House of Drumrany. Theobald, an ancestor of Michel Dillon, was the seventh Lord Viscount Dillon in the Court of James II of Ireland.[21] Dillon may have known that nobility existed in the early history of the Lapowskis in Poland (as well as earlier in Ireland) and may have liked the idea of being linked with that earlier nobility through the use of the title, "Baron." In other words, Dillon thought of himself as a baron.[22]

However, Douglas Dillon, Clarence's son, has no knowledge of nobility in the family, noting:

> The nobility heritage was not talked about to me; the Lapowskis were a good family that came over here to find their fortunes. . . . My father did have some photographs of one of his ancestors dressed very formally as a Polish official of some sort way back [but I doubt that indicated nobility]. . . .[23]

While the question of Dillon's nobility will never be answered satisfactorily, Dillon's social aspirations are acknowledged by all who knew him well. Philip Allen, Dillon's oldest grandson, notes:

> My grandfather had the brains but he always wanted to [become] socially acceptable and I think he married [my grandmother, Anne Douglass,] because she came from a very socially acceptable family in Milwaukee. . . . It was the one thing that he didn't have himself. So I think he was very conscious about doing things for himself and for his children and grandchildren to make them . . . socially acceptable. . . . I think he strived

hard . . . to achieve the pinnacle not only of business but also of society.[24]

Clarence was able to see more of the country than most boys of his age. To stock his various stores, Samuel Lapowski went to New York twice a year on buying trips and when Clarence reached nine years of age, his father began taking him on these trips. Also, to escape the brutally hot Texas summers, the Lapowskis vacationed in cool New Hampshire and Maine during the summer months. In New York, Samuel's business contacts advised him to send Clarence to an eastern school, preferably one of the more prestigious ones in New England, and then send him to a fashionable college.[25]

Lapowski subsequently sent Clarence to Worcester Academy, one of the elite prep schools in the Northeast. Worcester was considered a way station to several Ivy League colleges, with Clarence selecting Harvard as his primary choice. While at Worcester, Clarence made frequent weekend trips to see his Uncle Boleslaw in New York City to attend plays and to see the sights.[26] Boleslaw Lapowski, a younger brother of Samuel Lapowski, had emigrated to the United States in or about 1890 and had become a prominent doctor, settling in New York City. Boleslaw received his medical degree from the University of Warsaw (Poland) in 1885 and achieved prominence in his medical practice with three of his scholarly papers published in the New York Medical Journal.[27]

Clarence had difficulty entering Harvard especially with the Latin portion of the entrance examination. He described how he dealt with this crisis as follows:

> When I took my entrance examination for Harvard, I failed in Latin on account of misspelled English words. The college then was more magnanimous than it is today and I was accepted for the freshman class with the proviso that I would take the Latin exam again in the fall. Again, I failed on account of misspelled English. For this reason, I had to enter the scientific school working towards a BS degree for which Latin was not required. However at the end of the year, they allowed me to take the Latin exam once more. When I failed again—still on account of misspelled English—their patience was exhausted but instead of dropping me as they would today, they said, "Oh forget it." So I was transferred to the college and I received my AB degree in 1905.[28]

At Harvard, Dillon roomed with his old Worcester Academy school chum, William A. Phillips, at 35 Bow Street in Cambridge where he pursued his passion for poker with a small group of intimates. Dillon played poker in a friendly, unworried fashion. Often, when another player had raised him a few hundred, Dillon would expose his hand so all could see, and ask: "Do you think I am strong enough to call?" This ruse gave Dillon the opportunity to study his opponent's expression. That moment of appraisal almost invariably proved profitable to Dillon.[29] In similar fashion, he later employed many of his poker playing tactics to help drive hard bargains in his financing deals.

Dillon was an erratic student at both Worcester and Harvard. At Worcester he received grades of D in Latin and French, while excelling with As in science, mathematics and declamation (public speaking), with more Cs than Bs in his other courses. Similarly, at Harvard, while extremely intelligent, Dillon was not an outstanding student and showed scant interest in his studies although he developed a fascination with Napoleon and French history. He failed to make any of the prominent undergraduate societies, settling for the larger, less-exclusive Institute of 1770.[30]

One of Dillon's closest friends at Harvard was Armin A. Schlesinger. Like Dillon's father, Schlesinger's father was also an immigrant except that Schlesinger had emigrated from Germany and settled in Milwaukee where he became a manufacturer of mill machinery among other business interests. He offered Dillon a job in one of his businesses after graduation. During the next three years (1905-8) the two Harvard classmates were associated with various Schlesinger interests. Schlesinger married soon after graduation, and his wife introduced Dillon to Anne McEldin Douglass, scion of one of the founders of the R. G. Dun credit reporting firm. Soon Anne and Clarence were engaged.[31]

Years later, Dillon recollected his first meeting with Anne at a dinner party given by a friend of Schlesinger in 1905. After dinner they played roulette; Dillon banked and Anne lost one dollar. The next day Dillon received a note from Anne with a dollar reading: "Gambling debts, I understand, must be paid before sunset of the following day." Dillon immediately responded by sending Anne a bouquet of flowers with this short note: "I am sure that such payment must be acknowledged." After that, Dillon dined frequently at the Douglasses' large house overlooking Lake Michigan; Dillon recollected: "What I saved on food, I spent on flowers."[32]

Anne Douglass was born September 26, 1881 in Peoria, Illinois, the daughter of George Douglass and Susan (Dun) Douglass and was the youngest of a family of four children. Anne's forebears were members of the early colonial aristocracy with her earliest English ancestors, the Walkes, arriving in Virginia in 1662.[33] Her grandfather, Benjamin Douglass, and Robert Graham Dun together founded the mercantile agency, R. G. Dun & Company; Anne's father continued the family's interest in this business. There was a considerable amount of intermarriage between the two families with Benjamin Douglass and R. G. Dun each marrying the other's sister. There were other intermarriages in the subsequent history of the family.[34]

When Dillon was actively courting Anne, he suffered an accident in the summer of 1907 which nearly cost him his life; that he lived is a tribute to the determined efforts of the Douglass family doctor. Dillon had spent the weekend with Anne and her family at their summer resort on Pine Lake just outside Milwaukee.[35] On Monday morning, Anne and her mother accompanied Dillon to the railroad station where he was to board a commuter train to bring him to his office in Milwaukee.

That morning the Pioneer Express was running two hours late and thundered through the station desperately striving to make up for lost time. The train's cowcatcher hit a large Saint Bernard dog that had wandered onto the tracks and hurled its lifeless body through the air into the waiting crowd on the platform, striking Dillon broadside with such terrific force that he was knocked off his feet. Dillon was catapulted against an iron post and fractured his skull. Dillon's body struck Mrs. Douglass (who was standing just behind him) so hard that she was knocked down and broke her hip; she walked with a cane for the rest of her life.[36] Dillon was not at once knocked unconscious and he asked that someone telephone his office to tell them that he would be late! Gradually he passed out and remained unconscious for a week.[37]

The family's local physician, a Doctor Nixon, had Dillon put on a wagon and conveyed him with the least possible jarring to the Douglass home. Specialists hurried from Milwaukee to treat the two injured persons. The specialists wanted to turn Dillon over and examine him to see if his skull was broken. The old doctor rose up in arms. He issued an ultimatum to the Douglass family that if any of the specialists laid a hand on Dillon, he would withdraw as the attending physician. He explained to the Douglasses that if the patient's skull was broken, an examination might result in an internal hemorrhage, possibly causing severe complications.[38]

After Doctor Nixon succeeded in preventing the specialists from moving him, Dillon rested for several days in the living room of the Douglasses' home. Then Dr. Nixon had Dillon put on a stretcher and carried upstairs to a bedroom. So zealous was Dr. Nixon that he got down on his hands and knees under the stretcher and steadied Dillon's body with his bent back so that Dillon wouldn't be jarred as he was carried up the stairs.[39]

Dillon later recalled, "I was unconscious for eight or ten days with Anne watching over me," adding, "I have always felt that the stand that old doctor took probably saved my life."[40] For several months he was confined to bed. Anne Douglass nursed Dillon (and her mother) back to health, but the recovery was slow. Dillon's nervous system had been shaken by the accident. For the rest of his life, he suffered occasionally from an inner ear malady caused by the accident, resulting in occasional bouts of vertigo which may have contributed to his volatile temperament.[41]

The first thing Dillon did after he recovered was to marry Anne Douglass on February 4, 1908. The wedding took place in a Presbyterian church with Walter Jones, a classmate from college, Dillon's best man. They honeymooned in New Orleans, spending most of their time at the race track where Dillon made wagers of $2 to $5 on each race but only after thorough study of the records of the horses and of the dope sheets. Actually, Anne put $5 on a horse which was a 40-to-1 shot and won $200. They also spent a lot of time in New Orleans looking at antique furniture which became one of their enduring lifetime interests.[42]

After the Dillons returned to Milwaukee, Clarence was told by his doctors he would be unable to work for at least a year. The railroad awarded him a settlement of $8,000 for the accident, and with this Clarence and Anne took off for a post-honeymoon "health tour" of just under two years in Europe. While they were in Europe, they travelled up and down the Mediterranean coast from Nice to Grasse visiting many old villages high up in the Alps. Other trips included Naples, Pompeii, Sorrento, Capri, Amalfi and Paestum. Then it was on to Rome and Florence with day excursions to Pisa and other nearby towns, and then to Milan and Belaggio on Lake Como.[43]

After making this Grand Tour of Europe, Dillon and his wife settled down, dividing their time between Paris and Geneva, their favorites. During this period, Dillon became intensely interested in art and architecture. Although he never lost his interest in art, especially etching, he decided against becoming either a professional artist or an architect. In Paris, Dillon also developed a flair for gourmet cooking. Nitze recollects Dillon's describing his shopping trips to Les Halles to purchase fresh vegetables and the best fish, meats and poultry for gourmet cooking which he studied avidly at the Cordon Bleu in Paris.[44]

Ultimately, he used up all of his funds living the good life and in early 1910 was forced to return to the United States. Years later Dillon chuckled:

> I was awarded $8,000 damages by the railroad. I blew it all during those two years. . . . Although my wife's family was well-to-do, we lived very frugally except when her folks came to spend some time in Europe, when they took us along to swell hotels.[45]

Upon his return and eager for new challenges, Dillon founded a new firm, Milwaukee Machine Tool Co., with his brother-in-law, George Douglass, and became its president. Dillon's $10,000 half interest was financed by the sale of his father's land holdings in East Texas.[46] However, the business did not prosper due to Dillon's aggressive underbidding for a contract to reequip an automobile plant that had been badly damaged by a fire in 1913. Dillon's bid was too low and the fledgling firm lost a considerable amount of money completing the order.[47]

Dillon later recalled, "I was inexperienced and young. I got the order;

[but] I found out on my return to Milwaukee that we could not possibly make [money on the order]." Finally, two years later, Kearney & Trecker bought out Dillon and Douglass. It was a good deal for Kearney & Trecker because only a few months later, the first world war broke out and the demand for machine tools soared. Dillon and Douglass missed out on a killing by selling for cash instead of stock. In any event, Dillon was finished with the machine tool business, looking for new challenges and Wall Street beckoned with an irresistible opportunity.[48] The contacts he had developed in Milwaukee and Chicago would aid him greatly in his new endeavors in finance.

Notes

1. *Standard Blue Book*, Texas Edition, July 1921, vol. XIII, p. 176.
2. Mrs. Dorothy Dillon Eweson interview, October 1 and 4, 1991.
3. Douglas Dillon interview, May 23, 1991.
   Suzanne Campbell of San Angelo, Texas, who researched and wrote her master's thesis on the Jews of southwestern Texas in the nineteenth century, told the author that in the late 1800s, there was considerable agitation against eastern European Jews crowding into New York and other eastern cities. Accordingly, several Jewish leaders developed programs to disperse the Jewish population. One program called The Industrial Removal Office involved moving some 70,000 eastern European Jews from the Northeast to the Midwest and beyond. Another program called The Galveston Movement, encouraged new Jewish immigrants to enter the country through the port of Galveston in Texas from whence they migrated to Dallas and Houston and other cities in Texas. (Source: Suzanne Campbell telephone interview, January 7, 1992.)
4. Both sisters were much younger than the Lapowski brothers, with Bertha only seventeen when she married thirty-one year old Samuel Lapowski. According to family sources, Bertha and her sister were born in Denver, Colorado, but the 1900 Census records Bertha's birthplace as New York and Henrietta's as Texas. Their father, Gustav Stenbock, had taken his family as far as Denver but when he moved into a mining camp in Leadville, he decided that his wife and children should live elsewhere as a mining camp was not a proper place to rear a family. His wife and the two daughters went to live in Houston, Texas, while he worked his mines and prospected in Colorado. Stenbock made and lost a lot of money prospecting but ended up owning mostly dead mines. (Sources: Mrs. Dorothy Dillon Eweson interview, October 1 and 4, 1991 and "Family With No History Has Remarkable Story," by Dean Chenoweth, *San Angelo Standard-Times*, January 26, 1978.)
5. Mrs. Dorothy Dillon Eweson interview, October 1 and 4, 1991.
6. Duff, Katharyn, and Betty Kay Seibt, *Catclaw Creek, an Informal History of Abilene in West Texas*, Burnet, Texas, 1980, p. 133.
7. Clemens, Gus, *The Concho County*, San Antonio, Texas, 1981, p. 98.

8. "Abilenians Recall Dillon as Son of Early Merchant," by Don Norris, *Abilene Reporter-News*, April 1, 1956.
9. *Anne's Story.*
10. *Anne's Story.*
11. Mrs. Dorothy Dillon Eweson interview, October 1 and 4, 1991.

The Lapowski & Bro. store operation was the largest of its kind in western Texas. A reporter from the *Abilene Reporter-News* surveyed the Lapowski merchandising operation in the early 1890s as follows:

> Last week the Reporter . . . was invited to look through the wholesale and retail house of S. Lapowski & Bro., in this city, and see the immense stock of goods carried by this firm. The area of floor space covered by goods . . . is larger than that of any dry goods house west of Dallas, and sums up in round numbers to 12,400 square feet and every inch of the space is covered with goods.

> On the first or ground floor is displayed dress goods of every description and quality from the cheapest to the finest the eastern markets afford. Here also are the retail boot and shoe, clothing, notion and house furnishing goods departments, each and every one of them complete and containing stocks that would make large stores if each department was under a separate roof and . . . management.

> The wholesale department is located on the second floor where the wealth of goods, both staple and fancy, in a tasty and compact arrangement impresses the visitor and his first thoughts are "where in the world are all these goods to go, and who will buy them?" But we are assured that while the stock is immense, it is only what is needed by a live house to supply the constantly growing demand to this portion of the State.

> Mr. Sam Lapowski, the head of the house, was in fine spirits. He said the prospects for business were the best he had ever seen them and that they expected to sell during the season $150,000 worth of goods. (Source: "The Pride of Abilene County and the Largest Merchandising House in West Texas," *Abilene Reporter-News*, April 3, 1891.)

12. *Anne's Story.*
13. Paul H. Nitze telephone call, April 15, 1991, and interview, November 11, 1991.
14. Callahan, David, *Dangerous Capabilities: Paul Nitze and the Cold War*, New York, 1990, p. 20.
15. "Abilenians Recall Dillon as Son of Early Merchant," *Abilene Reporter-News*.
16. "Dillon's Father Spent Childhood Days in Abilene," *Abilene Reporter-News*, May 1, 1959.

The father, Samuel Lapowski, and all of his brothers, however, retained the Lapowski name. Clarence Dillon never denied his Polish Jewish ancestry and belonged to several Polish interest groups and actually seemed proud of his Jewish heritage. However, Dillon adopted the Episcopal faith as his religious affiliation. After the death of her husband, Dillon's mother, Bertha, also changed her name to Dillon as did her older daughter, Jeanie. (Sources: "Family With No History has Remarkable Story," *San Angelo Standard-Times*; also Joseph Haywood interview, October 28, 1991.)

17. Archbishop Dillon was a vigorous supporter of the *Ancien Régime* and was appointed president of the province of Languedoc as a royal reward by Louis XIV. He and his family opposed the divisive forces caused by the French Revolution and were forced into exile following the takeover of the French government by the revolutionary radicals. (Source: Bulletin de La Commission Archéologie de Narbonne, Années 1964 et 1965, June 28, Narbonne, 1966, hereinafter referred to as *Narbonne Archives.*)

18. *Narbonne Archives.*

19. Douglas Dillon interview, May 23, 1991 and Mrs. Dorothy Dillon Eweson interview, October 1 and 4, 1991.

20. Paul Nitze telephone interview, April 15, 1991.

21. *Narbonne Archives.*

22. Those who question whether there is nobility in the family, cite a number of theories as to how Dillon came to acquire the sobriquet, "Baron." One version has it that his Harvard classmates called him "Baron" because they found his given name not descriptive enough of him. As one of his classmates put it: "How could you `Clarence´ a fellow who sat up most of the night in a no-limit poker game, without benefit of tobacco or beer, and who won or lost (generally the former) the biggest stakes in the `Yard´?" Dillon was also addicted to horse racing and a great pacer of the time was named "Baron Dillon." Clearly, Dillon did not like the name, Clarence, and some of his close associates and partners thought "Baron" reflected his aloof but firm control of Dillon Read. (Sources: Sobel, Robert, *The Life and Times of Dillon Read*, pp. 35-6 and Winkler, *The New Yorker*, p. 29.)

23. Douglas Dillon interview, May 23, 1991.

24. Philip D. Allen interview, April 9, 1992.

25. *Anne's Story.*

26. *Anne's Story.*

27. *American Medical Directory*, New York City, vol. I, 1906, p. 640, published by the American Medical Association.

The papers included: "The Recent Investigations in Syphilis and their Practical Applications" (1907), "Diseases of Inguinal Glands and their Treatment" (1898) and "The Abortive Treatment of Syphilis" (1914).

Another brother, Nathan, emigrated to Texas from Poland in 1882 settling in Gainesville where he was engaged in the cattle business for several years and was also for a time engaged in his brothers' retailing operations. Seeking new adventures, Nathan became a member of Theodore Roosevelt's famed "Rough Riders" and participated in the successful attack on San Juan Hill in July 1898 during the Cuban campaign of the Spanish-American War. He continued to pursue his military career thereafter serving in the Philippines, in the 1916 Mexican border campaign (pursuing Pancho Villa) and in the first world war. (Source: "Colonel Lapowski, Pioneer, Dies at Home Here," *El Paso Times*, February 11, 1928.)

In 1906, Samuel Lapowski finally closed down the Abilene store and moved with his wife, Bertha, and their two daughters to El Paso managing another store in partnership with Jacob and his younger brother, Nathan. In 1910, Lapowski moved with his wife and older daughter to Salt Lake City where he was also engaged in the mercantile business. Two years later, he developed a brain tumor, suffered a stroke, and was hospitalized in San Francisco where he died four weeks later on June 23, 1912. Clarence was at the bedside when his father died. (Source: "Mortuary Record: Lapowski," *El Paso Times*, August 6, 1912.)

Thereafter, Lapowski's widow, Bertha, lived in Europe for more than twenty years staying in Lausanne, Switzerland, during the summers and wintering in Paris. She disliked housekeeping and stayed in plush hotels always accompanied by one of her daughters. In the late 1930s, Bertha came back to New York City where she lived at the Carlisle Hotel on Manhattan's elegant East Side until her death in the early 1950s in her upper eighties. (Source: Mrs. Dorothy Dillon Eweson interview, October 1 and 4, 1991.)

28. *Anne's Story.*
29. Forbes, Bruce C., "Clarence Dillon, The Man Who Bought Dodge," *Forbes*, p. 7.
30. Sobel, Robert, *The Life and Times of Dillon Read*, pp. 34-5.
31. *Anne's Story.*
32. *Anne's Story.*
33. The third governor of Virginia, who presided over the first House of the Burgesses, was a Walke. The Douglass family of Maryland were Scots tracing back to David the Bruce. The Duns were Scottish Presbyterians arriving in the late eighteenth or early nineteenth century. (Sources: Douglas Dillon interview, May 23, 1991 and Newman, Harry Wright, *A Branch of the Douglass Family with its Maryland and Virginia Connections*, Garden City, N.Y., 1967.)
34. Benjamin Douglass eventually became the owner of the business but later sold it to R. G. Dun. The business then prospered under Dun. Having no children of his own, Dun divided his estate among the children of his two sisters. The sister who married Douglass had four children with the other sister bearing six children. Since each child received one tenth of the estate, this led to later legal disputes between the two families. Benjamin Douglass's son, George, moved his family to Milwaukee in 1886 to manage R. G. Dun's office in that city, remaining there until he retired in June 1908. (Source: *Anne's Story.*)
35. "Again, Dillon." Time, January 11, 1926, p. 27.
36. Mrs. Dorothy Dillon Eweson interview, October 1 and 4, 1991.
37. "Again, Dillon," *Time*, p. 27.
38. Forbes, Bruce C., "Clarence Dillon, The Man Who Bought Dodge," *Forbes*, pp. 165.
39. Forbes, Bruce C., "Clarence Dillon, The Man Who Bought Dodge," *Forbes*, pp. 165 and *Anne's Story.*
40. *Anne's Story.*
41. Winkler, *The New Yorker*, p. 30.
42. *Anne's Story.*
43. *Anne's Story.*
44. Paul H. Nitze telephone interview, April 15, 1991.

45. *Anne's Story* and Forbes, Bruce C., "Clarence Dillon, The Man Who Bought Dodge," *Forbes*, p. 165.

46. Paul H. Nitze telephone interview, April 15, 1991.

47. Forbes, Bruce C., "Clarence Dillon, The Man Who Bought Dodge," *Forbes*, p. 165 and *Anne's Story*.

48. Forbes, Bruce C., "Clarence Dillon, The Man Who Bought Dodge," *Forbes*, p. 165 and *Anne's Story*.

3

Dillon Becomes a Wall Street Legend

In 1913, after the death of the co-founder of Dun's credit reporting business, a dispute arose amongst the Dun and Douglass heirs. George Douglass appointed Dillon and George B. Miller, an attorney in Milwaukee, to liquidate his one-tenth ownership in the business. The other nine-tenths majority share was centered in the Dun family of New York, who were opposed to any form of sale. Dillon and Miller went to New York in the spring of 1913 to try to work out a settlement with the Dun heirs.[1] The majority Dun holders were determined to buy out Douglass's minority interest at a low price and threatened to put the business up for auction to drive down the price unless Douglass agreed to their buyout offer. After many proposals and counter proposals, Dillon and Miller were able to secure a more favorable offer which George Douglass approved.[2]

George W. Wickersham, one of the New York attorneys handling the estate settlement, was very impressed with Dillon and arranged to introduce him to William A. Read, the banker, over lunch. Wickersham told Dillon: "Mr. Read is looking for bright young men and I told him you were one of the brightest I had met in a long time." Read, a bluff, hearty soul, took an instant fancy to Dillon.[3]

Moreover, it developed that William A. Phillips, Dillon's old school friend from Worcester Academy and Harvard, was a bond salesmen in the New York headquarters of Read's firm, where he excelled at selling bonds to large institutions.[4] Dillon and Phillips had kept in touch after graduation. For example, they had met in Milwaukee just a few months earlier when Phillips was seeking some bond orders from Dillon's in-laws. While in Milwaukee, Phillips advised his old friend, "This is no place for you. New York is where you belong—not out here in the sticks."[5]

After Dillon liquidated Douglass's interests in Dun's he actively pursued his own prospects in Wall Street. He met Read again who, aided by Phillips, soon persuaded Dillon to give banking a trial. Since Dillon's wife was reluctant to leave Milwaukee, Read offered him a position in the Chicago office, which Dillon accepted in the fall of 1913, with a starting salary of $250 a month. After a brief training course, Dillon began work as a bond salesman in the Chicago office under the supervision of W. Meade Lindsley Fiske.[6]

Dillon had suggested to Read that the firm tap the rich Chicago district where Dillon had developed numerous potential clients from his machine tool days in Milwaukee. He soon developed these prospects into important sources of business. Through Schlesinger and other friends in Milwaukee, Dillon was able to obtain interviews with several important investors in the upper Midwest, including William Horlick, president of Racine-based Horlick's Malted Milk. George Miller, Horlick's attorney, advised Horlick to put Dillon in charge of his portfolio, which Horlick did—a big coup for Dillon.[7]

As a reward for attracting substantial business to the midwest territory, Read promoted Dillon and moved him at the age of thirty-one to the main office in New York in the summer of 1914, with specific instructions to work with William Phillips to reorganize the New York main office sales force. After analyzing the situation, Dillon concluded that what was needed was to build up an aggressive sales force backed up by a large bonus compensation plan. Until then, the Read organization's specialty was its skill in buying securities issues, but its distribution system was limited. In essence, salesmen were regarded as inferior to the corporate finance staff.

Dillon got the sales force together and told them they would have the opportunity of becoming the most important end of the business and would be rewarded by a new system of compensation geared to performance. Dillon's new incentive-based marketing plan was an immediate success.

For his part, Dillon opened up new outlets for the firm through bank trust departments, brokerage concerns and other large wholesale outlets. Thus the selling organization both inside and outside the firm was thoroughly overhauled, with distribution and volume sharply improved thereafter.[8]

The Phenol Venture

After the onset of the first world war, Dillon made his first major killing by correctly speculating on wartime needs of the Allies. Through an old Harvard friend, Waddell Catchings, then at Goldman Sachs, Dillon learned that J. P. Morgan had become the American purchasing agent for the British government to procure critical materials for its war effort.[9] Dillon soon found out from his Morgan contacts that the British had a pressing need for picric acid, a scarce material essential to the manufacture of certain high explosives that only the Germans knew how to make. Dillon mentioned this to Read who advised him against it. "Don't bother with a thing like that —you will lose everything you put in it," was Read's warning.[10]

But Dillon persisted, discussing the proposed venture with his old Harvard friend, Armin Schlesinger, who immediately put his chemists to work on finding a way to make picric acid. Schlesinger's chemists discovered that it could be produced from phenol, which could be derived easily from benzene; this was readily available from Schlesinger's coal and coke facilities in Milwaukee.

With this technological breakthrough, Dillon put all of his energies to work amassing facts and figures to flesh out the proposed business venture including *pro forma* cash flow projections, very similar to a start-up business today in the venture capital field. Dillon's research on any proposed venture was always methodical and he decided to find out all he could about the chemical industry—its possibilities and pitfalls, likely dangers, potential customers and rewards, sources of supply, potential and actual competition—to determine if the probable success of the enterprise as a whole would overcome the risks of failure. Since the phenol operation was owned outright by Dillon and his Schlesinger associates, the profits flowed directly to them and not William Read & Co. Within two years, the phenol venture was a phenomenal success. Dillon and his associates became multi-millionaires almost overnight.

The Dillon approach, first utilized in a formal manner in the phenol venture, became his hallmark. "The devil lies in the details," said Nicholas Brady, a later Dillon Read managing partner, in describing Dillon's deal making style. "Clarence Dillon's style was to overwhelm the detail . . . to do the pick and shovel work to find where the devil might lie. Dillon's meticulous analyses gave him a tremendous edge," Brady added.[11] What to the public and Wall Street were major speculative gambles were to Dillon carefully thought out "investments."

Dillon's thoroughness was legendary on Wall Street. A Harvard classmate once said, "If Clarence Dillon wanted to buy a cattle ranch, he would read up everything on cows and before he closed the deal he would know more about the cattle business than the rancher himself." It was not unusual for Dillon to turn back an entire deal to be reworked if he was not completely satisfied with the thoroughness of the analysis. Moreover, if any of his partners had reservations about any deal, Dillon would refuse to go ahead with it. Reflecting his concern for thorough "due diligence," it was an accepted fact in Wall Street that the circulars issued by Dillon were the most complete.[12]

When the United States entered the war, Dillon and his partners turned over the phenol plant to the government to avoid any criticism of war profiteering, especially in light of Dillon's role on the War Industries Board. By then they had realized an enormous profit on their relatively small investments. After the war the plant reverted back to Dillon and his group and he sold his interest to his Milwaukee partners, who established a very profitable chemical company in which he had no interest. At the age of thirty-six, Dillon had accumulated a fortune worth about $8 million, largely from the phenol venture.[13] Unfortunately the episode convinced Dillon that he could function effectively as a business manager as well as a banker. Later, problems with running Goodyear and Dodge proved to him that bankers should not be involved in managing businesses they control.

Read was delighted with Dillon's rapid-fire achievements and astounded by his success with the phenol venture. As a reward, Read made Dillon a partner in the firm on April 1, 1916.[14] Dillon used some of the profits from the phenol venture to purchase his partnership. Whistling and jaunty after learning the news of his promotion, the Baron broke the news to a Harvard classmate and observed with a grin: "This game is more fascinating than no-limit stud poker." Dillon's development was rapid and he worked well with the other partners, who developed great trust and confidence in him. He was a good man to have around; no matter how frantic conditions became, Dillon always remained calm. The senior partners came to rely on him more and more to solve financing problems.[15]

However, just days after Dillon became a partner, tragedy struck the firm. William A. Read succumbed to pneumonia and died sixteen days later. Read, in death, was generous to his old firm and partners. The executors of Read's estate, probated at between $5 and $6 million, were permitted to loan up to $2 million to the firm at any time,[16] and Read left $25,000 to each of his partners.[17] Clarence Dillon wasted no time moving into Read's private corner office at 28 Nassau Street and immediately assumed the leadership of the firm although Dillon later claimed that he waited until the other partners asked him to take over.[18]

Just after the United States entered the first world war, Dillon underwent a serious operation which resulted in the removal of his left kidney and prevented him from going on active duty overseas. The normal way to perform this operation would have been to remove the stone from the kidney, but the attending surgeon was a major in the military service waiting for orders to sail for France; he told Dillon that removing the stone would keep Dillon in the hospital for another two weeks, delaying the surgeon's imminent departure for the war zone. Removing the kidney would be much quicker, taking only a week. Accordingly, the surgeon sought Dillon's approval of the speedier operation to remove his entire left kidney. Dillon agreed and his kidney was removed at New York Hospital. Dillon later sadly recollected, "with the war excitement, I very foolishly agreed and the doctor very unwisely removed the kidney."[19] Today, such a medical operation would have subjected the doctor to the risk of a major negligent practices suit.

After the kidney was removed, Dillon went to White Sulphur Springs to recuperate, with Anne taking charge of the children back home. He wrote Anne from there that General Pershing had cabled an offer to commission him as a lieutenant colonel, to go to France and unravel the bottlenecks blocking Allied war shipments. Dillon's condition, however, prevented him from sailing before the first of November. His assignment was to work as a troubleshooter under the commander-in-chief to break up supply bottlenecks.[20]

Later, fully recovered, Dillon reported for duty to Secretary of War Newton D. Baker in Washington. Baker told him it would be necessary to have a routine physical examination and that Dillon should go right over to the medical department that afternoon for his examination. When Dillon went into the examination room, the major sitting at the desk was none other than the surgeon who had performed the kidney operation! The surgeon had encountered delays in his overseas assignment and was still in the United States. The surgeon told Dillon, "You are out of luck, as medical regulations preclude any man with only one kidney from serving overseas in the Army." The major said, "If I had not known about your operation, it would have been a very perfunctory examination and you would have been commissioned."[21]

Despite this setback, Dillon became a major factor in the American war effort. To expedite war production, President Woodrow Wilson appointed Bernard M. Baruch to head up the newly formed War Industries Board (WIB) and Baruch immediately began to search for competent people to staff his new organization. Leading financiers including Jacob H. Schiff and Henry P. Davison recommended Dillon to Baruch, describing him as "capable and level-headed." With these credentials, Baruch logically asked Dillon to be his deputy and Dillon accepted the assignment.[22] Dillon had first met Baruch in William Read's corner office at 28 Nassau Street in 1915.[23]

Baruch selected three executive assistants to help solve production problems and act as his troubleshooters. In addition to Dillon, they included Harrison Williams, who later became the head of the nation's largest public utility holding company and Herbert B. Swope, the Pulitzer-prize-winning reporter for the *New York World* and later its editor.[24] Dillon used his new contacts profitably after the war's end. Harrison Williams's utility empire, North America Company and its affiliated companies, became a major Dillon underwriting client, accounting for $316.7 million in underwritings in the 1920s and $604.4 million in the 1930s and 1940s.[25]

Actually, Dillon's assignment at WIB paralleled the job Pershing had wanted him to perform, only Dillon was based in Washington in Baruch's office instead of at Pershing's headquarters in France. Dillon's job was to break up the bottlenecks in transportation within the United States and between ports in France and the United States which were strangling the flow of vital materials to our troops in the field. War *matériel* was piling up in the ports and freight yards and little was getting through to the fighting fronts. In the United States, Dillon unsnarled rail shipments by directing that non-vital loads be dropped off at way points and the empty cars rerouted to pick up vitally needed supplies.[26]

Two years in wartime Washington gave Dillon a world-wide perspective on economic and political conditions and greatly enriched his contacts. Dillon, as Baruch's assistant, interviewed many prominent businessmen, all seeking government contracts and procurement. Baruch's aide wielded his power with courtesy and diplomacy. Few of the mighty men of business who came to Washington daily asking for favors could visualize that this quiet, lean young man possessed the powers of those silent men who sat centuries ago in the chancelleries of Europe and ruled the world's trade routes.[27]

After the war, Dillon accompanied Baruch, who had been appointed a member of the American delegation, to the Versailles Treaty Conference concerned with German reparation payments. Thereafter, Baruch developed a close friendship with Dillon and became an important client and adviser of Dillon Read, helping to steer the Dodge deal to Dillon in 1925. Baruch was one of the most successful stock market speculators during the period between the two world wars and benefitted greatly from Dillon's investment insights.[28]

Returning to Wall Street in 1919, Dillon's grasp was now international and he soon had things humming in the old firm of William A. Read & Co. His key partners and staff were back in harness and raring to go. In rapid succession, Dillon launched a string of major financings in the 1920s that propelled his firm into the first rank of investment bankers just below J. P. Morgan and Kuhn Loeb.

After the war ended in 1919, the Read estate announced that it intended to withdraw its majority interest from the firm. The question was where the firm could get the capital to buy out the Read interests. According to Dillon's son, Douglas, his father used a portion of his profits from the phenol venture to help buy out the Read estate.[29] Actually Dillon, along with Henry Riter III, the firm's Philadelphia partner and branch manager, and William A. Phillips, put up the junior money, with the estate lending them an additional million dollars for one year to help them buy out the Read estate.[30]

The 1920s were an exciting and opportune time for aggressive men such as Clarence Dillon and his associates. The economy and the stock market were booming through most of the 1920s and Dillon made rapid strides in developing his financing programs. Within five years Dillon-led flotations compared favorably with those of the largest operations on Wall Street. Hugh Bullock, who ran several Dillon Read branch offices during his two year tenure in the firm in the 1920s, said he was always surprised that Morgan didn't hire Dillon from the beginning. Bullock added: "I have never met a man with the energy and sheer intellectual brilliance of Dillon. Dillon ran circles around Morgan, stole deals from right under his nose and was so fast that Morgan couldn't catch him or take business away from him."[31]

Dillon loved working on giant deals and upstaging the Wall Street establishment. Accordingly, he focused all of his efforts on bringing one or two mega-deals each year. But in doing so, few Wall Street houses researched deals as thoroughly as Dillon's; he refused to play long shots. Typically, he would accept only one or two out of every hundred deals brought to his attention. Douglas Dillon, his son, recalls his father's incredible energy and enthusiasm:

> In the twenties, he was downtown working his head off working late into the night [slamming together deals]. He'd work on Sundays . . . but he didn't bring his work home, leaving his business matters and dealings at the office. . . . My father didn't disregard his children even though he didn't see very much of us.[32]

Dillon utilized a client-oriented problem-solving technique in all of his deals. For example, he developed a major financing client, Youngstown Sheet & Tube, just after the first world war. The financing program began with a $5 million debt offering for Steel & Tube, a predecessor company created out of the Schlesinger family's holdings. This was followed by a $17.5 million preferred stock offering in 1919. Dillon soon lined up Allied Chemical and Dye as a major participant with an 18 percent interest. Then he restructured several of Schlesinger's other iron and steel interests into Steel & Tube financed by another $17.5 million preferred stock offering in 1920. Dillon followed that with a $10 million debt offering in 1921. All these financings were achieved without involving any commitment of capital by Dillon's firm; they flowed smoothly from the firm's carefully nurtured dealer syndicate that participated in all of Dillon's deals.[33]

Following the severe business recession of 1920-21, Dillon entered into a $5.3 million pool with Schlesinger to bring about in June 1922 the sale of Steel & Tube to Youngstown Sheet & Tube, a major steel company, for $33 million, making the company the fifth largest steel company in the country. The acquisition was financed by a debenture issue offered through the Dillon syndicate. Including the earlier financings, Dillon raised all told $100 million through his syndicate to finance the newly organized company.[34]

Another example occurred in 1926. After National Cash Register's rapid growth in the early 1920s, its founder, Frederick Patterson, was anxious to go public to cash in on his success. But the stock was owned by several family members with different objectives. Patterson wanted to cash in on part of his holdings if he could keep control; his sister, aunt and a cousin had other priorities—increased income in particular.[35]

Based on the publicity Dillon had received following his 1921 rescue of Goodyear, Stanley Allyn, Patterson's chief aide, recommended they contact Dillon to explore solutions to the problems associated with going public. After lengthy discussions, Dillon came up with a proposal to acquire the stock of the minority stockholders by recapitalizing the company under the laws of Maryland, which permitted stock provisions that preserved Patterson's control.[36]

Dillon's plan restructured the company's stock into two classes: 1,100,000 shares of "A" stock of no par to be offered at $50 a share to the public and 400,000 shares of "B" stock to be retained by Patterson. The "B" stock had the right to elect a majority of the directors as long as the company paid a $3-a-year dividend on the "A" stock. The Patterson family minority holders received Class "A" stock in exchange for their interests which afforded them a good dividend yield. In effect, so long as Patterson paid the $3-a-year dividend on the "A" stock, he would maintain complete control.[37] The 1926 public offering raised $55 million for the company and the Patterson family, the largest such common stock offering up to that time.[38]

Notwithstanding the intense pressure and rivalry of Wall Street, by the late 1920s Dillon would take several vacations a year usually involving one long trip to Europe, primarily France, for as much as three weeks where he pursued his business interests as well as indulged his taste for art and antiques. He foraged far and wide, searching in odd places for old furniture of simple design and looking for fine books. In between, Dillon enjoyed the leisure to think and reflect upon subjects far removed from the stock ticker.[39] He was fond of reading, especially biography and history. He had a fine collection of prints and etchings, including many Rembrandts and Whistlers. Occasionally he would indulge a weakness for sketching. His home resembled that of a literary man, an artist or a professor. The tables were strewn with etchings and prints.[40]

Dillon kept in physical shape by riding, walking and sitting-up exercises. Although he loved hunting and fishing, he rarely was able to pursue these hobbies because of the pressure of business. However, in August 1920, he did manage to take a hunting trip to Wyoming, camping in the woods and fishing and hunting with his son, Douglas. Their party included a guide, three wranglers and a cook.[41] Dillon also owned a salmon camp on the Restigouche River in New Brunswick, Canada, but he wasn't able to go there very often and it was sold in 1952. Along with three other men from college days, Dillon also had an interest in a shooting place in South Carolina but again, he didn't make much use of it. His main diversion from the frenetic world of Wall Street was quiet weekends with his family at his farm in Far Hills, New Jersey.[42]

Dillon considered new financing business at firm meetings which took place on most weekdays. Full assent of all partners was needed before new business would be accepted, and only if the partner involved was an expert in that area. This general rule permitted Dillon to participate in new, rapidly growing areas in which his associates had developed a special expertise.

One foray was in the energy field for which Dean Mathey had developed a special flair. Mathey had cut his teeth on energy investments with the development of Amerada, a Canadian company founded in 1920 by Lord Cowdray, a British investor, and headed by Everett Lee DeGolyer, the leading expert in oil field discovery methods, utilizing his knowledge of seismography and geology. Mathey was part of the Princeton crowd at Dillon Read. He was a tennis star at and after Princeton, defeating "Big Bill" Tilden in 1923 and coming within one set of defeating him again in the 1924 tennis championships.[43]

With Mathey and DeGolyer leading the way, Amerada soon forged ahead in the oil industry but DeGolyer advised Cowdray that as Amerada was foreign-controlled, it could not prospect for oil in Texas, the prime oil source in the mid-continental region. As a result, Dillon negotiated his firm's purchase of 51 percent of Amerada from DeGolyer, with Cowdray's approval in early 1926. Under the terms of the contract Dillon had absolute control for a period of ten years, with the right to name a majority of the board of directors![44] Dillon then organized his dealer syndicate to underwrite the initial public offering of 355,727 shares of Amerada at $26.[45]

Louisiana Land and Exploration Venture

While Amerada was a major success, the financing of Louisiana Land and Exploration Company, a venture capital deal done in early 1928, represented a mega-success story for Dillon and Mathey. As Mathey later related the story to one of his associates, "One day in the late 1920s this gentleman representing the ownership of Louisiana Land walked into Dillon Read's office and said they needed money." At that time, the company was a start-up speculation based on the prospects of developing oil and gas reserves on its 1,700,000 acres of swamps and bayous which lay across the southern portion of Louisiana. The company's only income consisted of modest fees paid by muskrat hunters for using the company's land holdings, which contained the nation's largest muskrat population.[46] The company also received income from shrimp harvested in the bayous;

they even sold brooms made from the stiff swamp grass.[47]

Mathey asked DeGolyer to test Louisiana Land's holdings to determine the prospects for oil. Through his oil prospecting subsidiary, Geophysical Research Corporation, DeGolyer explored over one million acres of Louisiana's lands and found them to have a high potential for a major oil find. Mathey recommended to Dillon that they provide initial financing for this promising start-up venture. Dillon agreed and then sold Louisiana Land bonds and common stock privately to the firm's investment trust, United States & Foreign Securities Corp., and to several of the firm's partners as well as several Dillon Read clients to raise money for the company in 1927.[48]

Then, in May of 1928, Dillon raised an additional $1 million in capital through an initial public offering of 500,000 shares of Louisiana common stock at $2 per share. Much to the partners' dismay, the offering was unsuccessful; as a result, Dillon's partners and the firm were obligated to take up the unsold shares, which they added to their holdings acquired the previous year. In the after market following the failed deal, the stock traded inactively and fell sharply in price.

Finally, in late 1928, the company contracted with the Texas Company (subsequently renamed Texaco) to explore and develop the company's oil and gas resources in return for a 25-percent royalty on all oil and gas produced from its lands. Thereafter, Texaco found a great quantity of oil and gas on the company's lands, and the discovery ranked among the major oil finds of all time. The resulting royalties caused Louisiana Land's earnings to soar, and Dillon's partners and other stockholders who bought shares in the embryonic company (and had the good sense to retain them) made fortunes. One Dillon Read secretary, at the recommendation of her boss, bought 3,000 shares of Louisiana Land stock in the late twenties at 50 cents a share; that investment soared in value to over $6 million by the early 1950s.[49]

Nitze also bought 300 shares when he joined the firm in 1929 with $1,000 his mother had given him for a birthday gift. This multiplied in the subsequent years with stock splits and stock dividends to 15,000 shares worth almost a million dollars. Louisiana Land was an aggressive Dillon venture, but as usual he insisted on painstaking research before he made a commitment. Nitze notes, "the prospects were so promising that it clearly qualified as an investment . . . a venture capital deal, yes, but not high risk; close to no risk."[50] Thereafter, Dillon became a leading oil industry financier with Standard Oil of California, Union Oil of California, Royal Dutch Petroleum and Texaco as major clients in addition to Amerada and Louisiana Land and Development.[51]

Although Dillon spoke slowly and softly with somewhat of a southern accent, he carried a big stick and he was ruthless. According to Nitze,

"Dillon ran the business with an iron hand; he was a hard boiled taskmaster." Nitze recalled that when he first joined Dillon, "I did a deal [poorly] involving United Light and Power, a large utility holding company, and I lost a couple of million dollars of the firm's capital as well as control of the venture." The day after that disastrous event became known, Dillon avoided contact with Nitze when he came into the office, refusing to have anything to do with him. "Dillon didn't know who I was; I was a `non-person.´"

In a way, Nitze's purgatory was the best thing that could have happened to him; it brought him into closer contact with Forrestal, Mathey and the other partners. They sympathized with Nitze saying, "this man is human; he has gotten into the same difficulties with the old man that we have had." Later, Nitze succeeded in regaining control of United Light and Power, recovering Dillon's investment in the process. That done, Dillon recognized Nitze again and he was released from purgatory but Dillon continued to be mean and unforgiving to his associates.[52] Dillon's grandson, Philip Allen, agrees that his grandfather "was a bit ruthless in his quest for fortune" adding, "I'm sure he stepped on some people's toes on the way."[53]

Bullock, another associate, said, "the stories about Dillon being a mean, tight-fisted, bastard were true," and added, "I have never met a man that was as tough and as hard boiled as Dillon. If you made a mistake he would raise hell and you would never hear the end of it. He was a taskmaster and very arbitrary and tight fisted. . . . Eberstadt got his mean streak from Dillon . . . but `Eber´ had a warm human quality underneath all of the hard exterior; Dillon did not—he was hard and inhuman." Even so, Bullock liked the old tyrant for what he was and for his incredible brilliance.[54]

Dorothy Dillon Eweson, Dillon's daughter, notes:

My father never had patience with stupidity. . . . When he was younger, he would blow up when he was working under pressure . . . [especially when an associate did something dumb]. He had a very explosive and short temper. . . . But I don't think that he . . . would even remember [the incident] two minutes later. There was no feeling that he didn't like that fellow. He would tell him he was dumb in a loud tone of voice [and that was the end of it].[55]

Marjorie Wellbrock, Dillon's private secretary, agrees that "Dillon had an explosive temper and would yell at people in the office on occasion [which would cause the entire office to stop in their tracks]."[56]

Douglas Dillon adds:

Well, like everybody, my father had all sorts of sides. In the office, he could be pretty tough. But, with me and my sister he never was harsh; he was very

easy and considerate. But in business, he was tough and drove a pretty hard
bargain. . . .[57]

While the public thought of Dillon as a swashbuckling robber baron in
the 1920s, his son, Douglas, counters this view with: "He always was very
careful, and . . . looked thoroughly into everything he touched." Eberstadt
later explained that "the public looked on our deals as speculations but all
of Dillon's deals were rooted in careful analyses based on known facts. [As
far as we were concerned,] they were investments—not speculations which
are based on chance."

Philip Allen, Dillon's older grandson, reflects:

> My grandfather was definitely a risk taker in those days but he was very
> smart himself and he had a group at Dillon Read that were equally smart
> who had been with him all the way. So that even though his deals and
> investments were definitely risky, he mitigated that risk . . . by really doing
> his homework.[58]

Dillon's thoroughness saved him from many of the disasters of the era.
For example, he never went along with Ivar Kreuger's schemes that
defrauded so many of the prominent investment banks and commercial
banks during the 1920s and 1930s.[59] Nonetheless, many of Dillon's closest
partners never really trusted him and his toughness led to many disputes
with unfortunate consequences. One example: Ferdinand Eberstadt, the
partner chiefly responsible for the spectacular growth of the firm's
European business, was fired in 1928 following a dispute over the size of
Eberstadt's share of the partnership's profits. Dillon's son Douglas, however,
thought that the split-up would have happened eventually given the strong
independent wills of both men.[60] Joseph Haywood, Dillon's long-time aide,
agrees: "Dillon had an explosive and volatile personality; it was in the
man's makeup."[61]

An anecdote underscores Dillon's autocratic control of the firm. In late
1920, he told the partners: "Gentlemen, I have brought in 85 percent of the
business here and henceforth the name of the firm shall be Dillon, Read &
Co. Those who do not like the arrangement can withdraw." Dillon's
partners talked it over among themselves and then decided to go along with
Dillon's plan. The partners realized that it weakened the public image of
the firm if the name of the principal partner was not in the firm's masthead.
Ford and Dodge typified the motor car business just as Westinghouse
typified the electrical industry. Thus, Clarence Dillon's name represented
a dynamic force in Wall Street which should be exploited in the firm's name.
Accordingly, on January 14, 1921, the name of the firm was changed to
Dillon, Read & Co., Inc.[62]

Dillon Read's main office at 28 Nassau Street (at the corner of an old fortress-like, block-square stone building) was not what one might have expected to house Wall Street's fastest-growing investment bank. The entrance was unimpressive, the carpets and furniture old and worn. Yet this was the global nerve center for Dillon's far-flung financings.

Dillon's private office, however, was the one exception to this austerity; it had been designed by Lewis Comfort Tiffany and featured a fireplace in which hickory wood was burned during cold weather. One day billows of smoke came out of all the floors up to the roof of the building because Dillon's fireplace chimney had not been cleaned. Nassau, Cedar and Liberty Streets were bumper to bumper with fire trucks and equipment and curious crowds. Fortunately for the staff, Dillon was not in the office that day.[63]

At 28 Nassau Street, Dillon would have the barber on the ninth floor of the building across the street come over to his office to give him a trim. Dillon's door was always locked shut; *no one* could enter unless Dillon released the lock by pushing a button on his desk. There were times when he had an important telephone call and the barber had to leave his office until he had finished the call; sometimes this happened repeatedly during the course of one haircut. After several of these frustrating incidents, the barber refused to come over to give Dillon his trim.[64]

In 1928, Dillon moved his private office and dining room onto the fortieth floor of the Equitable Building across the street, to insulate himself from the turbulent pace of the headquarters at 28 Nassau. His personal office had the atmosphere of the corner of a private club. His desk was a clean table with a single telephone. He was always cool, and sure of himself. A world globe located in a window recess and a few prints of old New York on the walls tastefully set off the room.[65] Later Dillon moved his private office and staff to 40 Wall Street.

Dillon had an incredible knack for separating fact from fiction, for seeing the truth even when the pace of activity approached chaos. For example, Nitze was out at Dillon's estate, Dunwalke, in the late 1930s when the Orson Welles NBC dramatization of an invasion by a Mars space ship was broadcast. At first, Chandler, the butler, came into the dining room and told Dillon excitedly about the news and urged him to leave for his safety. Dillon told him to check the news on the radio. When Chandler returned, he whispered in Dillon's ear that NBC was reporting the attack but CBS had nothing on it. With that, Dillon smiled and dismissed the reported attack as a hoax, adding: "Well, NBC wouldn't have an exclusive!"[66]

Clarence Dillon's success as a financier lay in his genius for getting the best out of his associates and using their initiative and knowledge to supplement his own abilities. He had a knack for inspiring his associates even though many of them secretly resented him and few trusted him. An example of Dillon's ability to develop new talent is James V. Forrestal, who emerged during the 1920s as perhaps the most dynamic of Dillon's new breed of investment bankers.

Forrestal was recruited by Dean Mathey when he was in his senior year at Princeton but Forrestal at first decided to try other fields without success. After serving in naval aviation during the first world war, Forrestal decided to get into the investment business to make his fortune.[67] After a short training program in New York, he started selling bonds working out of the Albany office, where he was outstanding from the start. His career thereafter was meteoric. Within a short period the business had expanded sufficiently that Forrestal was permitted to recruit a sales force to serve the rapidly expanding Albany branch which served all of the cities of upper New York State.

Based on Forrestal's success in upstate New York, Dillon called Forrestal back to New York to succeed Phillips as retail sales manager in charge of a retail sales force that had grown to over 900 men.[68] In addition, Forrestal was put in charge of new issue syndications and played a major role in pricing new securities offerings, a critical factor in securities underwritings. In today's investment banking business, Forrestal's role would be shared by any number of corporate finance specialists.

Forrestal worked hard at his new assignment, rarely leaving the office before 9 P.M. and often not until after midnight when a new securities issue was in syndication.[69] Dillon made Forrestal a partner in 1923 "because it was cheaper [than paying] him commissions," Arthur Krock later quipped. Eberstadt's son, Frederick, however, recalled his father's remark that Dillon regarded Forrestal as "the one [of all his young salesmen] with the dedication and chutzpa to make it big." Clearly, Dillon probably felt genuine affection for him.[70] After Dillon retired from active management in 1930, Forrestal took over the day-to-day management of the firm and became president in 1938 when he was only forty-six years of age.

While Morgan and Kuhn Loeb remained the twin pillars of finance in the 1920s, Dillon Read's collection of ambitious young turks (led by the Baron) pushed the firm forward into the front ranks of Wall Street.[71] Clarence Dillon's success possessed much of the romance of the many "Napoleons" of finance of the previous century, and he threatened to eclipse all his predecessors. Even with all his daring, Dillon was never guilty of doing anything inconsistent with the highest standards of banking of that era although many of his swashbuckling techniques later were outlawed by the SEC and the Congress.

During Dillon's most active participation in the firm, 1919 through 1929, total underwritings, including participations, came to $3.6 billion, about 7 percent of all such financings for U.S. corporations.[72] He continued to gain on his competitors during the second half of the decade, ranking just behind his arch rivals, J. P. Morgan and Kuhn Loeb in total originations. Although trailing the leaders in total volume, Dillon's deals were more profitable, and a partnership in Dillon Read fetched a much higher price than a partnership in Morgan or Kuhn Loeb in the late 1920s.[73] Clarence Dillon, the "Wolf of Wall Street" in Forrestal's respectful jeer, was on his way to the pinnacle of finance as the giddy decade drew to a close.[74]

The roaring twenties also witnessed important changes in the character of the securities markets. Some of these developments had been in the making from before the first world war, others grew out of the conflict itself, and still others were the result of postwar developments. Stocks, for example, became more popular than bonds; securities of new industries, such as radios, cars and energy, outranked those of railroads, and the distribution of foreign issues grew appreciably. The increase in U.S. foreign trade, moreover, called for new services from investment bankers and attracted the competition of other financial intermediaries. Dillon capitalized on many of these trends including the closed-end investment trust which enhanced Dillon's ability to finance his deals.

Closed-End Investment Trusts

Dillon pioneered investment trust flotations with twin offerings of his trusts, raising $90 million. Dillon's first investment trust offering, United States and Foreign Securities (US&FS), was made in 1924 and raised $30 million. US&FS was highly leveraged with three tiers of securities, consisting of two classes of preferred stock and one class of common stock. Dillon controlled a majority of the common stock and voting control; a second offering of a companion trust (also under Dillon's control) raised an additional $60 million in 1928.[75]

Copying Dillon's format, Wall Street's leading houses followed with a string of investment trust offerings; by 1929 total trust assets had soared to over $7 billion. Dillon promoted the trusts to the investing public as a way of getting the same investment advice and buying power as the very rich and powerful. Bullock stated that the Dillon-sponsored trusts gave the public an opportunity to tap in on Dillon's investment brains.[76]

Besides giving the public a superior investment vehicle, the trusts enabled Dillon to enhance the power of his syndicates through his power to use the trusts to purchase the firm's "undigested" (i.e., unsold) securities positions from earlier underwritings. The SEC later concluded that the trusts allowed the firm to unload underwriting positions that were hard to sell to the public.[77]

However, Dillon testified before the Pecora hearings in 1933 that only 7.8 percent of the trusts' purchases since their organization were of Dillon offerings and that the trusts realized net profits on those purchases of 10.5

percent.[78] But Dillon's use of the trusts' assets made a major contribution to some of the firm's important financings. For example, US&FS was included in Dillon's 382-member underwriting syndicate that executed the spectacular $146 million buyout of Dodge Motor Car Company in 1925.

In the 1929 market boom, the golden touch of Clarence Dillon and the trusts' built-in leverage extracted maximum benefits from the great bull market then exploding. US&FS's common stock soared, at one point reaching $72 a share in trading on the New York Stock Exchange. However, leverage is a two-edged sword, with deep downside risks as well as upside rewards—a fact that many investors learned too late in the 1929 Crash.[79] Following the Crash, US&FS common fell to a low of $2 in 1932.

The Crash hurt all the closed-end trusts because of the disastrous impact of leverage in falling markets. Goldman Sachs Trading Corp. was probably the most prominent casualty, falling from its leverage-induced 1929 high of $400 a share to only 12-1/2 cents a share in 1932. Many investors were wiped out, including the celebrated comedian, Eddie Cantor, who subsequently made Goldman Sachs Trading Corporation the regular butt of many of his jokes as part of his repertoire.[80] Eddie Cantor later filed a $100 million suit against Goldman Sachs. So many suits were filed against Goldman Sachs that brokers with a taste for black humor would call the firm and ask for the Litigation Department.[81]

US&FS net asset investment performance came back from the 1929 Crash and prospered in the postwar period when it achieved an average annual return of 14.1 percent compared with 12.8 percent for the *Standard & Poor's* 500 stock index.[82] However, in the early 1980s, it was still trading at a deep discount on the New York Stock Exchange from its asset value reflecting the loss of investor confidence in closed-end trusts following the 1929 Crash.

The Dillon family owned in the early 1980s approximately one-third of the US&FS common stock in various accounts acquired from the original flotations of the trusts in 1924 and 1928. Since the investment needs of the Dillon family interests had changed considerably after fifty years, many in the family wished to sell but refrained from doing so because the trust shares were still selling at a substantial discount from their book value. Merging with an open-end mutual fund, a procedure a number of closed-end trusts used to eliminate the discount, would have posed many legal difficulties and tax problems. Accordingly, the trust lawyers recommended liquidation as the least costly solution. A plan of dissolution was approved in late 1983 and the trust was dissolved by several liquidating dividends in 1984; the Dillon family interests received about $60 million in this dissolution.[83]

The market continued its sharp advance in 1928 and 1929, with a rising wave of speculative fever reaching a peak in October 1929, shortly before the end of the decade. Earlier, Dillon had exploited this boom by building up a large retail branch office system to back up his investment banking operation. By 1927, Dillon Read had over 1,000 salesmen in its various offices. Several branches, such as Boston, Philadelphia, Pittsburgh and Chicago were quite sizable. There were three large offices in New York City alone with well over 100 salesmen in each office.[84] Other branches were much smaller, some essentially one-man shops.

Due largely to the expansion prompted by the development of the retail business, the Dillon Read payroll more than doubled between 1922 and 1925. Dillon kept 40 percent of profits, which quintupled in the first half of the 1920s, dividing up the balance among the partners based primarily on his perception of each partner's value to the firm and performance over the previous year.[85]

New Dillon Read sales recruits entered a training class of perhaps thirty to forty recruits, where they would be briefed on the bond business and then given a desk and telephone in the office to which they were assigned. Forrestal conducted the Dillon Read sales training school which was among the best on Wall Street. In fact, some of the firm's retail clients offered to pay the firm to get their sons enrolled in the sales training program at Dillon Read.[86]

Dillon's salesmen differed from other securities brokers in that they offered only the issues underwritten by the firm; the firm did not provide a general investment service involving all securities available in the market. Each day the salesmen were told what merchandise was available and they would concentrate on placing these securities with customers. If a client wanted to buy or sell a security not originated by the firm but traded in the secondary markets, the Dillon salesmen would take the order and utilize Dominick & Dominick or Shields & Co., among others, to complete the transaction.

Although Dillon Read would make a market in its own originations, a client wishing to buy bonds in the secondary market would find that the spread between the bid and ask usually was quite large. Dillon kept abreast of the trading in all the securities originated by his firm. Whoever was working on the trading desk had the responsibility of keeping Dillon's stock and bond list of over 100 securities up to date at all times, as well as advising Dillon of any unusual trades that occurred.[87]

Augmenting the investment trust and domestic underwriting business, Dillon played a major role in the placement of foreign underwritten issues in the United States. The boom in foreign securities flotations started after the implementation of the Dawes Plan for Reparation Payments in 1924. Thereafter, American investors purchased $4.6 billion in foreign issues, of which Dillon's firm accounted for about one-third. At the same time, foreigners increased their purchases of new American issues so that there was a two-way flow of capital between the United States and Europe. The outflow from the United States, however, greatly exceeded the inflow from abroad. To handle the huge wave of foreign financings, Dillon opened an office in Paris at 39 rue Cambon, directly across from the Ritz Hotel, with an extensive staff to find new issues of foreign securities which were then syndicated by the New York office to the American market. (See Chapter 6 for a detailed discussion of Dillon's foreign financing activities.)

Despite this hectic business pace, Dillon managed to further his social aspirations maintaining a number of stately residences from which he sought to achieve access to society. In 1919, he rented a thirteen-room apartment with four bedrooms that comprised the entire seventh floor of 635 Park Avenue; the apartment was grandiose, with views in all directions. The family stayed there for nine to ten months of the year during most of the 1920s. For the rest of the year, the Dillons lived at the family mansion in Far Hills, New Jersey, or at their summer place at Dark Harbor on Islesboro off the Maine coast.[88] Dillon also maintained a small apartment at the Ritz Tower on Park Avenue. Dillon stayed mostly in this apartment in the summers during the 1920s when the pressure of business prevented him from spending much time in Maine—it being too far to commute.[89]

Reflecting his new-found wealth and power, Dillon and his wife decided to rent a townhouse in 1926 and 1927 to expand their foothold in society. The next year, they bought several adjoining lots on fashionable East 80th Street just off Park Avenue as a potential building site for a townhouse of their own. They then tore down three small houses on their land, using two of these lots at 124 East 80th Street for their new house[90] and selling the third to George Whitney, J. P. Morgan's senior partner, to complete the site on which Whitney built his own townhouse in 1930.[91]

Dillon began building his townhouse in 1928 from plans by the noted architect, Mott B. Schmidt; it was completed in 1929. Dillon adopted the same Georgian style he had used for the main house at Dunwalke in Far Hills as well as the large homes he built there for his son and granddaughter. William Vincent Astor, the real estate tycoon and great-great grandson of John Jacob Astor, also built a neo-classic Greco-Roman-style white limestone townhouse next door to the Dillons.

When the Dillons moved into the townhouse on East 80th Street, they increased their house staff from about five to fourteen to take care of the thirty rooms.[92] In addition to this staff, there was a night watchman plus a motorcycle guard who came several times each night to check security. All of this precaution was caused by the continuing fear of terrorism following the bomb attack on Morgan's office building on Wall Street in September 1920. To protect against such attacks, Dillon also hired five ex-marines as armed security guards at Dillon Read's offices at 28 Nassau Street. At East 80th Street, the police kept "No Parking" signs in front of the Dillon, Astor and Whitney townhouses for security purposes so that only Dillon and his immediate neighbors were permitted to park their limousines—in effect free parking courtesy of the Police Department![93]

The East 80th Street townhouse fitted nicely into Dillon's social aspirations with two chieftains of finance and society living next to him—Astor on his right and Whitney on his left. One might question whether he felt comfortable, living between the senior partners of two competitors. Nitze quipped: "Dillon loved it."

Dillon also was very careful to gain favorable public attention by acting on behalf of public-spirited causes—especially if these could be financed at nominal cost. Such was the case with his dramatic move to replace the burned-out and gutted locker house at Harvard following a devastating fire. The previous all-wood locker house burned down early in the morning on January 14, 1930. After the fire was put out, Dillon's son, Douglas, a Harvard junior at the time and the next year's football manager, phoned his father in New York and got him to pledge $500,000 to build a new all-brick field house also in Dillon's signature Georgian style (appropriately named the Dillon Field House) on the same site where the old one had stood.[94] Reflecting concern for academic traditions as well, Dillon endowed two professorships as a fitting additional touch.[95]

Notes

1. *Anne's Story.*
2. *Anne's Story.*
3. Forbes, Bruce C., "Clarence Dillon, The Man Who Bought Dodge," *Forbes*, p. 166.
4. Secretary's Fourth Report, June, 1920, *Harvard College Class of 1905*, p. 251.
5. *Anne's Story.*
6. *Anne's Story.*
7. *Anne's Story* and Forbes, Bruce C., "Clarence Dillon, The Man Who Bought Dodge," *Forbes*, p. 165.
8. Forbes, Bruce C., "Clarence Dillon, The Man Who Bought Dodge," *Forbes*, p. 165.
9. Sobel, Robert, *The Life and Times of Dillon Read*, p. 41.
10. *Anne's Story* and written comment from Paul H. Nitze received in January 1993.
11. "Nicholas F. Brady: The New Deal-Maker at the Old Guard Firm," *Business Week*, May 15, 1978, p. 45.
12. Perez/Willett, *The Will to Win*, p. 60.
13. *Anne's Story.*
14. Winkler, *The New Yorker*, p. 30.
15. Winkler, *The New Yorker*, p. 31.
16. "William A. Read, Death and Career," *New York Times*, April 8, 1916.
17. "Asked to Construe Read Will Clause," *New York Herald*, April 28, 1916.
18. Mathey, Dean, *Fifty Years of Wall Street*, pp. 4-5.
19. *Anne's Story.*

20. *Anne's Story.*

21. *Anne's Story.*

22. Winkler, *The New Yorker*, p. 31.

23. *Anne's Story.*

24. Baruch, Bernard M., *The Public Years*, p. 80.

25. Author's survey of Dillon Read financings.

26. *Anne's Story* and Douglas Dillon Interview, May 23, 1991.

27. Winkler, *The New Yorker*, p. 31.

28. Mathey, Dean, *Fifty Years of Wall Street*, pp. 6-8.

29. Douglas Dillon interview, May 23 and October 29, 1991.

30. *Anne's Story.*

31. Hugh Bullock telephone interview, April 11, 1991.

32. Douglas Dillon interview, May 23, 1991.

33. Hoopes/Brinkley, *Driven Patriot*, p. 53 and Sobel, Robert, *The Life and Times of Dillon Read*, pp. 53, 55, 80 and 81.

34. Hoopes/Brinkley, *Driven Patriot*, p. 53 and Sobel, Robert, *The Life and Times of Dillon Read*, pp. 53, 55, 80 and 81.

35. Allyn, Stanley C., *My Half Century with NCR*, New York, 1967, pp. 56-7.

36. Allyn, Stanley C., *My Half Century with NCR*, pp. 56-7.

37. Allyn, Stanley C., *My Half Century with NCR*, pp. 56-7.

38. Sobel, Robert, *The Life and Times of Dillon Read*, pp. 130-1.

39. Forbes, Bruce C., "Clarence Dillon, The Man Who Bought Dodge," *Forbes*, pp. 163-4.

40. Winkler, *The New Yorker*, p. 33.

41. *Anne's Story.*

42. Forbes, Bruce C., "Clarence Dillon, The Man Who Bought Dodge," *Forbes*, pp. 163-4.

43. "Dean Mathey, 81, Banking Official," *New York Times*, April 17, 1972 and *New York Sun*, June 2, 1924.

44. Mathey, Dean, *Fifty Years of Wall Street*, pp. 42-5.

45. "Dillon Read Buys Control of Amerada," *New York Times*, February 2, 1926.

46. Perez/Willett, *The Will to Win*, pp. 119-20.

47. Marjorie Wellbrock interview, October 30, 1991.

48. Sobel, Robert, *The Life and Times of Dillon Read*, p. 89.

49. Perez/Willett, *The Will to Win*, pp. 43-4.

50. Paul H. Nitze interview, November 11, 1991.

51. Testimony of James V. Forrestal before Senate War Investigating Committee, *Congressional Record*, March 31, 1948, p. 3805.

52. Paul H. Nitze interview, November 11, 1991.

53. Philip D. Allen interview, April 9, 1992.

54. Hugh Bullock telephone interview, April 11, 1991.

55. Mrs. Dorothy Dillon Eweson interview, October 1 and October 4, 1991.

56. Marjorie Wellbrock interview, October 30, 1991.

57. Douglas Dillon interview, May 23, 1991.

58. Philip D. Allen interview, April 9, 1992.

59. *Anne's Story* and Douglas Dillon interview, May 23, 1991.

60. Douglas Dillon interview, May 3, 1984.

61. Joseph Haywood interview, October 28, 1991.

62. "The Way of the Winner," by Walter P. Barclay, *Wall Street Journal*, April 13, 1925 and *New York Times*, January 14, 1921.

63. Joseph Haywood interview, October 28, 1991.

64. Joseph Haywood interview, October 28, 1991.

65. Winkler, *The New Yorker*, p. 32.

66. Paul H. Nitze telephone interview, April 15, 1991.

67. Paul H. Nitze interview, November 11, 1991.

68. *Anne's Story.*

69. Mathey, Dean, *Fifty Years of Wall Street*, p. 63.

70. Hoopes/Brinkley, *Driven Patriot*, p. 54.

71. Hoopes/Brinkley, *Driven Patriot*, pp. 54-5.

72. Author's survey of Dillon Read financing.

73. Winkler, John, *The New Yorker*, p. 29.

74. Janeway, Eliot, "Balancing the Books," *Barron's*, June 4, 1990.

75. In the first offering in 1924, Dillon Read purchased all of the 50,000 shares of second preferred stock for $5 million and received as a bonus an additional 750,000 shares of the one million shares of common stock, for which it paid the nominal sum of $100,000. Thus, Dillon achieved control of the new trust's assets for just $5.1 million. US&FS was run as a separate unit from Dillon Read's other operations although it was initially domiciled in Dillon Read's offices.

The second trust offering in 1928, United States and International Securities (US&IS), also consisted of three tiers (500,000 units of two classes of preferred stock and common stock). Dillon used $10 million in accumulated profits from the first trust to purchase effective control of the second trust. US&IS was operated as a majority-owned subsidiary of US&FS and later formally merged into US&FS by exchange of stock. (Sources: Carosso, Vincent, *Investment Banking in America*, Cambridge, Mass., 1970, pp. 290-91 and *Moody's Manual of Banks and Finance Companies*, 1960 edition, p. 571.)

76. Bullock, Hugh, *The Story of Investment Companies*, New York, 1959, p. 20.

77. Sobel, Robert, *The Life and Times of Dillon Read*, pp. 88-9, Note 39, pp. 369-70.

78. United States, 73rd Congress, 1st session, Senate, Committee on Banking and Currency, *Stock Exchange Practices*, pt. 4, Dillon, Read & Co., October 3-13, 1933; hereinafter referred to as "The Pecora Hearings."

79. Phalon, Richard, "O Death, Where is Thy Sting?" *Forbes*, December 5, 1983, p. 199.

80. Brooks, John, *The Takeover Game*, New York, 1987, pp. 81-2.

81. Chernow, Ron, *The House of Morgan: An American Banking Dynasty and the Rise of Modern Finance*, New York, 1990, pp. 319-20, hereinafter referred to as Chernow, Ron, *The House of Morgan*.

82. US&FS annual reports for year ending December 31, 1983, p. 7 as supplemented by US&FS data contained in *Moody's Bank & Finance Manual*, 1960 edition, p. 572. *Standard & Poor's* 500 Stock Return from "Stocks, Bonds, Bills and Inflation," by Roger G. Ibbotson and Rex A. Sinquefield, *The Financial Analysts Research Foundation*, 1977, as updated by Ibbotson Associates in 1992.

83. Phalon, "O Death, Where is Thy Sting?" *Forbes*, p. 200.

84. Joseph Haywood interview, October 28, 1991.

85. Sobel, Robert, *The Life and Times of Dillon Read*, p. 136.

86. Joseph Haywood interview, October 28, 1991.

87. Joseph Haywood interview, October 28, 1991.

88. *Anne's Story.*

89. Dorothy Dillon Eweson interview, October 1 and 4, 1991.

90. Mrs. Dorothy Dillon Eweson, written comments received May 12, 1993.

91. *Anne's Story* and "Clarence Dillon Buys Site on East 80th Street for Home," *New York Times*, April 15, 1927.

92. Mrs. Dorothy Dillon Eweson interview, October 1 and 4, 1991.

93. *Anne's Story.*

94. "Clarence Dillon Gives New Field House to Harvard University," *New York Times*, January 16, 1930 and the "People" column, *Time*, January 27, 1930, p. 58.

95. *Anne's Story.*

4

The Dodge Coup

Clarence Dillon's rise to fame had been meteoric and by the mid-1920s he had become a major force to reckon with on Wall Street. His penchant was for spectacular mega-deals, focusing his financings on new rapidly expanding growth fields. By far, his most spectacular financing was his $146 million cash buyout in mid-1925 of Dodge Brothers, the number three auto maker. The buyout, the largest cash transaction ever, shocked Wall Street and was heralded by the press as the deal of the century.

By the 1920s, major innovations had transformed the motor car from a rich man's toy to the most sought after possession on the American market. Most of the founders of major automobile companies were still alive and active and the public regarded their products as not only automobiles but the personification of human beings, read about in newspapers and magazines and seen in newsreels. Earlier in the decade, Dillon had become a part of this folk hero cult through his inspired rescue of Goodyear Tire, then tottering on the brink of financial bankruptcy as a result of the severe depression of 1921 (see Chapter 1).

Just before the Goodyear rescue, on January 1, 1920, two of the most flamboyant entrepreneurs in the motor field, John and Horace Dodge, made their way to the Ritz Carlton Hotel on Manhattan's Madison Avenue. Six years before, they had established Dodge Brothers, Inc., and the company had been flooded with more than 22,000 applications for dealerships based on Dodge's role in supplying major components for the legendary Ford Model T.

The Dodge brothers had been in the manufacturing business together in the Detroit area since the beginning of the century, establishing their own machine shop in 1901 in Detroit with a work force of eleven men initially making parts for Oldsmobile.[1] At that time, Henry Ford had developed the prototype of the low-cost Model T and was trying to organize a company to produce it. He struck a bargain with the Dodge brothers by which each brother received a $5,000 interest in the business paid in Ford stock for producing 650 chassis. Thereafter, the Dodge Brothers Company grew along with Henry Ford.[2]

In 1914, the Dodge brothers began producing their own car. The Dodge cars proved sturdy and reliable and sales reached 18,000 in 1915, the first full year of operation. The Dodge car was so rugged that the following year the U.S. Army ordered several Dodge trucks for General Pershing's fruitless campaign to capture Pancho Villa, the Mexican bandit guerilla leader. A young cavalry lieutenant, George S. Patton, Jr., reported to his superiors: "The motor car is the modern war horse." Following Dodge's early success, the French army reequipped its mobile forces in the first world war with a hastily requisitioned fleet of Dodge vehicles.[3] The two military campaigns proved the Dodge automobile's value. Later, the development of the U.S. Army tank corp (a military offspring of the automobile) led to spectacular victories for the United States and its allies in the second world war.[4]

Over the years since their start in 1914, the Dodge brothers had built up a dealer organization of formidable loyalty, designed and produced a sturdy car for it to sell, and basked in the resulting profits. In the days when a Cadillac engine purred and a Ford engine still rattled, the Dodge engine did neither: it chugged. The Dodge car was small, black, unfashionable, and gadgetless, but so were the times in which it moved. Dodge advertising stressed the Dodge car's dependability and Dodge owners loyally stood behind the Dodge brand.[5]

After the end of the war, Dodge launched a major expansion financed in large part by the $25 million the Dodge brothers received in 1919 from Ford in settlement of their stockholder suit.[6] By 1920, Dodge sales soared to 145,389 cars with $161 million in revenues and a net profit of $18.6 million; sales more than doubled by 1926.[7]

The Dodge brothers weren't prepared for the enormous wealth suddenly thrust upon them. Joseph Thompson, one of the original Dodge dealers in 1914, noted they were "pretty crude," best remembered for their off-duty antics—usually performed by John, the elder of the two. Once he smashed all of the light bulbs in the chandeliers of the banquet hall in Detroit's Book-Cadillac Hotel; on another occasion, in a drunken rage, Dodge pulled a gun and forced a saloon operator to dance while he smashed glasses against the bar mirror. Then, in another temper tantrum, John Dodge called the publisher of the *Detroit Times* out of his home and knocked him unconscious in retaliation for critical comments about Dodge that had appeared in his paper.[8]

On Saturday, January 3, 1920, the annual automobile show opened at

Grand Central Palace on Lexington Avenue in mid-town New York City and the Dodge brothers were in town to attend the big show and exhibit their automobiles.   It had been extremely cold and raw with the thermometer falling to 10 degrees in the morning and hovering in the low twenties all afternoon. After returning to the Ritz in the evening, the chilled brothers opened a bottle of bootleg liquor (prohibition was in full force).

Shortly afterwards, the world was shocked to learn that John Dodge lay near death and his brother was seriously ill from wood alcohol poisoning.[9] John died first, succumbing at half past 10 o'clock on January 14.   His brother, Horace E. Dodge, lingered longer, finally passing away eleven months later from the after effects of cirrhosis of the liver.[10] After twenty stormy years, death had suddenly ended the lives of these two brothers who had always been inseparable.[11]

After the death of the founders, the Dodge company continued to expand in the early 1920s but there was fear for the estates of the two widows of the founders. While the estates were valued at well over $100 million, dynamic changes in the motor car business caused the widows to favor a sale of the business and that news leaked out into the market place. The widows had remarried men preoccupied with the theater and they soon lost interest in the automotive business; moreover, none of the Dodge children were engaged in the business.[12] Soon no less than three Wall Street houses were pursuing a buyout including J. P. Morgan; there is some indication that Dillon may have also shown an interest in making a bid at this point.[13]

Then, at the suggestion of Bernard Baruch, the family agreed to meet with A. Charles Schwartz, a New York broker interested in arranging for the sale of the company. Baruch and Schwartz were close friends, even sharing a box seat at Madison Square Garden; they also co-ventured several daring and successful speculations. Against the advice of Dodge's senior management, Schwartz persuaded the widows to give him an option to purchase Dodge Brothers. The option gave Schwartz an inside track into arranging a buyout.

When Schwartz asked Baruch for advice on what to do next, Baruch replied, "Go to my friend, Clarence Dillon." Baruch knew Dillon from his work as his deputy on the War Industries Board in the first world war and he knew Dillon would exploit the opportunity. So Schwartz took the option to Dillon, who agreed to pay him a finder's fee based on a percentage of the purchase price in the event Dillon got the deal. They recorded that agreement in a formal memorandum of understanding.[14]

Not aware of the Schwartz option, J. P. Morgan & Co. dispatched representatives to the Dodge facilities in Hamtramck, Michigan, just outside Detroit. Morgan had some experience in the industry, having financed several auto companies, and would later serve as General Motors's investment banker. Morgan believed Dodge would make an ideal fit into General Motors's family of cars. As an added incentive, buying Dodge would permit General Motors to sell to Dodge immense quantities of parts: 200,000 radiators and carburetors a year, for instance, as well as a myriad of other parts. Dodge was a prize well worth striving for and the house of Morgan gathered its ablest financiers for advice on the figure to be bid. Earlier, General Motors had offered Dodge $100 million but the Dodge management deferred a decision.[15] The Morgan bankers were confident that $132 million would win the prize, and they believed the Dodge company was theirs.

When the Morgan partners learned that Dillon was also negotiating with the Dodge widows, they told Clarence Dillon to step aside as Morgan was intent on acquiring Dodge for its client, General Motors. Today such an intervention would be a clear violation of antitrust regulations, but in 1925 it was normal and accepted practice in Wall Street as well as an expression of Morgan's power and preeminence.[16] Reacting to the Morgan ultimatum, Dillon countered by proposing a competitive bidding procedure whereby all interested parties, including the Morgans, would have a chance to bid on the Dodge business. Morgan agreed to Dillon's plan and the bidding finally narrowed down to Morgan and Dillon. The two financiers engaged in a clandestine battle of wits; rumors grew daily and filled the media.

Backing up his proposed buyout, Dillon had formed a syndicate of securities firms (including US&FS) from all parts of the country ready to commit $150 to $200 million to buy an undisclosed company (secrecy was critical at this point).[17] The syndicate granted Dillon authority to make the final decision on the buyout bid. Thus, the money was in hand when Dillon made his bid, the syndicate functioning as a blind pool.

The bidding process was complicated by the difficulty of valuing the assets and earnings of the privately-held Dodge Corporation as there was no public market for the stock. Much of the process by which investment bankers inspect target companies is known as "due diligence" which requires that confidential documents be produced and executives made available to discuss how to improve company operations in connection with a takeover. Dillon and Morgan had teams of accountants, lawyers and investment bankers, crawling over Dodge until every nook and cranny of the business was evaluated with assets earmarked to be jettisoned, pared or increased.

Although the procedures used in the 1920s differ from those employed today, the methodical and unexciting chore of due diligence was the key to the success of Dillon in calculating his takeover bid.[18] While the public heard of the Dodge deal overnight, it had taken several months and hundreds of trained men to complete the appraisal.[19] To the public, Dillon appeared to buy Dodge Brothers as casually as a housewife purchases ten pounds of potatoes. In reality, he and Charlie Schwartz, his secret intermediary, along with a shoal of experts devoted eight months in the bitter battle with the Morgan-led General Motors group.[20]

The Dillon and Morgan final offers contrasted sharply both in price and form. The Morgan bid actually consisted of two proposals, one offering $125,650,000 in cash; the other was for $155 million, but only $65 million would be in cash, the rest in notes, to be paid back, without interest, at the rate of $10 million a year, out of anticipated profits over the next nine years. The Dillon bid of $146 million, all cash, was compressed into about a half dozen lines written on ordinary letter-paper; Morgan's proposal was much more complex.[21] Moreover, Dillon sweetened his final offer by allowing the widows to retain an additional $14 million from Dodge's cash assets so that Dillon's all-cash bid swamped the Morgan-led bid by General Motors. In terms of today's purchasing power of the dollar, Dillon's $146 million bid was the equivalent of $1 billion.

Dillon's cash offer exceeded the company's $90 million book value by $56 million and was based on a wholly new theory of corporate valuation whereby he calculated the discounted present value of Dodge's future earnings, earmarking the premium paid as corporate "goodwill." For the first time in Wall Street history a new issue of securities was priced on the basis of the company's expected "future earning power" rather than on its assets. James Forrestal, now recognized as the firm's expert on pricing new issues, played a major role in the negotiations.[22] After a brief conference, the Dodge widows formally accepted the Dillon offer with the closing taking place on May 1, 1925.[23]

Feigning indifference, Dillon stayed in his office in New York rather than journeying to Detroit for the presentation and opening of the bids for Dodge. Actually, Dillon had the "inside track" all along since Schwartz maneuvered himself adroitly with the widows and secretly learned the amounts being offered by the other bidders. Exploiting his "in" with the two Dodge widows, Schwartz connived and worked directly with William A. Phillips, Dillon's deputy, to secure the business for Dillon. A Dillon Read associate of the era, who requested anonymity, said that he retrieved discarded notes from Phillips's waste basket containing Schwartz's memoranda reporting on how he was faring in persuading the Dodge widows to turn over their interests to Dillon Read.[24]

Dillon's coup startled Wall Street and the press heralded the sale with major front page stories. Within eight days, Dillon's high-powered 382-member dealer syndicate, led by Forrestal, offered and sold to an eager public $160 million of new Dodge securities consisting of $75 million of bonds plus $85 million of preferred stock, including a share-for-share bonus of Class A non-voting stock. The press reported that the Dillon Read syndicate received subscription orders nearly five times greater than the $85 million of preferred stock actually offered, and twice the $75 million debenture issue offered at the same time.

Dillon retained for its managerial services 650,000 shares of the Class A stock and all of the 500,000 shares of Class B voting stock which represented voting control.[25] The Dillon syndicate netted a quick $14 million profit from the public offering. Based on *pro forma* market values, Dillon's retained holdings had an indicated value of $34.5 million which, when added to the profits on the underwriting, brought total potential profits to $48.5 million for Dillon and his syndicate.

The Dodge transaction was a classic Clarence Dillon operation—bold, audacious, and carefully planned, with a minimum danger of failure and financial exposure. Dillon's investment had been time, effort, expenses, and most important, imagination and intrigue. Dillon had bested Morgan and had captured the attention of the tabloid and financial press, which told the dramatic story of a titanic struggle between the old warrior, Morgan, and the new challenger.[26]

Dillon thought of himself as a lonely competitor pitted against the giants. Paul Nitze, his later long-time personal assistant and confidant, believes that Dillon preferred to think of himself as the underdog, adding: "in the garden of his Far Hills, New Jersey, estate, Dillon had a statue of David `drawing a bead on Goliath.'" Dillon thought of himself as the David from Texas who was to slay the Goliaths of Wall Street. Dillon's buyout victory did not create any hostility with the Morgan group since neither firm was acting as Dodge's investment banker at the time. The two firms stayed friendly and Dillon participated in Morgan syndicates regularly thereafter.[27]

Dillon was a master of public relations and understatement. When the press came to interview him the morning after he won the Dodge deal, Dillon's desk was uncluttered and he was reading a Greek classic. Dillon quietly told the reporters that he had signed a check to the widows for $146 million and announced that he was transferring Edward Wilmer from Goodyear to become president of Dodge. The ease with which Dillon seemed to direct such vast undertakings deeply impressed the financial press and they soon surrounded him with a "sacerdotal aura" which was never dissipated during his lifetime.[28] He was a good actor as well as a financier.

One journalist, Bruce Forbes, who was Dillon's next door neighbor out in Far Hills and knew him intimately, described Dillon as the new "Napoleon" of finance. As related by Forbes:

> Dillon's greatest asset . . . is the faculty he has . . . of getting opinions . . . from all sources and weighing . . . the value of each and fusing them all into a final decision. He is indifferent to external criticism once he has made up his mind . . . in whatever he is doing. The qualities which have contributed

mainly to his success are: a great native flexibility of mind combined with powers of clear analysis and ability to have [talented] men around him . . . who believe in his . . . courage [and character]. . . .[29]

In the 1933 Pecora hearings, Senator James Couzens of Michigan subjected Dillon to intense questioning on the sale of Dodge Brothers to a Wall Street firm.[30] Couzens had been Henry Ford's closest business associate for twelve years in the earlier part of the century and was instrumental to a large degree for the sensational success of the Ford Motor Company, launched in 1907.[31] Reflecting his inbred hostility to Eastern bankers, Couzens prodded Dillon on how he arrived at his winning bid for Dodge Brothers.

"That's a long story," Dillon answered.

"I just want to know the principles on which you base it," returned Senator Couzens.

"The past earning power largely controls," explained Dillon.[32]

After the Dodge deal was completed, Schwartz stood to receive $10 million for his role in aiding Dillon in the takeover.[33] When Schwartz came to collect his reward, Dillon told him: "Charlie, it strikes me that that amount . . . is far in excess of what you're really entitled to."

Schwartz retorted: "Clarence, you and I have a deal on that."

And Dillon replied: "I know we have a memorandum agreement but I'm talking reality now and this is real money."

Whereupon, Schwartz took the memorandum out of his pocket, tore it up and threw it down at Dillon's feet snorting: "Clarence, if that's what your word means, then this is what I think of your written contracts!"

Cornered, Dillon backed off snarling: "You'll get your money."[34] (Dillon may have paid off Schwartz by transferring to him part of the common stock he received from Dodge for his efforts in organizing the purchase and sale of the Dodge company to the public.)

After he made his killing, Schwartz acquired a huge apartment and a staff of servants. Schwartz was a flamboyant character much in tune with the heady times of the 1920s. He had been very proud of the fact that while Dempsey was in training for the Firpo match, Schwartz had been his sparring partner for five or six rounds. To celebrate his new found wealth, Schwartz gave a formal dinner to which he invited Clarence Dillon. Dillon discreetly declined the invitation sending instead his partner, Ferdinand Eberstadt, as his personal representative. Eberstadt recalled that all of the rich and powerful were at the party; there was a footman behind every chair and all the servants were dressed in livery.[35]

It was about the most elegant affair that Eberstadt had ever attended; that is until the Chinese cook, brandishing a meat cleaver, burst out of the kitchen running after one of the footmen. That pretty well broke up

Schwartz's celebration party but he continued to live "big," dabbling in race horses among other expensive interests and trying with some success to spend his new found wealth in his own lifetime.[36] Reflecting his gratitude to Dillon Read, Schwartz named one of his race horses after a partner of the firm.

However contrived Schwartz's manipulations, Dillon's acquisition of Dodge Brothers in 1925 established his credentials as a superb financier who could calculate accurately the intrinsic value of even the most complex transaction. The Dodge deal elevated Dillon to the pinnacle of Wall Street, unquestionably one of the greatest financial virtuosos,[37] and made his firm the equal of any investment house on the Street. The sensational coup revealed to critics and admirers Clarence Dillon's fertile imagination and cold, calculated daring. Many of Dillon's rivals had considered the Goodyear rescue in 1921 a stroke of luck; after the Dodge coup, few of them denied that Dillon was a true financial genius.[38]

Notes

1. May, George S., *A Most Unique Machine: The Michigan Origins of the American Automobile Industry*, Detroit, 1979, p. 272, hereinafter referred to as May, George S., *A Most Unique Machine*.
2. "John Dodge Dead." *New York Times*, January 15, 1920.
3. Cray, Ed, *Chrome Colossus: General Motors and Its Times*, New York, 1980, p. 147.
4. Crabb, Richard, *Birth of a Giant: The Men and Incidents that Gave America the Motorcar*, Philadelphia, 1970, p. 355.
5. "Chrysler," *Fortune*, August 1935, p. 36.
6. Seltzer, Laurence H., *A Financial History of the Automobile Industry*, Boston, 1928, p. 112.
7. *Poor's Industrials*, 1927 edition, p. 851 and company annual reports and Dillon Read offering prospectuses.
8. May, George S., *A Most Unique Machine*, p. 272.
9. "Dodge Brothers Ill," *New York Times*, January 12, 1920.
10. "Horace Dodge Dead," *New York Times*, December 11, 1920.
11. May, George S., *A Most Unique Machine*, p. 272.
12. Sobel, Robert, *The Life and Times of Dillon Read*, p. 122.
13. Telephone interview with Alexander Schwartz, son of Charles Schwartz, on May 1, 1984.
14. Hoopes/Brinkley, *Driven Patriot*, p. 58.
15. "Auto Merger Proposed; Detroit Hears Dodge Brothers May be Absorbed by General Motors," *New York Times*, March 19, 1925.
16. Mathey, Dean, *Fifty Years of Wall Street*, p. 13 and Hoopes/Brinkley, *Driven Patriot*, p. 58.
17. Hoopes/Brinkley, *Driven Patriot*, p. 59.

18. Burroughs, Bryan, and John Helyar, *Barbarians at the Gate: The Fall of RJR Nabisco*, New York, 1990, pp. 301-2.
19. Williams, Frank J., "A New Leader in Finance: Clarence Dillon," *American Review of Reviews*, February 1926, pp. 146-9.
20. Winkler, *The New Yorker*, p. 29.
21. Forbes, Bruce C., "Clarence Dillon, The Man Who Bought Dodge," *Forbes*, p. 223.
22. Hoopes/Brinkley, *Driven Patriot*, p. 59; Rogow, Arnold A, *James Forrestal: A Study of Personality, Politics, and Policy*, New York, 1963, p. 82; Perez/Willett, *The Will to Win*, p. 41; "Dodge Deal," *Literary Digest*, April 25, 1925, pp. 80-2 and interview with Hugh Bullock, April 18, 1984.
23. Seltzer, Laurence, *A Financial History of the American Automobile Industry*, p. 242.
24. It is astonishing to realize that over the past four centuries exploiting inside information was scarcely challenged anywhere. In fact, the possession of inside information was looked upon as a tribute to the enterprise of the possessor. All but universal approval of the use of insider information proceeded well into the present century when it gradually ended as the public demanded tighter controls to curb the practice leading to its ban under provisions of the Securities Act of 1934 which provides severe civil and criminal penalties for violations. (Sources: Brooks, John, *The Takeover Game*, pp. 317-9; Ferris, Paul, *The Master Bankers*, p. 272 and "Clarence Dillon Who Arranged Dodge Bros., Inc. Sale; Portrait," *New York Times*, April 12, 1925, Sec. IX, p. 5.
25. Seltzer, Laurence, *A Financial History of the American Automobile Industry*, p. 243.
26. Sobel, Robert, *The Life and Times of Dillon Read*, pp. 128-9.
27. Paul H. Nitze interview, November 11, 1991 and Sobel, Robert, *The Life and Times of Dillon Read*, p. 44.
28. Jereski, Laura, "Clarence Dillon: Using Other Peoples Money," *Forbes*, p. 274 and Hoopes/Brinkley, *Driven Patriot*, p. 59.
29. Forbes B. C., "Clarence Dillon: The Man Who Bought Dodge," *Forbes*, p. 186.
30. Mathey, Dean, *Fifty Years of Wall Street*, p. 14.
31. Barnard, Harry, *Independent Man: The Life of Senator James Couzens*, New York, 1958, pp. 7, 84-5, 99-100.
32. The Pecora Hearings.
33. Telephone interview with Alexander Schwartz, son of Charles Schwartz, on May 1, 1984.
34. Interview with Robert G. Zeller, May 1, 1984.
35. Zeller interview, May 1, 1984.
36. Zeller interview, May 1, 1984.
37. "Wall Street Itself," *Fortune*, June 1937, p. 74.
38. Hoopes/Brinkley, *Driven Patriot*, p. 59.

5

Dillon's Dream House: Dunwalke

The Dunwalke mansion and estate was Dillon's life-long dream. It engaged his attention from shortly after his marriage to Anne Douglass to its final completion twenty-five years later. Dillon created the Dunwalke name from a combination of two of his wife Anne's colonial ancestors, the Duns and the Walkes.

The project was complex, involving finding the ideal land site to build the mansion and acquiring the furniture and silver to furnish the completed masterpiece in lavish fashion. To find the right location, the Dillons lived in several rented homes in different areas during their first ten years in the New York metropolitan area; they finally settled on the Far Hills-Peapack hunt area of New Jersey which provided all the features they had been seeking.[1]

The Far Hills estate area dates from before the turn of the century when James Cox Brady, the son of Anthony Nicholas Brady—the tycoon who built a $100 million fortune in utilities and trolley cars—acquired huge tracts of farmland. Brady then sold off some of his holdings to other affluent people who wished to become involved in breeding race horses and prize-winning cattle and other livestock.[2] The Bradys continue to be the dominant landholders in the area with about 3,200 acres bordering the Dillon estate on two sides.

The Bradys also created Maxwell Motor Co., later absorbed into Chrysler Corp. The Maxwell-Chrysler merger in 1924 was financed with $15 million advanced by the Bradys who controlled Maxwell. The Bradys later lent a helping hand to Dillon in the negotiations leading to Chrysler's acquisition of Dodge Brothers Motors in 1928.[3]

A Sotheby's real estate brochure described the Far Hills area in the early

1990s:

> Reminiscent of the picturesque, unspoiled English countryside, the Far Hills
> area embraces a lush bounty of beautiful rolling meadows laced with
> hedgerows and peaceful lanes. With its rich heritage of historic estates and
> large equestrian properties, steeped in the traditions of this celebrated horse
> and fox hunting country, the area represents one of the most sought-after
> locations in the Northeast.

In the fall of 1923, Clarence Dillon bought his first property in Far Hills
consisting of a house, stable and about 200 acres of land. The Dillons
moved into that house in 1925.[4] Then they bought the farm that adjoined
them on the west, then the farm bordering them on the south and other
properties, stopping only when they came to main roads. Aided by the
Bradys, Dillon continued to acquire land in the area during the 1920s, until
he finally owned about 1,200 acres.[5]

The gentlemen farmers in the Far Hills area had a unanimity of purpose,
namely to develop large estate areas insulated from the outside world.
William Phillips, Dillon's close friend from Harvard and Worcester
Academy days and partner in the investment banking firm, also purchased
some land with a house from Dillon and took up residence adjacent to the
Dillons. Later, however, Phillips gave the property to his wife as part of
their divorce settlement. She then chose to sell it to others, refusing to
reoffer it to Dillon, feeling that he had unfairly sided with her husband
during her divorce from him. Subsequently, Phillips married his secretary
at Dillon Read and left the firm, relocating with another investment firm in
Virginia in the mid-1930s.[6]

After Dillon had finished assembling his large land holdings in Far Hills,
it took five years to complete the main house at Dunwalke. Much of that
time was spent in planning the design of the building and in searching for
the materials to complete it. The actual construction time took two years.[7]

The site for Dunwalke was so barren that Dillon determined to move in
large elm trees collected from the surrounding countryside. He and his
wife searched for trees of a particular size and shape that they liked. More
than one hundred elms were moved on special equipment built by Dillon
and planted along the entrance roadway. In addition, Dillon moved fifty
pin oaks to the property, as well as fifty great maples and several beech
trees. Then they moved a complete orchard of about twenty apple trees,
choosing each tree largely for its shape.[8]

They searched the area for boxwood bushes and made a box garden.
Dillon arranged with truck drivers with regular routes through New Jersey,
Maryland and other nearby states that whenever they saw a piece of
boxwood, they should photograph it; if the Dillons acquired the shrub,

Dillon would pay the trucker a bonus. Unfortunately, the extremely cold winter of l934 killed off these shrubs.[9]

In choosing an architect, Dillon first talked to Mott B. Schmidt, who had built their cottage at Dark Harbor in Maine. Schmidt made a scale model of his proposal for the mansion. Dillon's problem with that was that he wanted the five rooms on the first floor so arranged that no room opened onto another. Another architect, a friend by the name of John Cross, happened to be lunching with Dillon, who told him of the trouble he was having arranging the rooms on the first floor.

Cross asked, "What is it you want?" and Dillon told him.

Cross took a pencil and sketched a floor plan on the tablecloth with five rooms, none of them opening onto any other.

With that, Dillon said: "You've got a job."[10]

The Dillons also wanted a house of red brick, but all that was available was new brick which didn't have the weathered, antique look that Dillon wanted. They searched and found the ruins of a red brick colonial house in Virginia gutted by fire. The brick walls were intact and still standing. It was called Hayfield and had been built in the eighteenth century by Lund Washington, a cousin of George, with brick that had been brought over from England as ballast in sailing ships. Dillon bought the exterior brick walls and shipped them intact to Dunwalke, where they were used to face the entire house and some of the garden walls. The house was built with a concrete inner shell including the floors of each of the house's three stories, with the brick exterior walls and the interior finishes added later. Subsequently, Dillon found a local foundry where he was able to have the weathered brick copied, so that the new brick on the other buildings at Dunwalke and the outside garden walls resembled the old brick used on the main house.[11]

The first floor included a large 36' x 20' dining room with a music room of about the same size across the hall. The stair hall had a circular staircase which looked as if it were suspended in air (but it is actually connected to the wall at two places). Anne's morning room had colonial period panelling from a house on the James River in Virginia. On the second floor, there were seven master bedrooms, six with fireplaces, and all with private baths. Clarence Dillon's bedroom was 22' x 24' with two large windows and a large glass door leading out onto a deck; Anne's bedroom was somewhat larger.[12]

Dillon maintained tight security at Dunwalke with an armed ex-marine as a bodyguard, twenty-four hours a day. The guard, however, had to wear bedroom slippers at night so as not to disturb any one. Dillon at one point wanted to build an atom bomb shelter but did not want anyone to know about it. His aide, Haywood, contacted the president of a top engineering firm in New York to discuss building the shelter. A new well was drilled for water and new equipment was purchased, along with food and instruments to read radioactivity and periscopes to monitor activity above ground. Halfway through the project the *New York Times* and a few other papers became aware of it. The press reports attributed the building project to Dillon's son, Douglas, who was then Secretary of the Treasury; Douglas was furious about the reports and the bomb shelter project was quietly dropped shortly thereafter.[13]

In 1937, Dillon built a house for his son Douglas on the site of the original house at Dunwalke which had been torn down. The house, now known as Dunwalke East, is of brick similar to that used in the main house. Dillon reverted to his Dark Harbor architect Mott Schmidt, who designed the house in the Georgian style.[14] In 1991, Douglas Dillon decided to put Dunwalke East up for sale through Sotheby's for an asking price of $5 million.[15] The offering brochure describes the house and grounds of Dunwalke East as follows:

> Secluded amidst thirty-three acres of carefully tended grounds, Douglas Dillon's residence stands regally among beautiful and rare specimen trees, ornamental shrubs, and gardens. A profusion of flowers including tulip, daffodil, rose, peony, lily, and lilac provide a constant bloom of color throughout the spring and summer months. The property includes a sunken rose garden with fountain, stone-walled tulip garden, birch and spring bulb garden, fruit orchard, pink chestnut trees and a large vegetable garden and raspberry row. Superbly constructed, the home has . . . a total of eight working fireplaces. . . . There are ten principal or family rooms including seven bedrooms each with bath. In addition, the house includes ample staff quarters including six small bedrooms and two bathrooms as well as a five-car garage with a work room and a three bedroom cottage.

In 1958, Dillon's granddaughter, Phyllis (Douglas's elder daughter), also built a red brick American colonial house at the northwest corner of Dunwalke. She subsequently sold that to her cousin, Philip Allen, and she now lives in Fairfield, Connecticut.[16] In the late 1950s, Dillon's daughter, Dorothy, built her house at the northeast corner of Dunwalke in rural French design furnished with the boiseries and parquets which her father and mother had given to her from their Paris apartment on rue Barbet-de-Jouy. There is a walled entrance courtyard as in a French farm house.[17]

Removing the boiseries and parquets and shipping them from the Paris apartment to Far Hills for Dorothy's new house involved a complex project supervised by Joseph Haywood, Dillon's trusted project coordinator. All of the panelling and flooring had to be shipped by air; several members of Dillon's New York and Paris offices were assigned to help make up detailed lists of the materials and make final arrangements for the shipments. The boiseries and parquet flooring were stored in a barn at Dunwalke pending construction.[18]

Even though the architects went to Paris to measure the materials, they underestimated the materials needed and the builders didn't have enough panelling and parquets to finish the walls and floors. When he learned of the mistake, Dillon flew into a rage and shouted, "What could have happened?"

Haywood said, "I don't know . . . but there are craftsmen [locally] who can duplicate the panelling."

"It won't be the same," Dillon snapped.

Haywood, who is a fine wood craftsman himself, said, "I guarantee it will be the same . . . craftsmen can duplicate it perfectly and if I have to, I will make it myself."

"Well," Dillon retorted angrily, "if you say so, but if it is not right. . . ."

Fortunately, Dillon couldn't tell the difference between the old and new boiseries and parquets after they were installed.[19]

The balance of Dunwalke's acreage, known as Dunwalke Farm, is given over to farming and cattle raising. In 1924 and 1925, Dillon made several trips to the Isle of Guernsey where he purchased the seed stock to form his cattle herd at Dunwalke Farm. The cattle had to be quarantined for some time before the Dillons were allowed to bring them into the country. The cattle barns were three-quarters of a mile north of the main house alongside the old sheep barns and were extensive, with the main barn housing about thirty cows, each with its own box stall. Adjoining the main barn, there is a calf barn with fifteen separate boxes. Another calf barn to the west also has fifteen separate boxes.[20] The Guernsey herd for many years produced all the milk, butter, cheese and cream needed for the Dillon household and its staff.[21]

The cattle herd numbered about 150 head, and in the bull pens Dillon had four bulls, with younger bulls for sale. There was also a small herd of Hereford and Black Angus, with many of the bulls gaining national reputations. These herds became too large for Dunwalke during the late 1930s, so Dillon bought four farms in Maryland and moved the Angus herd there. Roger Derby, a friend from Harvard days, subsequently moved down there and took over the management of these farms. Later, the farms were sold and the Angus herd dispersed.[22]

After it was determined that the cream of the Guernsey cow contained a high level of cholesterol and therefore was injurious to health, the Guernsey herd was sold in 1954, but Dillon kept the younger stock to maintain a small herd because he liked the creamy milk they produced despite the health problems.[23] In the early 1970s, after the Guernsey herd was finally dispersed, Dunwalke's emphasis switched to breeding Polled Herefords.[24]

Dunwalke now has a Hereford herd of over 400 head with cattle sales scheduled every two years to dispose of about a quarter of the herd.

Douglas Dillon relates, "we have a big cow sale every two years and then we start again to rebuild the herd; these sales are all very fancy. For example, we sold a bull last spring for $100,000."[25] Between cattle sales, the farm breeds enough new offspring to build up the herd again for the next sale.[26]

Dillon maintained a number of pigs at the farm which were slaughtered for pork. He built a smoke house, which while modern and convenient was very old fashioned in operation. They also slaughtered cattle for veal and beef. In addition, Dunwalke Farm had turkey and hen houses, a pond for ducks, and a number of brooder houses for chickens, turkeys, pheasants, quail, mallard ducks, chukar, partridge and puddle ducks; all of the game birds were put out in covered runs, where a native habitat was provided. They flourished there. The farm usually raised about one hundred chicks and ninety to ninety-five pheasants, quail or mallards.[27]

In the Far Hills area, there is a large population of red fox, weasels and hare, ideal for hunting. Dillon also had a large horse stable as his children and later his grandchildren were active riders.[28] As members of the Essex Fox Hounds Club, the Dillons periodically hosted hunt breakfasts at Dunwalke.[29]

Water has always been a problem at Dunwalke. Dillon initially drilled many wells around the property but they proved inadequate to provide the water needed for the main house, the farm and the grounds. So Dillon went five or six miles west, found a water source to which he was able to acquire water rights, and built a dam to collect the water. Then, Dillon built a pipeline through the village of Pottersville and thence on to Dunwalke two to three miles further southeast. He negotiated a contract to supply water to that village and several houses on lands just to the west of Dunwalke; the pipeline provided all the water needed for the various activities at Dillon's estate. The Dillons ran this water company for fifty years, but after the war a large regional water company took it over and now maintains it.[30]

Animals and birds were well taken care of at Dunwalke. Hay, feed and apples were placed along the roadways during the winter for the deer. There was a pond with a platform and feed for the Canada geese. A large kennel housed a number of prize French poodles with a separate staff to care for them. The estate greenhouses produced flowers twelve months of the year, which were displayed in every room in the house.[31]

Today, farming at Dunwalke is taken seriously and not as a hobby. Dillon's son, Douglas, has taken an active interest in maintaining the farm and he notes:

> I'd say that this farm at least breaks even. . . . [The grazing cattle] keep the
> land in good shape [which] provides . . . grass silage and corn to feed the
> herd. . . . I think eventually, when the time comes to sell the land, it will be

worth more. . . .[32]

In the spring of 1991, Douglas Dillon turned over the running of Dunwalke Farm to his sister's son, Philip Allen.[33] Allen runs Dunwalke Farm with a special focus on research to maintain its position as a world-class breeder of Polled Herefords, a tribute to the emphasis on excellence demanded by his grandfather in all his activities.

Besides selling the animals, Dunwalke Farm sells the eggs and the semen from the bulls to other breeders both here and in South America. Dunwalke Farm is basically trying to improve the genetics of the Hereford breed, matching the best bull to the best cow. Philip Allen notes: "There is some science and a lot more of luck to it but in any given year we may have . . . ten calves that [become] terrific cows with two or three of them [winning trophies as the best in their class]."[34]

There are seventeen houses at Dunwalke, including the main house and the houses of Dorothy, Douglas and Philip Allen; the others are occupied by people working on the estate as well as retirees. For many years at Christmas time the Dillons held a party in the tennis court building at Dunwalke for the staff, the farmers and their families with the chauffeur, Fleming, dressed up as Santa Claus and handing the presents to the children. The last one held was in 1955; thereafter the Dillons spent all of their holidays at High Rock on Montego Bay in Jamaica.[35]

In the early days, the Dillons had a permanent house staff of fourteen at the townhouse in New York and at Dunwalke, consisting of two footmen, a cook, two kitchen helpers, two chambermaids, a parlor maid, a laundress, Dillon's valet, Anne's maid and a houseman. There were also two chauffeurs. In addition to the people who worked on the farm, the Dillons also had an engineer at the house, two men for the lawns, grooms and stable boys, a kennel man and the man who looked after the poultry and game. The footmen wore green tailcoats, green-and-gold waistcoats and white gloves; their buttons were engraved with the Dillon initials, "C & A" overlaid. Their job was to answer the door and at meals one stood behind Anne Dillon's chair and the other behind Dillon's, changing plates and so forth; afterwards they would also help out in the pantry.[36]

The Dillons were avid collectors of antiques during their entire marriage. Their collections became so extensive that Dillon had to lease a warehouse in lower Manhattan to store them for future use.[37] In the 1920s the Dillon's furniture acquisitions took on a heightened degree of urgency as the final building plans for Dunwalke moved forward. Dillon went to many auctions, frequently taking along his daughter, Dorothy, who shared her father's interest in antiques and "found the auctions very exciting." Dorothy remembers that at some of the auctions her father sat next to William Randolph Hearst and they frequently competed for the same piece.

Dorothy adds, "They had all kinds of devices to indicate what their bid was, including crossed legs, handkerchiefs in or out of pockets, etc."[38]

Dillon's will bequeathed the main house and 125 acres of land to Princeton University as a retreat and conference center with a multimillion-dollar endowment to provide maintenance.[39] While Dillon gave Dunwalke to Princeton, his will stipulated that all of the furniture be given to his children and grandchildren.[40]

Dillon's development of Dunwalke is a tribute to the methodical approach which he utilized in all his enterprises. He spared no expense in its evolution from a barren, treeless hilly site into a lush estate. The rocky knoll presented just the kind of stimulating challenge that Dillon loved to overcome; he personally supervised and planned every detail of this vast undertaking. The Baron was determined that Dunwalke would become his feudal domain.

Notes

1. *Anne's Story.*
2. *Anne's Story*
3. "Nicholas F. Brady: The New Deal-Maker at the Old Guard Firm," *Business Week,* and "The Quiet Crusader: Nick Brady's Plan to Curb Fast-Buck Management and Deal Mania," *Business Week,* September 18, 1989.
4. Mrs. Dorothy Dillon Eweson interview, October 1 and 4, 1991.
5. *Anne's Story.*
6. Mrs. Dorothy Dillon Eweson interview, October 1 and 4, 1991 and written comments received May 12, 1993.
7. *Anne's Story.*
8. *Anne's Story.*
9. *Anne's Story.*
10. *Anne's Story.*
11. *Anne's Story.*
12. *Anne's Story.*
13. Joseph Haywood interview, October 28, 1991.
14. *Anne's Story.*
15. Douglas Dillon interview, October 29, 1991.
16. Philip D. Allen interview, April 9, 1992.
17. *Anne's Story.*
18. Joseph Haywood interview, October 28, 1991.
19. Joseph Haywood interview, October 28, 1991.
20. *Anne's Story.*
21. Philip D. Allen interview, April 9, 1992.
22. *Anne's Story.*
23. Douglas Dillon interview, May 23, 1991.

24. Philip D. Allen interview, April 9, 1992.
25. Douglas Dillon interview, October 29, 1991.
26. Philip D. Allen interview, April 9, 1992.
27. *Anne's Story.*
28. Philip D. Allen interview, April 9, 1992.
29. *Anne's Story.*
30. Douglas Dillon interview, October 29, 1991.
31. Joseph Haywood interview, April 9, 1992.
32. Douglas Dillon interview, October 29, 1991.
33. Douglas Dillon interview, October 29, 1991.
34. Philip D. Allen interview, April 9, 1992.
35. *Anne's Story.*
36. *Anne's Story.*
37. Mrs. Dorothy Dillon Eweson interview, October 1, 1991.
38. Mrs. Dorothy Dillon Eweson interview, October 1, 1991.
39. Clarence Dillon's probated estate, April 25, 1979.
40. Douglas Dillon interview, October 1, 1991.

6

Foreign Financing

In the early 1920s, Dillon knew that he could not meet J. P. Morgan and Kuhn Loeb head on domestically, but he saw a risk-free shot—the kind he liked—to beat them both on Wall Street's new frontier in Europe which would benefit from its industrial revival following four years of devastation during the first world war.

Earlier, Dillon had met Henning Plaun, a director of the Landsman Bank of Copenhagen on a return trip from Europe in 1919, and had discussed financing opportunities in Russia and Siberia. Dillon carefully considered entering into a joint venture with the Landsman Bank but nothing came of this because of the murky nature of Russian politics and business.[1] Dillon's primary interest was to exploit the financial opportunities presented by the rebuilding of the war-torn economies of Europe, especially Germany.

Clarence Dillon was convinced there were major financing opportunities beckoning private capital to Europe. In 1922, Dillon told the *New York Times*:

> Our opportunity lies in industrial Europe. . . . The railroad and public utility financing that is to be done in Europe is tremendous, and . . . lucrative. . . . We will lend, but we will lend with care. We must be thoroughly `sold´on a loan before we will make it, and I would say that it is much harder to sell us on a loan than it is for us to sell the bonds to investors here.[2]

Dillon personally opened up this financing field for the firm with extensive travel to the Continent during the early 1920s. He also sent Ralph Bollard, one of his key partners, to Germany on a fact-finding mission. Dillon went to Europe again in 1922 to hold meetings with J. Henry Schroder & Co., an important London-based merchant bank with offices in Germany and the United States and with Max M. Warburg, head of an important private bank in Hamburg. Schroder became Dillon's major European underwriting partner.

In addition to the Warburgs and Schroders, Dillon had business relations with the Rothschilds and Baring Brothers in London and he maintained contact with Montague Norman, the lordly head of the Bank of England.[3] Dillon invariably went to Europe for a month or more each year, with most of his trips connected to his business dealings there. On each of his trips, Dillon would always stop to cement ties with these bankers.[4]

At first, Dillon believed that he could obtain a significant part of the foreign business by working with Morgan and other banks. He had been encouraged by a meeting he attended in October 1919 with senior partners from Morgan and National City Bank, along with representatives from Guaranty Trust and Bankers Trust. According to Dillon's diary entries, these bankers wanted to "talk the matter over . . . and get our advice and views," looking toward the launching of a $250 million investment trust, but the position offered to Dillon was too small and he declined. Since Morgan dominated the English and French markets, Dillon would have to find some other way to become a principal in these markets and his search uncovered Germany as the prime prospect. In the meantime, Dillon participated in Morgan syndicates originated in the United Kingdom and France.[5]

Morgan had few financial interests in Germany other than its role in financing the Dawes reparation payment plan in 1924. By the same token, Dillon had no involvement in the United Kingdom and only minimal exposure to French government business. Although other competitors, notably National City, provided intense competition, Dillon's quest succeeded in Germany, once the political situation was stabilized.[6]

Germany had been devastated by the war and the victorious French were intent on taking their pound of flesh in tribute, demanding reparations that would assure that Germany would never again pose a military or economic threat to France. The French insisted that the Versailles peace treaty contain a stiff schedule of German reparations which Germany found difficult to meet.

The political quarrel between France and Germany had been complicated by economic considerations. During the 1920s, Dr. Gustav Stresemann emerged as the leading political figure in Germany. He was a dedicated German but more importantly he believed peace could be achieved by Germany's settling its long-term differences with the French.[7] A successful German stabilization was the key to European recovery, but France's position on reparations, hardened by U.S. insistence on repayment of the Allies' war debts, stood in the way.[8]

In 1921 the Allied Reparations Commission shocked Germany by informing its government that it would have to pay the Allies $33 billion in reparations on a deferred-payment basis. The German economy was so weak that obtaining funds through exports was out of the question. The result was reliance by the Germans upon the printing press to help pay the reparations, which resulted in hyperinflation and a major flight of capital out of the country.

Germany did manage a first payment of $250 million in 1921 but was obliged to ask for a one-year moratorium before the year was out. When payments were not resumed in 1923, French and Belgian troops occupied the Ruhr District, the heart of Germany's industrial economy. The German economy collapsed and German workers went on a general "passive" strike that persisted for months. The German government tottered and inflation skyrocketed. By September 1923, the mark was literally worth less than the paper on which it was printed.

So much money was required for reparations that the German government had to commandeer newspaper presses to keep pace. Moreover, thirty paper mills worked around the clock to satisfy the need for paper for bank notes. Prices soared so fast that wives would meet their husbands at factory gates, collect their wages, and then rush off to buy goods before the next round of price increases took effect. In January 1922, about 200 marks equalled one dollar; but in November 1923, it took over five *billion* marks to buy a dollar. A stamp on a letter to the United States cost a billion marks. At the end, in the final absurdity, prices doubled hourly.[9]

U. S. Secretary of State Charles E. Hughes set the stage for the eventual solution to the reparations problem in a speech in New Haven, Connecticut, on December 29, 1922 stating:

> We have no desire to see Germany relieved of her responsibility for the war or of her . . . obligation to make reparation. . . . On the other hand, we do not wish to see a prostrate Germany. There can be no economic recuperation in Europe unless Germany recuperates. . . .[10]

Hughes recommended that:

> Men of the highest authority in finance should be called . . . who can point the way to a solution . . . free . . . from any responsibility to . . . obey political instruction.[11]

The Reparations Commission agreed with Hughes's suggestion and appointed a group of experts headed by Brigadier General Charles G. Dawes to work out a solution. Owing partly to extensive French propaganda, the belief was widely held that Germany possessed inexhaustible wealth. It was a relief to Stresemann when a neutral and unprejudiced committee was convened, under Dawes, to investigate Germany's capacity for payment. More important, the United States (which had previously resisted all requests for intervention with the reply "No European Troubles") was represented on this committee and was committed to finding a solution to the European imbroglio.[12]

The Dawes Plan drastically scaled back reparations, tying them to Germany's capacity to pay, secured by a lien on the revenues of the German State Railways and its major industries. The German government consented to the appointment of an Agent General for reparations payments who was given far-reaching supervisory powers over German economic policy. The German government was required to balance its budget, reparations included. Germany, in effect, was mortgaged to the allies and under foreign control, a situation that would later provide a propaganda bonanza for the Nazis.[13]

In April 1924 the German government accepted the Dawes Plan, and the program began on September 1, 1924, when a Morgan-led syndicate floated a $110 million loan in England and the United States, in which Dillon Read participated. The acceptance of the Dawes Plan marked the commencement of German liberation, as France and Belgium were compelled to evacuate the Ruhr District with the last foreign troops leaving on July 31 of the following year.[14]

With the Dawes Plan in place, the way was cleared for considerable investments of American private capital in German industries. Dillon went to work to capture a share of this, hiring Colonel James A. Logan, the unofficial American observer to the Reparations Commission, to take prime responsibility for developing Dillon Read's financings in Europe.[15] Logan had been in the running for Agent General but lost out to Parker Gilbert. Thereafter, he met with Dillon who liked Logan's ambitious and aggressive energy.

Logan had excellent connections in France and England which Dillon believed would open doors for his firm in a market otherwise closed to a banker with little reputation in Europe. But Logan was too aggressive and crude; he lacked the diplomacy needed for success in delicate financial negotiations. Moreover, Logan rubbed raw the nerves of Morgan bankers and other competitors as well as potential clients.

As Dillon's representative, Logan clashed repeatedly with Morgan interests and came to be viewed as the cutting edge of the growing Morgan-Dillon Read rivalry. Although Dillon conceded that Morgan had established the United Kingdom as its "fiefdom," Dillon's goal was to establish a major financing base in France as well as in Germany. In a meeting held in early 1926, Morgan's senior partner, Thomas Lamont, complained to Dillon about Logan's "poisonous propaganda" and denounced Logan's activities.[16]

Dillon retorted: "I will not countenance . . . such things" and asked for concrete examples of Logan's offending behavior so that he could confront

Logan with the exact situation. Dillon emphasized that he would not tolerate any type of offensive behavior by any of his representatives.[17] However, Dillon made it clear that he would continue to pursue financing opportunities in Germany, France and in the rest of Europe.

Earlier in the decade, Ferdinand Eberstadt, then a young attorney at Cotton & Franklin, had been working closely with Dillon Read helping to negotiate German deals.[18] Eberstadt demonstrated outstanding qualities and was already bringing new business to Dillon from his German contacts. As the Dawes Plan neared completion, Eberstadt prepared an in-depth paper on the economic and investment implications of the Dawes Plan that Dillon Read published and distributed to its clients. With Eberstadt's Dawes brochure, Dillon pressed forward aggressively with financing programs in the German market.[19]

As Logan faltered, Dillon relied more and more on Eberstadt. Eberstadt's background and personality, as well as his fluency in German and French, suited him eminently for the job of managing Dillon's German financings. Short, wiry, intense, and vain, Eberstadt was a close friend of Forrestal whom he had met at Princeton and had invited to become an editor of the campus paper, *The Daily Princetonian*. At Princeton, Eberstadt was considered one of the most prominent members of his class and was voted by his classmates the "one most likely to succeed."[20]

Eberstadt had deep roots and contacts in Europe and especially Germany. After graduation Eberstadt spent a full year in Europe studying politics and economics at the University of Berlin and the Sorbonne. The German Jewish families were close knit and had considerable influence in finance. For example, Eberstadt's grandmother was related to the Paris Rothschilds. Moreover, Eberstadt's grandfather, as mayor of Worms, had arranged for Solomon Loeb to emigrate to the United States where he established with his brother-in-law, Abraham Kuhn, the prominent investment banking firm of Kuhn Loeb & Co. in 1867.[21]

In addition, Eberstadt's first cousin was none other than Otto Kahn, the head of the same Kuhn Loeb, which had become the second most powerful firm in Wall Street; Morgan was number one. Kahn's influence extended well beyond Wall Street, he became a major patron of the Metropolitan Opera hiring the widely-acclaimed Arturo Toscanini in 1908 as conductor which helped propel the Met into the first rank of opera houses in the world.[22] Obviously, these family connections would help Eberstadt during the 1920s, when he began operating in Europe.

At the beginning of the decade of the 1920s, Clarence Dillon initiated the deals in Europe and Eberstadt did the tough negotiating—doing the dirty work that had to be done with the middle and upper managers to complete the deals—as well as prospecting for new deals.[23] Ever on the alert, Eberstadt developed the German electrical giant, Siemens & Halske, as a

Dillon Read financing client in late 1924.[24] Founded in 1847, Siemens created the telegraph and telex systems and was one of the largest industrial concerns in Europe.[25]

Dillon finally turned to Eberstadt in late 1925 and offered him a partnership in the firm to take charge of European financing. Although Eberstadt regretted leaving his law firm, Cotton and Franklin, where he had become a partner, he was enthusiastic about the prospects for developing European financing business for Dillon Read. Besides, he would continue to maintain his contacts with Cotton and Franklin, which was Dillon Read's principal legal firm. Logan was quietly let go.

Although private financing prospects in Germany were almost non-existent, amounting to only $10 million in 1924, they picked up sharply in 1925 in anticipation of the implementation of the Dawes Plan. The key German financing began with a Dillon-syndicated loan of $15 million for August Thyssen-Hutte in early 1925 in a very difficult and turbulent market. Rumors were circulating that the Allies would seize the Krupp works and other German factories because of reports that hundreds of cannon had been found hidden at the Krupp works. Krupp had been in the process of offering $10 million in bonds through Chase National and the offering was disrupted by the adverse rumors which proved to be false. But the Krupp issue still overhung the market when Dillon Read brought out the Thyssen loan in January 1925; Dillon's ability to organize a syndicate in the face of such uncertainties did much to embellish his firm's prestige in German industrial circles and led to additional business.[26]

The growing attitude that it had now become safe to invest in Germany was confirmed in October 1925, when at Foreign Minister Gustav Stresemann's suggestion representatives of the major European powers met in Locarno, a small town in Switzerland, and agreed that all future disputes would be settled through negotiations. Stresemann pledged Germany would never seek revisions of the Treaty of Versailles through force.[27] Reflecting his role in reestablishing cordial relations with France, Stresemann was awarded the Nobel Peace Prize in 1926.

In pursuit of Dillon financings, for the next three years Eberstadt shuttled back and forth between his office in Paris and the Hotel Adlon in Berlin. With a lawyer's precision, he would dispatch lengthy letters to Dillon at 28 Nassau Street, sketching conversations he had with business and government leaders, analyzing political and economic trends, and suggesting investment and underwriting strategies and tactics.[28]

The purpose of the private financings of German companies was to make Germany more productive and therefore in a better position to make the reparations payments. Eberstadt met with Stresemann on July 11, 1926, and told the German statesman that he thought Dillon Read "would be [able] to negotiate [the purchase] . . . of one [billion] dollars worth of . . . [German] bonds in the next three or four years, if Germany would undertake the payment of interest and France [guarantee] security for it. . . ."[29]

Though Stresemann appreciated Eberstadt's qualities, Hjalmar Schacht and several other German bankers perceived Dillon Read as too young and inexperienced and therefore inferior to Morgan. Eberstadt countered by relating the long history of the predecessor firm, Vermilye & Co., dating back to the 1830s and citing its impressive financing gains in the 1920s compared with J. P. Morgan, National City and Harris Forbes. The Dillon total in the previous twenty months came to $818 million against $770 million for Morgan. As for German financing, Dillon was far ahead, with $160 million versus $110 million (entirely made up of the massive Dawes Loan) and $79 million for National City. Eberstadt performed his tasks well.[30]

Eberstadt suggested to Stresemann that there was no question that Dillon Read was the only banking house that could challenge Morgan. He noted that by the end of 1926 Dillon Read would probably have issued over $100 million dollars of German industrial obligations, which had impressed observers in Berlin. A few days later, Stresemann asked Eberstadt what Dillon's relations were with the Morgan group. Eberstadt replied that the Morgan group was welcome to participate in Dillon Read's German syndications but Eberstadt suggested that Dillon Read, in effect, become Germany's exclusive banker and its liaison with Wall Street, representing its interests.[31] Although Dillon Read never quite became Germany's exclusive banker, the business expanded considerably during Eberstadt's tenure.

The most important German business for Dillon was the creation of the Vereinigte Stahlwerke (United Steel Works) in 1926. The financing began in mid-1925 when Dillon Read and Schroder bought a half interest for $4 million each in the Deutsche Luxemburgische Company, which with Siemens and two other mining companies comprised the Rheinelbe Union, the largest producer of coal, coke, iron and steel in Germany. Functioning as a cartel, Vereinigte Stahlwerke then assimilated Thyssen, Rheinelbe Union, Phoenix, and Rheinstahl with combined capital estimated at $150 million. To finance these acquisitions, Dillon headed underwriting syndicates for $30 million in bonds in June 1926, followed up by an additional $30 million syndication of bonds a year later and with a final $4 million offering in July 1927.[32]

While Dillon Read emerged as the most powerful American banking firm for German industrial concerns in the 1920s, Dillon remained a smallish player elsewhere in Europe. Dillon was frustrated in France probably as an ironic consequence of Eberstadt's success in Germany as well as by the dominant position of Morgan in French finance. However, the German business overall made Dillon Read the third-largest American bank in foreign flotations, behind Morgan and National City but ahead of Kuhn Loeb and Seligman.[33]

Dillon's financings involved raising funds for European countries as well as private companies. For example, Dillon took an active hand in stabilizing Poland's fragile economy. In the mid-1920s Poland's coalition government came to power but its economic future was in doubt. The Treasury was almost empty, the shortage of private capital was acute, unemployment was rife and the Polish currency, the *zloty*, continued to fall.[34] Poland desperately needed foreign help and Dillon provided it.

In the early summer of 1924, Dillon went to Poland to discuss with the Polish government his firm's possible role in negotiating a loan with western capital sources. The Poles treated Dillon lavishly, furnishing him with a special train for his travel convenience in Poland. Premier Grabski gave a dinner for Dillon and his associates and the minister of foreign affairs, Count Alexander Skrzynski, gave a ball in a palace lighted by crystal chandeliers and attended by the leading people of Warsaw.[35]

Then Dillon and his aides traveled in this special train to Lancut, in Galicia, 150 miles south of Warsaw and the seat of the domain of Prince Alfred Potocki, where the negotiations continued. On descending from the train in Lancut, a red carpet was rolled out for Dillon on the station platform. Potocki handled the four in hand himself and as the carriage set down the road the peasants turned and bowed their heads. The carriage finally drove through the gates of the castle into a covered court. In the castle, Dillon and his group dined in a different dining room every evening during the three days they were there.[36]

Potocki had extensive stables of Arabian horses and a large dairy herd, and he owned a liquor distillery in Lancut. The Potocki holdings had been left undisturbed during the first world war, as the family was related to both the German and Russian royal houses. In the twilight of its century-old prominence, the Potocki family was still living more or less as they had always lived. The Potockis went to great lengths to maintain their level of culture. All of the ladies of the court sent their lingerie by coach to Paris to be laundered rather than risk it to local peasant laundresses.[37] Dillon admired the level of culture in this land of his forefathers and his Dunwalke estate contains many of the elements of the baronial estates he visited in Poland and elsewhere in Europe.

Eberstadt had a hand in completing the negotiations of the Polish loan. Dillon's visit had left many detailed questions that needed to be negotiated and resolved, and he assigned to Eberstadt the difficult task of hammering out the final details of the loan terms with Count Potocki at his estate. Eberstadt was treated as warmly as Dillon had been the year before although he was not given the use of a private railroad car.

Upon arrival at the castle, Eberstadt was taken aback by the palatial interior of the great hall of the castle where a sumptuous ball was under way with scores of beautiful women, lavishly dressed, footmen carrying champagne and great heaps of caviar and other exotic foods on silver trays, all accompanied by music from wandering minstrel groups and string orchestras playing waltzes. Everyone was dancing, eating and drinking and having a fine old time which continued to dawn. At this point, the story reminds one of Prince Orlofsky's party in Johann Strauss, Jr.'s comic opera, *Die Fledermaus*.

The following day the men mounted their horses and went off to hunt wild boar for exercise and to rid themselves of their hangovers from the night before. The following evening another gala took place; revelry appeared to be the normal state of life in the castle—contrasting sharply with the austere peasant surroundings outside the castle grounds. As Frederick Eberstadt recalls his father's account: "The Polish cavaliers rode out early each morning, eager for sport, in spite of night after night of drinking and wenching."

In betwixt all this cavorting and merriment, Eberstadt finally sat down with Count Potocki to go over the points of negotiation that he had in his briefcase and the other instructions that Clarence Dillon had sent him from New York. Having reviewed these points, other questions were raised, causing further delays while Eberstadt cabled Dillon for instructions.

Following several more complex negotiating sessions, Eberstadt finally wrapped up the $35 million deal with Count Potocki and after sending a confirming cable to Dillon from Lancut, he took the next train for the gruelling return trip to Berlin via connecting train in Warsaw.[38]

Back in Berlin, Stresemann subsequently cautioned Eberstadt regarding the Polish government stating that he was "exasperated" with the lack of progress after a year and a half of negotiations with Polish officials. He told Eberstadt that "insofar as the standing of the house of Dillon Read was concerned in Germany he thought it would be a mistake for them to get out [any further] Polish loans." Heeding Stresemann's warning, Dillon Read did not underwrite another Polish issue for the rest of the 1920s, this despite Dillon's Polish heritage.[39]

In January 1928 Eberstadt was able to explain to his United States-based associates at their general sales meeting just how significant the German accomplishments were, by going over the important criteria Dillon Read used in selecting financing prospects:

> The most critical factor we value [is whether] . . . the company generates or has access to its own foreign exchange. If it has adequate foreign exchange, you can sleep quietly irrespective of any transfer crisis because no German . . . government is going to reach into the pocket of its own citizens and take their foreign exchange. The companies financed by Dillon Read have this

access to foreign exchange. . . .

Meanwhile, Germany and other world-trading nations had received an unexpected boost by an event which took place in London in 1925. Winston Churchill, as Chancellor of the Exchequer, announced Britain's return to the gold standard but in so doing he set the parity between gold, the dollar and the pound sterling at the same level of $4.86 per pound that had prevailed for upwards of fifty years prior to the first world war. This substantially overvalued the pound which proved disastrous for British trade during the 1920s. Foreign importers avoided buying artificially high-priced British goods and instead shifted their purchases of goods to other exporting nations including Germany, France and the United States.

The overvaluation of the pound led to a persistent erosion in the British trade position and was a major factor in planting the seeds of the worldwide depression that developed after 1928. But in the mid-1920s it meant that business conditions were exceedingly favorable for German exports, including the iron, steel, coal and electrical equipment industries. Dillon's newly revitalized corporate finance staff aggressively pursued financing for those industries from their Paris base.[40]

While Dillon focused his main energies on developing financings in Germany and elsewhere in Europe, he also made major inroads in South American finance, raising $178 million for Brazil, his major Latin client, during the 1920s. Dillon especially favored deals in the emerging Brazilian economy. A Dillon analysis found that the Brazilian government had a surplus of revenues over disbursements in 1923 and that the financial reforms instituted by the Bernardes regime qualified Brazil as a promising emerging area for foreign investment.[41]

While London merchant banks continued their presence in Latin American finance in the 1920s, Dillon and other American bankers threatened to undermine this dominance.[42] In 1921 Dillon Read dared to cut out a piece of business from under the noses of the English Rothschilds. While the English bankers were haggling over terms Clarence Dillon stepped in and undertook to market a loan of $50 million to Brazil.

This was followed one year later by another Brazilian loan for $60 million, which was underwritten by Dillon and Schroder, using a coffee valorization plan whereby coffee comprised the security for the loan. Agreements were drawn up under which the Brazilian government would supervise the marketing of the coffee crop and, from the proceeds, gradually amortize the loan. A novelty at the time, it was subsequently copied with variations by other banks. Including the Brazilian financing, Dillon raised $244 million for Latin American countries. Dillon also moved aggressively into Canadian financing, raising almost $300 million for the Canadian railroad system plus $133 million for Canadian provincial and municipal governments in the 1920s.[43]

Foreign governments bestowed honors and decorations on Dillon for his role in helping to finance the troubled nations of Europe. For example, a loan to the Belgian government in 1921 was followed by a reception given by King Albert in Brussels at which the Belgian Order of the Crown was awarded to Dillon by the King. In the summer of 1922 he helped to finance certain harbor improvements in Palermo, Sicily, for which King Victor Emmanuel II gave him the Italian Order of the Crown. He was made a Grand Officer of Polonia Restituta with Star by Poland following the $35 million loan negotiated for that country in 1925.[44]

Sometimes these awards would create bizarre occurrences. When Dillon was in Paris in 1938, he was made a Commandant of the Legion of Honor upon the recommendation of Marshal Pétain and was invited to give a speech before the Franco-American Society. Dillon had his speech translated into French and his reading of it was carefully rehearsed. The audience assumed he was fluent in French. At the conclusion of his speech, members of the society came up to him and started speaking in French, which caused Dillon some embarrassment and forced him to "wing it," feigning understanding.[45]

In the late 1920s, Eberstadt became disenchanted with the prospects for continued growth in the German economy, a view which Dillon also began to accept as the decade came to an end.[46] Stresemann's health faded, and he succumbed to a stroke in 1929; Hitler gained in political strength thereafter. As the long shadows of anti-Semitism, extreme nationalism, violence and ultimate world war lengthened, the investment prospects were becoming less attractive and the outlook for a democratic Germany faded.[47]

Paul Nitze shared Eberstadt's concerns about Germany's economic and political outlook. After Nitze graduated from Harvard in 1928, he began working for a Chicago securities firm which was considering entering the lucrative German securities business. They asked Nitze to make a field trip to Germany to explore the situation and prepare a report. A Harvard classmate suggested he contact Dillon, who met with him and gave him letters of introduction to several German bankers and industrialists; in return, Nitze agreed to give Dillon a copy of his report. Nitze's survey concluded that the economic situation in Germany was such that any slight disturbance elsewhere would cause a big depression in Germany. The Weimar Republic couldn't hold up in a serious economic crunch and it was likely that Germany would politically fall apart.[48]

When Nitze returned he visited Dillon and gave him his report. Dillon began to look at the question again and came to the tentative conclusion that Nitze and Eberstadt were probably right.[49] Although Dillon did not curtail all of his German financing activities immediately, he became more cautious and refrained from making any new commitments in Germany.

By then, Dillon had hired Nitze as his personal assistant. The thunderous crash of the New York Stock Exchange on October 24, 1929 confirmed Nitze's and Eberstadt's worst premonitions, and Germany defaulted on most of its external debt obligations. Moreover, almost all of the Latin debt issues financed by Dillon Read in the 1920s went into default and were repudiated by the governments involved, with huge losses for American investors in the early 1930s.

Dillon retained only Siemens & Halske and Vereinigte Stahlwerke (United Steel Works) as his major German corporate clients in the 1930s after Hitler seized power. Nonetheless, Dillon maintained the Paris office staffed by W. Meade Lindsley Fiske, F. Y. Steiner and Dillon's nephew, Seymour Weller, closing the office only after the war broke out in the fall of 1939. Dillon revived his European operations after the war at 16 place Vendome, not far from the earlier office Dillon had maintained across from the Ritz in the 1920s and 1930s.[50]

As for reparations, Germany paid 36.1 billion marks to the Allies but actually borrowed 33 billion marks from foreign bankers, notably American houses such as Dillon Read and Morgan, to make these payments. Thus the German net payment on reparations came to only about 3.1 billion marks. Not surprisingly, the reparations program was most successful during the period of the greatest volume of German financing—between 1924 and 1931, the period when Dillon Read built its reputation in German finance.

Notes

1. Sobel, Robert, *The Life and Times of Dillon Read*, pp. 93-5.
2. "Clarence Dillon Says Private Loans to European Countries Will Replace Government Loans," *New York Times*, July 19, 1922.
3. *Anne's Story*.
4. "Clarence Dillon Will Visit Germany," *New York Times*, August 2, 1924.
5. Sobel, Robert, *The Life and Times of Dillon Read*, pp. 97-8.
6. Cleveland, Harold van B., and Thomas F. Huertas, *Citibank, 1812-1970*, New York, 1985, pp. 148-9, hereinafter referred to as Cleveland/Huertas, *Citibank, 1812-1970*.
7. Stresemann, Gustav, *Essays and Speeches on Various Subjects*, Reprint Edition 1968, pp. 50-51.
8. Cleveland/Huertas, *Citibank, 1812-1970*, pp. 148-9.
9. Chernow, Ron, *The House of Morgan*, pp. 248-9.
10. Dawes, Charles G., *A Journal of Reparations*, London, 1939, p. 241.
11. Dawes, Charles G., *A Journal of Reparations*, pp. 242-4.
12. Sutton, Eric, editor and translator, *Gustav Stresemann: His Diaries, Letters, and Papers*, vol. 3, London, 1935-40, pp. 405-6.

13. The post of Agent General for Reparations was an international position of cardinal responsibility to receive and allocate world war reparation payments from Germany and to stabilize the German currency. S. Parker Gilbert, former Undersecretary of the Treasury and a former Cravath partner, was appointed the Agent General by the Reparations Commission. During his five years in Berlin as agent general, Gilbert oversaw the transfer of $2 billion in reparations. As Germany's economic czar, he was a stern taskmaster constantly pressing the Germans to curb fiscal extravagance. Gilbert's reports on Germany's financial condition won him widespread respect in Anglo-American financial circles; he became a figure of worldwide influence in the 1920s. (Sources: Chernow, Ron, *The House of Morgan*, pp. 252-3 and "S. Parker Gilbert," *National Cyclopaedia of American Biography*, Book 28, p. 331.)

14. Stresemann, Gustav, *Essays and Speeches on Various Subjects*, pp. 50-51.

15. *New York Times*, May 31, 1925.

16. Draft Memorandum of Ferdinand Eberstadt, dated June 29, 1926, Clarence Dillon's private papers.

17. Draft Memorandum of Ferdinand Eberstadt, dated June 29, 1926, Clarence Dillon's private papers.

18. Eberstadt got his start in German financing following his return to the law firm of Cotton and Franklin after the end of the first world war. Eberstadt was dispatched in 1920 to Germany to handle war claims for several clients. Other German legal business quickly followed. This brought him into close contact with Dillon Read which used Cotton and Franklin as its law firm. (Sources: Perez/Willett, *The Will to Win*, pp. 29-31 and Dorwart, Jeffrey, *Eberstadt and Forrestal, A National Security Partnership, 1909-1949*, College Station, Texas, 1991, p. 13.)

19. Dorwart, Jeffrey, *Eberstadt and Forrestal*, pp. 22-3.

20. Christman, Calvin Lee, *Ferdinand Eberstadt and Economic Mobilization for War, 1941-1943*, Ph.D. dissertation, pp. 2-3.

21. Perez/Willett, *The Will to Win*, p. 17.

22. Matz, Mary Jane, *The Many Lives of Otto Kahn*, New York, 1963, pp. 9, 13, 55-144.

23. Douglas Dillon interview, May 23, 1991.

24. Sobel, Robert, *The Life and Times of Dillon Read*, p. 105.

25. "Hermann von Siemens, Director of German Concern for 27 Years," *New York Times*, October 15, 1986.

26. James Forrestal, comments in Record of Addresses to General Sales Meeting Held on January 6-7, 1928, Clarence Dillon private papers, Far Hills, N.J.

27. Stresemann, Gustav, *Essays and Speeches on Various Subjects*, p. 238.

28. Sobel, Robert, *The Life and Times of Dillon Read*, p. 108.

29. Sutton, Eric, editor and translator, *Gustav Stresemann, His Diaries, Letters and Papers*, vol. 3, pp. 165-7.

30. Letter from Ferdinand Eberstadt to Clarence Dillon, November 20, 1926, Eberstadt private papers, *Seeley G. Mudd Manuscript Library*, Princeton University.

31. Letter from Ferdinand Eberstadt to Clarence Dillon, November 4, 1926, Eberstadt private papers, *Seeley G. Mudd Manuscript Library*, Princeton University.

32. "[Dillon] Reported as Joint Buyer with J. H. Schroder & Co. of London of Stinnes Stock in Deutsche Luxemburgische Co.," *New York Times*, July 28, 1925 and "Dillon Read Offers Bonds to Finance German Steel Merger," *New York Times*, January 15, 1926.

33. Ferdinand Eberstadt comments at General Sales Meeting Held January 6-8, 1928, Clarence Dillon private papers.

34. Poland, *Encyclopaedia Britannica*, Vol. 18, 1964 edition, p 148.

35. *Anne's Story*.

36. *Anne's Story*.

37. *Anne's Story*.

38. Frederick Eberstadt interview, September 9, 1987.

39. Letter from Ferdinand Eberstadt to Clarence Dillon, November 4, 1926, Eberstadt private papers, *Seeley G. Mudd Manuscript Library*, Princeton University.

40. Perez/Willett, *The Will to Win*, pp. 34-5 and Chernow, Ron, *The House of Morgan*, pp. 275-7.

41. "Dillon Read Reports Gain in Brazilian Government Finances," *New York Times*, July 14, 1923.

42. Marichal, Carlos, *A Century of Debt Crises in Latin America*, Princeton, 1989, p. 171.

43. "Dillon Read, Agent for Arranging $100 Million Stabilization Loan," *New York Times*, April 8, 1927 and Author's survey of Dillon Read financing.

44. *Anne's Story*.

45. *Anne's Story*.

46. Although the business made him rich, Eberstadt was appalled by the money pouring into Europe, especially since so little of it was earmarked for productive enterprises. (Source: "Ferdinand Eberstadt," *Fortune*, April 1939, p. 74.)

47. Perez/Willett, *The Will to Win*, p. 38.

48. Paul H. Nitze interview, November 11, 1991.

49. Paul H. Nitze interview, November 11, 1991.

50. Sobel, Robert, *The Life and Times of Dillon Read*, pp. 207-9, 266.

Clarence Dillon with his wife Anne, his son Douglas, and his daughter Dorothy, in New Jersey, circa 1919. *(Photo courtesy of Mrs. Dorothy Dillon Eweson)*

Rear view of the Dunwalke mansion, Far Hills, New Jersey. *(Author's photograph)*

Barns and other farm buildings at Dunwalke Farm. *(Author's photograph)*

James Forrestal took over the day-to-day management of
Dillon Read in the mid-1930s after Dillon withdrew from
active participation. (*A/P Wide World*)

Ferdinand Eberstadt was primarily responsible for building
up Dillon's German financing in the 1920s. (*Photo courtesy of
John Payne*)

Dean Mathey combined deal making at Dillon Read with his second career as a top-seeded tennis player defeating "Big Bill" Tilden in 1923. (*Bettmann Archives*)

After leaving Dillon Read in 1938, Paul H. Nitze became involved in national defense serving as an advisor to every president from Harry S Truman to Ronald Reagan. (*A/P Wide World*)

Dillon's Paris office in the 1920s was located at 39 rue Cambon, directly across from the Ritz Hotel shown here in the early 1990s. (*Author's photograph*)

Dillon's granddaughter, Phyllis, inherited Dillon's cottage at Dark Harbor, Maine. (*Author's photogragh*)

Anne Dillon in her garden at the Dillon cottage in Dark Harbor, Maine, circa 1930. (*Photo courtesy of Dorothy Dillon Eweson*)

Dillon talks with Ferdinand Pecora (*left*) during a break in the 1933 Senate hearings on stock market practices in the 1920s. (*Bettmann Archives*)

Dillon (*center*) and Forrestal meeting with senior navy officers in Washington to report on the $10 million Navy Relief Campaign that Dillon headed during World War II. (*Photo courtesy of Mrs. Dorothy Dillon Eweson*)

Chateau Haut-Brion, Dillon's celebrated wine estate in Bordeaux, France, during harvest time in 1985. (*Chateau Haut-Brion Archives*)

The new ambassador to France, Douglas Dillon (*center*), accompanied by French President Vincent Auriol (*left*) and Foreign Minister, Georges Bidault, presents his credentials in March 1953. (*Bettmann Archives*)

Dillon's daughter, Mrs. Dorothy Dillon Eweson, at the front entrance to the Dunwalke mansion, in the early 1990s. (*Author's photograph*)

7

The Chrysler-Dodge Buyout

In 1925, Dillon bought Dodge from under Morgan's nose; this was heralded by the press as the deal of the century (see Chapter 4). After acquiring control, Dillon moved Edward G. Wilmer from Goodyear and installed him as head of the auto maker. However, the automobile business was entering a period of withering competition; Dodge's earnings began to go down hill and Wilmer was not able to sustain Dodge's position. Thus, Dillon's interests in Dodge stock were worth far less in 1928 than in 1925 when Dillon first brought Dodge public. Despite these setbacks, Dillon continued to claim: "Buying the Dodge was one of the soundest acts of my life."[1] However true that may be, by 1928 Dillon was desperate to sell Dodge but that had become exceeding difficult. From Berlin and Paris, Eberstadt would wryly ask his associates, "Is it better to issue the Dodge or dodge the issue?"

Dillon's management of Dodge provides a near-classic case study of the limited ability of financiers to run a business. Investment bankers of those years were generalists, adept at analyzing a broad array of companies but with little ability to run any of them. Investment bankers excelled at deal-making and when one was completed they turned quickly to the next venture, moving from one deal to another. Investment bankers covered all fields of economic activity; they were the "kingmakers."[2]

Perhaps because of this attitude, investment bankers tended to treat business management as a by-product of financing, not significant in itself nor requiring specialized talents. Bankers believed a capable manager in one field could effectively transfer his abilities to a totally different field. The same attitude dominated Wall Street's strategic planning during the ill-founded conglomerate merger boom of the 1960s with similarly devastating results.

In the first months of Dillon Read control, Dodge possessed strong internal management headed by Frederick J. Haynes but after he and other key managers retired some months later, Edward Wilmer took direct charge of running the company. After initial setbacks at Dodge, Wilmer resigned his Dillon Read partnership in July 1926 to focus all of his attention on auto making. Wilmer's initial talk to the Dillon Read sales organization in April 1925 indicates his lack of a clear understanding of the automobile business in general and Dodge in particular. He had a simplistic view of automotive technology and markets and of the major competitive forces which would soon overwhelm the industry. This was in sharp contrast to his approach at Goodyear, where he relied on the operating management of George Stadleman and Paul Litchfield, with Wilmer concentrating on finances.[3]

Wilmer was destined to make damaging errors. Under the old management all Dodges were powered by rugged and economical four-cylinder engines. Shortly after his arrival, Wilmer ordered a crash program to develop a more powerful six-cylinder model together with a major streamlining of Dodge's lackluster design. At the same time, Wilmer introduced a new installment purchase plan to spur sales coupled with a stiff increase in prices. Wilmer did not wait for the new models to be available before raising prices which backfired with sales sagging badly; reversing himself, Wilmer then cut prices drastically, pushing sales to record levels but at lower profits.[4]

Moreover, the new models introduced in late 1926, while more stylish, soon developed mechanical problems which dismayed customers used to Dodge reliability. Wilmer again raised prices to recover the costs of the new models which were repositioned to compete against Buick, not Ford and Chevrolet. Again, Wilmer's strategy failed resulting in confusion for the dealers and the car buying public. Although Dillon defended Wilmer's management of Dodge, he knew better. The new Dodges, hastily developed and poorly built, were priced at $1,500—three times the price of the soon-to-be-introduced Ford Model A. Dodge cars piled up on dealer lots, demoralizing the dealer organization. Finally, Dillon realized he was in trouble and needed to sell Dodge Brothers.[5]

One persistent rumor that had circulated around Wall Street during 1927 had William C. Durant heading a group to buy out Dodge and several other auto companies to create a major competitor for General Motors. Of all the colorful men who led the United States into the automobile age, William Crapo Durant was perhaps the most flamboyant. A handsome sporty man with a winsome grin and a flair for invention, Durant had started out by developing the largest horse carriage company before the turn of the century. Then in 1904, Durant acquired Buick rescuing it from almost certain failure.[6] Following the Buick acquisition, Durant merged Olds (also on the brink of failure) and Buick in September 1908 to create the original General Motors.[7] Durant was a persuasive character—"he could coax a bird right out of the tree," Walter Chrysler once said—but he was a disastrous manager, and his own worst enemy. Soon Durant overextended General Motors and was ousted. However, he had a charmed life and was able to regain control of GM after a withering and scandalous proxy fight.[8] Finally, Durant was ousted for good after his hastily-formed pool failed to corner the stock of minority interests who opposed his ruthless methods.[9]

Accordingly, Durant was no person with whom Clarence Dillon wanted to be associated. However, the Wall Street rumor mills insisted that Dillon was negotiating an ambitious plan with Durant to group together in one unit a number of automobile manufacturers to form a new organization to rival Durant's former company, General Motors. Encouraging the speculation, Durant had let it be known that he would issue a "startling statement" in April, but Dillon spiked these rumors by flatly denying any interest whatsoever in any business venture involving the maverick Durant.[10] To create interest in the Dodge situation, however, Dillon probably floated a number of these and other rumors regarding potential buyouts.

Anxious to sell, Dillon apparently first approached General Motors, assuming it was the only company large enough to relieve him of his white elephant but GM's head, Alfred Sloan, declined as its expansion program had eliminated the need for additional car-producing facilities. Instead, Sloan recommended that Dillon sound out Chrysler, who desperately needed both Dodge's production facilities and dealer organization to break into the industry's "Big Three."[11]

One of Chrysler's early innovations was designing and bringing out a new model which he called the Chrysler Six and which featured the nation's first high-compression engine and hydraulic brakes, developed by his bright young automotive designer, Fred M. Zeder. The manufacture of a new car, however, requires major financing and public showing, and Walter Chrysler had neither. The Automobile Show, which allots space on the basis of sales in the preceding year, would allot none for his prototype of the Chrysler Six. Moreover, the bankers told Chrysler two months before the 1924 Automobile Show (held that year in New York's Grand Central Palace) that the proposed $6 million new financing could not be carried out. Besides, Chrysler's new car was unconventionally short and carried a relatively high price usually associated with longer touring cars.[12]

Not to be denied, Chrysler leased the main lobby of the Commodore Hotel to display his new automobile model. Chrysler's move was an immediate success. From morning until late at night, a crowd was densely packed around the Chrysler models in the Commodore lobby—attracting more attention than any automobile on display at Grand Central Palace. By the end of the first day Chrysler knew that his new models would be a sales success if he could produce them in volume.[13]

After a few days, the bankers realized the new car was a sensation and they agreed to advance $5 million to Chrysler to finance the manufacture of the new car. Thereafter, the Chrysler Six became an instant sales success and soon propelled Chrysler into the fifth-largest producer in the industry. The demand, however, caused production problems and Chrysler soon had trouble obtaining parts to meet his rapidly expanding production schedules. Construction of a new plant would have cost $75 million and probably would have forced Chrysler to close down as Ford had when he tooled up the new Model A.[14]

Acquiring Dodge was the logical solution. Chrysler was already buying parts from Dodge, which had a modern, efficient, but not fully utilized plant just down the road from the Chrysler plant in Detroit. A merger of the two companies would resolve Chrysler's problems and at the same time extricate Dillon from an extremely difficult situation.

General Motors continued to have a latent interest in acquiring Dodge but at a much lower price than Dillon was willing to accept. Other potential buyers were lined up; from Berlin, Eberstadt received an indication of interest in acquiring Dodge from bankers representing Mercedes Benz but Wilmer told Eberstadt to put those negotiations on hold for the time being, as Wilmer still hoped for a turnaround.[15] Meanwhile, Dillon focused all of his efforts on unloading Dodge on Chrysler. As Eberstadt put it, "One day God appeared to us in the guise of Walter P. Chrysler mercifully [agreeing] to buy the Dodge Company."[16]

This was the setting of the stage for the entrance of Chrysler and the beginning of the deal of the century. There are as many versions of that deal as there are narrators to tell them, but it was actually Walter Chrysler who opened negotiations with Dillon with an abortive offer in 1926 but nothing materialized. Chrysler had become acquainted with Clarence Dillon shortly after the latter bought Dodge in 1925.

After Dodge's fortunes declined, Dillon approached Chrysler in early April 1928 and in the course of conversation asked if he was in the mood for "some trading." However, Chrysler played coy even though he knew he had an urgent need to purchase Dodge to put himself within range of his lifelong hero, Henry Ford.[17]

"Hell, Clarence, I don't want your plant. What'll I do with it?" was Chrysler's tongue-in-cheek response.[18]

But Dillon knew Dodge would mesh nicely with the kind of company Chrysler was creating; both men knew that Chrysler and Dodge would make a good fit. The conversation was inconclusive but Dillon was certain that he could convince Chrysler that Dodge would become the springboard to propel Chrysler into the big time.

However, a few days later when Dillon returned to talk price, Chrysler put him off, demanding a much lower price, noting: "When a big outfit like [Dodge] starts slipping, it can go down fast."

Dillon retorted: "We're doing splendidly, only I think your crowd could do better with it."

Dillon, ever the master salesman, did not leave right away. He talked for a couple of hours about the Dodge plants and dealer organization; Chrysler listened closely but tried to conceal his evident interest.

Finally, Dillon got up to leave, adding: "I'm going back down to talk this over with my associates."

Chrysler retorted: "All right, Clarence, come in again, at any time."

In a few days Dillon came back. Chrysler was gruff, and put him off again with: "Its too much money; we aren't interested unless it was a bargain—but it's not. So what's the use of talking?"

But Dillon came right back: "Now Walt, don't shut your eyes to this. How else are you going to make Chrysler Corporation a first-rank competitor of Ford and General Motors?"

Chrysler replied: "Clarence, we are doing pretty well—show me a company with a record to compare with the Chrysler Corporation."

Dillon snapped: "That's true, Walter, but you've got your head pretty close to the ceiling right now, unless. . . ."

Chrysler repeated: "It's too much money, Clarence. You keep right on worrying about Dodge; maybe it will come on the market a year from now a lot cheaper."

Dillon kept supplying Chrysler with information for a month or so and then one day he came to Chrysler's office, obviously distressed. He moaned: "Walter, bankers got no business trying to run a great big industrial enterprise. What do I know about making automobiles and selling them? Why don't you take this Dodge business and . . ."

Chrysler looked at Dillon for a minute and said: "Clarence, you're wasting your time and you're wasting mine. Put your proposition down on paper and don't forget: you had better make it tempting."

Dillon came back after ten days, bringing this time a considerable number of typewritten data sheets with all of the critical financial information. Chrysler called in his assistants and lawyers and went with Dillon and his team to the Ritz where they closeted themselves in a suite of rooms.

Chrysler told Dillon: "You may get a sore throat from talking before we are finished, but we'll stay in this suite until we come to a conclusion, until one of us says yes or no."

From the outset, Chrysler insisted on obtaining the assent of 90 percent of all the classes of Dodge shares for the takeover, since he did not want to be troubled by damaging lawsuits from minority stockholders such as had occurred with Dillon's earlier Goodyear rescue. Chrysler's demand for an almost unanimous vote of the Dodge stockholders would avoid costly and troublesome lawsuits. Dillon concurred.[19] With that, the two men shook hands and the final negotiations got underway.

At one point, Dillon's attorneys advised him that a legal snag had developed that would delay the deal. Dillon called Chrysler to inform him of the delay and Chrysler, in a rage, shouted: "We will have to renegotiate . . . as soon as possible" and with that he stormed down to Dillon's office.

Dillon resorted to one of his poker playing ploys and decided to call Chrysler's bluff. Dillon called Forrestal into his office and told him: "Get all the reporters to come to our office for important news."

When Chrysler arrived he was shown into Dillon's famed corner office without delay. Chrysler immediately asked: "Who are all those men in the reception room?"

"They are reporters," said Dillon.

Chrysler retorted, "What are they doing here?"

"We are going to tell them our deal is off!" Dillon replied.

Chrysler said, "No we are not! We will walk out of here [arm-in-arm] and tell the reporters there will be a slight delay, but we have an agreement."

Dillon's bluff worked and the negotiations went forward.[20]

After five days of marathon bargaining, arguing, eating, smoking, sleeping, talking and trading at the Ritz, Dillon and Chrysler finally came to terms. All of them had bloodshot eyes from weariness but there was a sense of triumph at having found a way of doing the deal. Chrysler agreed to acquire Dodge in exchange for $170 million of Chrysler stock and the assumption of Dodge's debentures and other debt, but Dillon was forced to agree to produce proxies approving the merger from holders representing at least 90 percent of all outstanding Dodge common and preferred stock.[21] Obtaining 90 percent approval of Dodge's diverse stockholders, however, proved elusive and the Chrysler deal appeared in jeopardy. At this point, however, Dillon had not given up hope of selling Dodge to General Motors if the Chrysler deal fell through. GM had indicated a willingness to pay Dillon $125 million for the business. While Dillon did not reject their offer outright, he strung GM along; if the Chrysler negotiations failed, Dillon could still accept GM's bid.[22]

The Dillon 1925 buyout of Dodge followed by the 1928 merger into Chrysler bears amazing similarities to the RJR Nabisco leveraged buyout in 1989. The bidding in both deals took on a lot of the poker playing tactics for which Dillon was renowned, with bidding and counter-bidding escalating the stakes to then unheard of levels. In both battles, the competing sides shuttled between different groups closeted in different suites attempting to raise the ante.[23]

With the merger terms finally set, Dillon and his partners locked themselves in their offices and began the lengthy process of cajoling Dodge stockholders to provide the stock needed to complete the terms of the merger. However, obtaining the required 90 percent of each class of Dodge outstanding shares proved a formidable obstacle. Dillon, Phillips, Forrestal, Eberstadt, Mathey, Bermingham, and others worked full time at obtaining proxies. The offering was made public on June 1, 1928, and was to expire June 30, but Dillon Read had to ask three times for extensions, with the final deadline extended to July 30.[24]

The *New York Herald Tribune* reported on July 23 that Dillon had 86 percent of the preferred stock, 76 percent of the Class "A" common, and all but a small fraction of the Class "B" stock, most of which was owned by Dillon Read. Time and again, as the difficulty of securing 90 percent of each class of stock—held here, there and everywhere, at home and abroad—became more evident, Dillon begged to be let off from his commitment to deliver to Chrysler 90 percent of each class.

"Good grief, Walter," Dillon pleaded, "I've got 85 percent of the stock. That's more than has ever been brought in on a deal of this kind."

But Chrysler, pacing the floor with his long Kansas stride, replied: "No, Clarence, I can't do nothing for you."[25]

Dillon persisted, pointing out: "One of the largest [Dodge] stockholders is in Paris and she can not get that stock in our hands in two days. That's why I can't put my hands on that 60,000 shares."

When Chrysler again flatly refused, Dillon rushed out of the office in despair. Even Chrysler's own lawyers looked at him with reproachful eyes.[26]

The difficulties seemed insurmountable, but Dillon refused to concede defeat. At this critical juncture, just before time ran out, Eberstadt and Forrestal came up with a brilliant but daring plan that saved the deal. Their plan was approved by Dillon and the next day Wall Street was astounded to learn that Dillon Read had gone into the open market and bought up a sufficient amount of Dodge preferred shares and Class A common stock for its own account to satisfy Chrysler's 90 percent requirement.[27]

To hedge the firm's position (involving about $5 million in purchases or one-third of Dillon's liquid capital) they offset their long position by simultaneously selling short the same amount of preferred stock and Class A stock. They accomplished this by discreetly borrowing the needed stock from "Street Name" accounts with Dominick & Dominick and other friendly firms in the Street able to lend Chrysler stock to Dillon. The arbitrage was critical to obtaining the shares needed to meet Chrysler's condition while at the same time hedging Dillon's long position.[28]

With this cunning last-minute move, the firm made good on Chrysler's demand for a 90 percent minimum by the final deadline. Eliot Janeway says that Dillon, always cautious and conservative, was scared stiff that the arbitrage strategy would not work and as the pressure mounted, "he literally wet his underpants worrying about the risk."[29] Despite Dillon's concern, the Eberstadt-Forrestal tactic paid off: Dillon had scored another major coup. With the 90 percent minimum met, the deal was closed with Chrysler's paying $170 million in stock for Dodge's securities and assuming Dodge's outstanding debt of $66 million, bringing the total purchase to $236 million. The deal was consummated at 5:30 on the afternoon of Monday, July 30.

Both Dillon and Chrysler benefitted handsomely from this deal. Dillon Read made about $40 million in profits from the sale of Dodge to Chrysler[30] and the firm was finally divorced from an operation which produced nothing but headaches. Dillon quickly cashed in by selling or distributing to his partners all of the Chrysler shares the firm received as part of the merger. Moreover, Dillon realized the profit on his Dodge investment a full year in advance of the Stock Market Crash of November 1929. Chrysler, meanwhile, acquired Dodge's manufacturing facilities and dealer organization which enabled Chrysler to penetrate the auto industry's "Big Three."

The Chrysler-Dodge deal marked the end of Dillon's forays into merchant banking. Never again would he install his own management in a company that he bought out, relying instead on the entrenched management or bringing in new management, but in either case allowing them to operate the business autonomously. Wilmer returned as a partner of Dillon Read but would not again be placed in a managerial role.

The merger constituted the biggest consolidation in the automobile business up to that time. The new corporation had a manufacturing capacity of 700,000 cars and trucks annually, a gross business of $500 million a year and a potential annual earning power of $40-50 million, with a total capitalization of $450 million. For a bargain price, Chrysler Corporation gained Dodge's facilities and 12,000-man dealer organization intact, a key ingredient in Chrysler's subsequent success, and the Dodge name plate was soon restored to its former luster.

Notes

1. Sobel, Robert, *The Life and Times of Dillon Read*, p. 154.
2. Perez/Willett, *The Will to Win*, p. 106 and "Oral History of Douglas Dillon," John Luter, *Columbia University Oral History Department*, 1973.
3. Sobel, Robert, *The Life and Times of Dillon Read*, p. 143.
4. Sobel, Robert, *The Life and Times of Dillon Read*, p. 144.

5. Sobel, Robert, *The Life and Times of Dillon Read*, pp. 144, 146, 147.

6. Chernow, Ron, *The House of Morgan*, p. 223.

7. Unlike Henry Ford who stamped out endless Model Ts, Durant favored a diversified product line. He wanted to adjust to the constant and sudden shifts in public tastes by offering as wide a choice of models and as wide a range of prices as possible. Durant's idea was long lasting and became the basis for nearly all subsequent automobile development, even including Ford.

8. Durant had organized a new car company and had brought over Louis Chevrolet from France to produce a utilitarian car to compete with Ford. The Chevrolet was an instant success and Durant was soon in a position to wage a proxy contest to reacquire GM through an exchange offer of Chevrolet stock for GM stock. Durant's proxy contest was successful and he regained control of GM employing all the devious tricks of a flim-flam artist to bring it off.

9. After regaining control of GM, Durant determined to punish his former GM allies. Just before the 1920 business recession, Durant formed a secret pool, borrowing heavily to buy and drive up GM's stock price in an attempt to corner the stock thus squeezing out the shorts. But the tactic backfired; GM's stock plummeted as its unsold cars piled up on dealer lots. The bankers then forced Durant out buying up all of his GM shares at well below his cost. An unreconstructed plunger, Durant lost most of his remaining net worth in the 1929 Crash. (Sources: May, George S., *A Most Unique Machine*, pp. 324-5, Chernow, Ron, *The House of Morgan*, pp. 223-5 and Cray, Ed, *Chrome Colossus*, p. 140.)

10. "Dillon Read Denies that It Is Interested in W. C. Durant's Automobile Merger Plans," *New York Times*, March 29, 1927.

11. Cray, Ed., *Chrome Colossus*, p. 258.

12. "Chrysler," *Fortune*, August 1935, p. 34.

13. Chrysler, Walter, *Life of an American Workman*, pp. 184-5.

14. "Chrysler," *Fortune*, p. 37.

15. Eberstadt diary entries, October 12, 13 and 24, 1927, Eberstadt private papers, *Seeley G. Mudd Manuscript Library*, Princeton University.

16. Perez/Willett, *The Will to Win*, p. 40 and "Chrysler," *Fortune*, pp. 31-2.

17. "Chrysler," *Fortune*, pp. 36-7.

18. The account of the bargaining for the sale of Dodge to Chrysler between Clarence Dillon and Walter Chrysler is drawn mainly from Chrysler, Walter, *The Story of an American Workman*, pp. 192-6.

19. "Chrysler," *Fortune*, p. 37.

20. Joseph Haywood interview, October 28, 1991.

21. Chrysler, Walter, *The Story of an American Workman*, pp. 195-6.

22. "The Upheaval at Dillon Read," by Tim Anderson and Stephen Bronte, *Euromoney*, September 1982, p. 257.

23. Burrough, Bryan, *Barbarians at the Gate, the Fall of RJR Nabisco* , pp. 398-9, 413-21, 449-95.

24. Perez/Willett, *The Will to Win*, p. 41.

25. "Chrysler," *Fortune*, p. 37.

26. Chrysler, Walter, *The Story of an American Workman*, pp. 195-6.

27. "Dodge Stock Buying Caps Chrysler Deal," *New York Times*, July 31, 1928.

28. Perez/Willett, *The Will to Win*, p. 41.
29. Eliot Janeway interview, April 4, 1991.
30. Winkler, *The New Yorker*, p. 29.

8

The End of an Era

The press trumpeted Dillon's outstanding success in merging Dodge into Chrysler, welcoming "the new colossus of the automotive industry." However, Dillon was not a man who enjoyed sharing either glory or profits with his partners, and he was predictably restrained in thanking his two brilliant young partners, Eberstadt and Forrestal, for their role in saving the deal with their eleventh-hour stock arbitrage scheme. "They saved Dillon's ass," Eliot Janeway said many years later, "but got little thanks for it."[1]

Eberstadt was particularly bitter even though his and Forrestal's fame on Wall Street increased dramatically thereafter. While Clarence Dillon greatly admired Ferdinand Eberstadt, the two were headed on a collision course. Eberstadt had previously been displeased with his status and compensation at the firm and he demanded satisfaction. Although Dillon increased Eberstadt's partnership interest in 1927 and again in the spring of 1928, Eberstadt wanted more.

Eberstadt finally determined to leave the firm and had talked to his old friend and colleague, James Forrestal, about joining him and Robert Christie, Jr., Dillon Read's treasurer, to form a new firm to be known as Eberstadt and Forrestal. Forrestal would be the "inside" brains and Eberstadt the "outside" brains. Eberstadt would get the deals and Forrestal with his intellectual brilliance would create the financial techniques and ideas to merchandise them to the public. Together in their own firm, Eberstadt and Forrestal would become an unbeatable team. As Charles Murphy, a former editor at *Fortune* who knew both men quite well, put it:

Eberstadt's relationship with Forrestal was, in many ways, a balance of opposite qualities. Eberstadt was brilliant, quick of thought and assertive.

89

. . . Forrestal was intuitive, hesitant, reserved and assailed privately by doubts and misgivings. However, separately and together, Eberstadt and Forrestal towered above the senior financial leaders of their day.[2]

The proposed Eberstadt-Forrestal venture was not without problems. Eberstadt was temperamental and explosive, often firing people one day and then rehiring them the next. Most people found him fascinating but many found him impossible to work with; he was undeniably arrogant. Janeway, in one of his colorful asides, referred to him as "a real nut-cutter."[3]

Characteristically, Eberstadt had leased office space for the new firm in the fall of 1928. He told Forrestal that "the die is cast." Forrestal, however, was reluctant to abandon what amounted to a clear shot at becoming the head of Dillon Read, since Dillon was reducing his participation in the firm's day-to-day activities and seemed determined to withdraw completely. Forrestal had become increasingly important to Dillon.

Although Dillon was only forty-six years old in 1928, he was beginning to show signs of boredom with investment banking. He was spending more of his time engaged in farming, cattle raising, painting, and other pursuits at Dunwalke. If Dillon withdrew, Phillips and Forrestal would be the leading candidates to succeed him until Douglas Dillon was prepared to assume command. As a result, Forrestal pulled out of the new venture telling Eberstadt: "Why don't we wait another year and see how things work out?"[4]

While Eberstadt wanted to set up his own firm at that point, the withdrawal of Forrestal from the venture forced him to reconsider his options. He decided to make one last effort to achieve financial success by demanding a steep increase in his partnership interest from Dillon as well as a change in the name of the firm to Dillon Read and Eberstadt, with Eberstadt assuming a greater role in the management. If Dillon would meet his conditions, he would stay—otherwise he would strike out on his own.

As was his custom, Eberstadt came to New York in December for the holidays. While there, he went to the office every day and tended to necessary matters, hoping that Dillon would call him into his famous corner office to discuss business conditions—but Eberstadt waited two weeks in vain; Dillon in effect ignored him. Finally Eberstadt came in one morning, hung up his hat and coat, walked into Dillon's office and, after greeting him, began recounting all of the deals that he had done—the millions and millions in German bond issues that he had negotiated and had brought to the firm for sale in the U. S. market; the millions in American bond issues that he had successfully placed with the so-called Jewish banks in Europe.

Eberstadt reminded Dillon of his critical role in bringing off the Chrysler-Dodge merger and in the legal defense of the firm in the Goodyear litigation. He knew exactly how much money Dillon Read had earned on every one of those deals—he had it right down to the penny. Finally Eberstadt threw down the gauntlet and told Dillon he thought his cut in the partnership should be increased to 10 percent from 3 percent, along with the other demands.

Without blinking an eye, Dillon growled: "You're fired."[5]

Dillon was unwilling to share the leadership with Eberstadt or anyone else. According to Marjorie Wellbrock, Dillon's personal secretary, "both Dillon and Eberstadt were strong willed and martinets—leaders who projected an irresistible force and vibrations of power."[6] Eberstadt and Dillon were fighting over the division of the spoils. Dillon largely kept that decision to himself. He made the division and no one knew by what formula.

Dean Mathey later remarked to Peter Wastrom, one of his junior associates:

> Eber was a very tough and uncompromising person and very difficult to work with [but] if you think Eber was tough, you should have known Clarence Dillon. He was probably . . . the meanest man that ever lived as far as his partners were concerned. To this day, I don't know whether he cheated us at the end of the year in divvying up the pie. He just called you in and told you what you were going to get with no rhyme, reason, or calculations—very arbitrary.[7]

As an example of Dillon's arrogance, Forrestal told Eliot Janeway, the columnist and economist, that he didn't know where he stood when he left the firm in 1940. Mathey added: "Forrestal never knew what his final share of the profits was, even after he had been down in Washington for all those war years; he went to his death without knowing his final wealth."[8]

Eberstadt's decision to leave the firm may have been influenced partly by the sharp drop in profits of the firm after 1925 and Eberstadt's need for additional resources to finance the ambitious estate he was building on 80 acres of prime land in Lloyd's Neck along the Gold Coast on the North Shore of Long Island. Eberstadt wanted to build a mansion to rival the lavish estates of other multimillionaires—including Dillon's Dunwalke estate and the palatial eighty-room French chateau built for $4.5 million in 1917 by his first cousin, Otto Kahn, on 700 acres in neighboring Cold Spring Harbor. Kahn's mansion perfectly complemented his lavish Italian palazzo on Fifth Avenue.

Many years later, Eberstadt had second thoughts as to the wisdom of his abrupt demand and departure and tried to make peace with Dillon. A letter dated October 2, 1968 from Eberstadt to Dillon seems to bear this out. He wrote:

Dear Baron:

It is a long time since I have seen you and I miss you and I hope you will give me a ring some time when you are in town so that we can get together. If that is not convenient, let me know and I can run out to see you . . . [at Dunwalke]. I have nothing in mind except to confess and seek absolution. As ever,

Sincerely,

Ferdinand Eberstadt[9]

But Dillon never answered Eberstadt's letter and Dillon's secretary, Marjorie Wellbrock, states that she had no record that Eberstadt ever visited Dunwalke or that there ever was any further contact between the two men. Apparently, Dillon's stubborn grudge with Eberstadt caused him to ignore him. Nitze adds: "I don't think that old man Dillon was ever a very forgiving man." Nitze also recalled Dillon's resentful behavior whenever he crossed swords with rivals. For example, Louis Strauss, an investment banker at Kuhn Loeb and an early member and later, chairman of the Atomic Energy Commission, offended Dillon in a press interview with negative comments about Dillon and Dillon Read & Co. Dillon was furious but contained his anger.

When *Time* magazine featured Strauss in a cover story, Dillon cut out the *Time* cover photo of Strauss and put it in a drawer in his desk. Nitze asked Dillon, "Why are you doing that?" Dillon answered: "Whenever one of these people that I know is no good, becomes [the subject of a feature article], I put the article about him in this desk and when he falls on his face, I take the article out and throw it in the waste basket."[10]

After the breakup with Dillon, Eberstadt started his own firm in the teeth of the depression in 1931 and went on to become one of the most profitable entrepreneurs in Wall Street, financing his "little blue chips" in the 1930s and thereafter launching several spectacular buyouts in the drug and chemical field which brought him and André Meyer of Lazard Frères incredible profits in the 1950s and 1960s.[11] Nitze admired Eberstadt, noting "you couldn't put Eberstadt down for long; he kept on fighting . . . he had that inner strength."[12]

As aforementioned, financing activity declined at Dillon Read after 1925 with the firm's relative share of total American underwritings declining from 7 percent of the total to just above 3 percent, the lowest relative level for the firm since 1919. Dillon correctly anticipated problems ahead and was retrenching in preparation for them. In 1933, Dillon attributed the firm's post-1925 policy "in no small measure to [our] careful examination applied to prospective issues . . . and our rejection of many proposals for new financing presented to us."[13]

One Dillon Read legend has it that in 1928, Dillon ordered his partners to cut back on activities and personnel just before leaving for his annual summer vacation. When he returned in the autumn and saw that the cutbacks had not been made, Dillon abruptly ordered his partners to fire every third person.

In late September 1929, Nitze had been invited by Dillon to Dunwalke for the weekend. Nitze's visit coincided with the beginning of the stock market's first sharp declines. On the long drive through New Jersey out to Dillon's estate in his chauffeur-driven Rolls Royce, Nitze asked Dillon if he thought the market decline an omen of hard times ahead.

Dillon answered: "No, I don't. I don't think it portends that at all."

Nitze said, "Well, what do you think it indicates?"

Dillon thought for a few minutes and replied, "I think it presages the end of an era." Dillon continued emphasizing that the change would not be merely a retrenchment, but a major overhauling of the securities industry and its institutions.[14]

Dillon noted that students of history recognize that ultimate power sometimes rests with the military, sometimes with men of God, sometimes political figures, and sometimes with men of wealth. But he noted that in the power structure of the great civilizations—ancient Greece, Rome, the city-states of Italy during the days of the Medici, for a time in France and in Austria—the periods when men of private wealth held power were relatively short and ultimately power would shift to one of the other groups. Dillon noted that in the United States, men of wealth in Wall Street had held power from the end of the Civil War through the 1920s, an exceptionally long period of time.[15]

Dillon also told Nitze that the U.S. power structure was going to change from that point forward—that we would have a long depression of immense depth, and that the Washington political power structure would take control and would dominate Wall Street and the economy. Nitze asked how Dillon planned to meet the new order.

Dillon told him, "I have already acted." Just two days before, he had ordered wholesale reductions in the Dillon Read staff, from a total of nearly seven hundred down to fewer than one hundred, including termination of the entire retail sales operation. "Because I acted now, they can all find other jobs," Dillon said. "If I had waited six months, they would face unemployment." Similarly, at about the same time, Charlie Merrill closed down most of the original Merrill Lynch brokerage business selling its extensive retail branch office system to E. A. Pierce & Company.

Thus Dillon coldly braced his firm to meet the market crash that came six weeks later and to weather the long years of the depression that followed.[16]

Actually, Henry Riter III, his partner and manager of the Philadelphia office, agreed to take over all of the retail branch offices. Dillon helped Riter by investing in his new retail firm, which prospered for many years and survived well into the postwar period.[17]

As November 1929 approached, Dillon completely unloaded the firm's securities inventory and the firm had no bank loans.[18] Dean Mathey, one of Dillon's most trusted partners and chairman of Princeton University's investment committee, picked up the same cue; in 1928 he had shifted Princeton's portfolio out of stocks and into bonds because he also was fearful of the outlook for the economy and the stock market. For one full year his decision proved dead wrong, with the market continuing to make new highs. Then the Crash hit, and the Depression. Mathey's switch to bonds, a shrewd deflation hedge, was a classic move.[19]

Later, exhibiting the nimbleness of the tennis star that he was, Mathey played both ends of the investing cycle. With the stock market languishing five months after Pearl Harbor, Mathey acted resolutely again, selling 80 percent of the university's bonds and replacing them with common stocks. The chairman of the trustees' finance committee denounced Mathey's move as reckless and irresponsible, pointing out that bonds were the only prudent and conservative investment for a college endowment fund. Forced to defend what proved to be an incredibly correct investment move, Mathey wrote in reply: "The only true test of conservatism is to be right in the future."[20]

Nitze recalled Dillon's ordering him to sell 5,000 shares of Alcoa from the US&FS portfolio in late 1929. Nitze sold 100 shares of this block at 502; then 100 shares more at 480. When the broker told him that the bid had dropped to 460, Nitze pulled back and said:

"I think I'd better check this."

He went in to Dillon, told him what he had sold and what the market was, and asked him what he should do.

"I told you to sell it all," Dillon said. "Sell it!"

So Nitze went back to the broker and sold it all but the last trade went through at 350. Dillon drove the market down by relentlessly selling Alcoa and other holdings in a falling market. Thus Dillon's decision to sell at any cost accelerated the drop in the securities markets and deepened the depression. He wanted to get out of the market, regardless of the consequences.[21]

By late 1929, the economy was beginning to crumble; the gross national product, $103.1 billion in 1929, declined to $58 billion in 1932 and unemployment multiplied nine-fold, representing 24.1 percent of the labor force. The value of all shares listed on the Stock Exchange declined from $90 billion in 1929 to under $16 billion in 1932.[22] While Dillon did not panic, he acted as a person who believed that utter disintegration lay just ahead.

Later, most of Dillon's remaining key partners left the firm either to start up their own firms or to make a mark in Washington working in government. Nitze, after taking a six-month sabbatical in the late 1930s, also left for government service in the National Security Organization, serving as an advisor to every president from Truman to Reagan.[23] For the balance of the 1930s and 1940s Dillon systematically reduced the importance and presence of the firm he had so carefully built up in the 1920s.

Thus ended the era of the 1920s.

Notes

1. Hoopes/Brinkley, *Driven Patriot*, p. 61.
2. Letter from Charles J. V. Murphy to author, May 26, 1984.
3. Hoopes/Brinkley, *Driven Patriot*, p. 62.
4. Eberstadt interview with Calvin Christman, July 17-18, 1969.
5. Peter L. Wastrom interview, March 29, 1984.
6. Marjorie Wellbrock interview, October 30, 1991.
7. Peter L. Wastrom interview, March 29, 1984.
8. Eliot Janeway interview, April 3, 1984 and Peter L. Wastrom interview, March 29, 1984.
9. Eberstadt private papers, *Seeley G. Mudd Manuscript Library*, Princeton University.
10. Paul H. Nitze interview, November 11, 1991.
11. "Ferdinand Eberstadt," *Fortune*, April 1939, p. 72 and Perez/Willett, *The Will to Win*, pp. 83-6.
12. Paul H. Nitze interview, November 11, 1991.
13. *Anne's Story*.
14. Paul H. Nitze interview, November 11, 1991.
15. Paul H. Nitze interview, November 11, 1991.
16. Hoopes/Brinkley, *Driven Patriot* , p. 72.
17. Nitze, Paul H., *From Hiroshima to Glasnost*, New York, 1989, p. xviii and *Anne's Story*.
18. *Anne's Story*.
19. Knowlton, Christopher, "Money & Markets: How the Richest Colleges Handle Their Billions," *Fortune*, October 26, 1987, p. 106.
20. Knowlton, Christopher, *Fortune*, p. 106.
21. Paul H. Nitze interview, November 11, 1991.
22. Sobel, Robert, *The Life and Times of Dillon Read*, p. 168.
23. Barringer, Felicity (interview), "After the Thaw, Who are Our Enemies?" *New York Times*, February 4, 1992.

9

The Crash and the Pecora Hearings

Dillon rode the wave of Wall Street's incredible bull market to its crest in the late 1920s, amassing a huge fortune for himself and his partners. Stock prices more than doubled during the first eight years of the 1920s, not much out of line with the growth of corporate profits during the same period. It was only during the final year of the Coolidge administration that the market began to exhibit manic qualities by doubling again, which led to the epic crash of 1929.[1] The year 1929 began quietly and gave little indication of the fireworks that lay ahead. Trading was listless initially but roared to all-time peaks by early September.[2]

Along with the trading markets, public underwritings soared with new issues totalling $9.4 billion in 1929, nearly double the average annual volume of the previous five years, and a record that stood for three decades thereafter. Common stock issues in 1929 bulged to $6.7 billion, 71.3 percent of total underwritings, and nearly four times the annual average of the prior five years.

The methods used by investment bankers in the 1920s differ strikingly from today's practices, and many of the procedures common in that era have become illegal nowadays. Dillon and his colleagues operated well within the ethical and legal boundaries of the era which featured stock pools and preferred lists and control of public trust accounts. In fact, business leaders and other influential people rushed to get into stock pools and onto preferred lists as well as the trusts in order to receive the benefits of the inside price on the private offerings of these deals. Investors knew the stock market was being manipulated but that only spiked their desire to get into the action. The exploits of stock market insiders such as Jesse Livermore, Mike Meehan, Joe Kennedy and others, filled the press. Most of these operators ran pools organized to push issues one way or the other, rumors of which frequently sent the price of a stock soaring or plummeting.

Pools had developed over the 1920s as the most prevalent of the various schemes traders conjured up to entice the public into speculating in stocks, with Dillon Read a major player. From 1927 to 1931, Dillon's firm organized and managed sixty-five pools while participating in forty-eight pools managed and originated by other firms.[3] Stock pools were regarded as racy and glamorous; they attracted cocktail party sophisticates and their progress was regularly covered in the press. These syndicates blatantly manipulated stock prices; some would hire publicity agents or even bribe reporters to "talk up" a stock. By October 1929 over one hundred stocks were being openly rigged by these market operators.[4]

Without question, the RCA pool was the most famous and successful. The RCA pool was conceived by a small group of wealthy investors in early 1929 who sought to rig the market and make large profits with little risk. The group enlisted Michael J. Meehan, the stock exchange floor specialist for RCA stock, to carry out the manipulation. The Meehan pool purchased one million shares of RCA at an average cost of 90. Utilizing fake publicity stories, Meehan brought in thousands of unsuspecting buyers who helped to drive up the price of RCA stock to 109, even though the company had never paid a dividend. At that point the insiders in the pool sold, locking in millions of dollars in profits while leaving the public to fend for itself; thereafter, the price of RCA stock quickly settled back to 87.[5]

In contrast to most of Wall Street, however, Dillon anticipated trouble ahead by reducing his underwriting commitments. He also reduced the risk in his securities portfolio by selling off huge chunks of the most vulnerable positions during the year before the Crash. In Dillon's memoir, he states: "As we approached November 1929, we completely unloaded our [securities] inventory and we had no bank loans anywhere."[6] However, Dillon's relentless selling before the Crash contributed to the precipitous drop in the market thereafter.[7]

On "Black Thursday," October 24, 1929, price levels melted away quickly after the opening trades; then followed a tidal wave of panic, not a gradual loss of confidence. By 10:30 a.m. the New York Stock Exchange was in pandemonium. Prices dropped $5 and $10 per trade. Bids for less-active stocks disappeared completely. Shortly after the opening of the Exchange the streets of the financial district were in an uproar, as investors heard of the disaster and, desperate to gain information first hand, went directly to the Exchange to view the action. Thousands of people milled about at the intersection of Broad and Wall streets.

The Federal Reserve Board, brokers, and bewildered customers had to rely on flash reports from the Exchange floor to keep track of prices during the day. The ticker tape was useless; it was sixteen minutes late at 10:30

a.m., forty-seven minutes late at 11:30, and ninety-two minutes late at 1:00 p.m. The 3:30 p.m. closing prices were not available until 7:35 p.m. There were 12,894,650 shares traded in 974 issues during the day—both records.[8]

At about 12:00 noon the first organized effort to support the market began at J. P. Morgan's corner office at Broad and Wall streets, across from the New York Stock Exchange. Several leading bankers assembled for the meeting. This small group, from then on known as "the Bankers' Pool," initially committed $125 million to buy stocks. At midday Richard Whitney, the Morgan broker, strode to the Exchange post for U.S. Steel and bid $205 for 25,000 shares (over $5 million) when it was trading at $195. Whitney moved to place bids at the top of his voice in other stocks, and support bids appeared throughout the list.[9]

The effect was electrifying: stocks that had been down 15 to 20 percent now bounced back in leaps of $2 to $5 at a time. Later in the trading session, however, stock prices weakened again and finished lower for the day. The bankers' support effort failed, although the pool continued to meet daily to try to stem the tide.[10] After three weeks of liquidation, the panic selling began to subside and the market finally stabilized but few realized it was over. While the panic phase of the Crash had ended, the Dow continued to decline thereafter, reaching its ultimate bear market low of 41 three years later, a whopping 89.3 percent lower than the 1929 high.[11]

The Crash set off a flurry of activity in Washington, with a number of bills to regulate corporate finance introduced and a number of Congressional hearings held to determine the cause of the collapse. The hearings led to further calls for a broader investigation. Hoover finally came out in favor of a wide-ranging probe of financial dealings, and on April 11, 1932, the Senate Banking Committee established a special subcommittee to conduct the investigation into stock exchange practices. The hearings were subsequently led by a fiery former assistant district attorney from New York, Ferdinand Pecora.

Pecora craved elective office and hoped the exposure would help him achieve his goal. The hearings had been stalled for six months but with the appointment of Pecora, the hearings acquired new and irresistible momentum. They would afford a sobering *post mortem* that would blacken the name of bankers for a generation.[12] Pecora punctuated his courtroom appearances with vigorous jabbing of his stubby index finger. Even when his prosecutorial manner was mild, he had a talent for withering asides, and he was fearless and incorruptible.[13]

At one stage during the Pecora hearings a midget was put on J. P. Morgan's lap as a publicity stunt. When Dillon got word of that, he decided to have his staff prepare detailed studies in advance of his appearance. For this job, he chose Nitze, as he had not been involved with the deals under investigation, along with Dillon's trusted personal attorney, John Cahill, of

Cotton and Franklin.

The urgency of the hearings caused Dillon to put aside his differences with his former partner, Eberstadt, who was called in for guidance along with the journalist David Lawrence, a friend of both Forrestal and Eberstadt from *Daily Princetonian* days. Lawrence and Eberstadt both recommended that Dillon would make the best spokesman for the firm but that Dillon's staff should prepare him for Pecora's likely cross-examination by staging mock hearings as a dress rehearsal.[14] Finally, Nitze and Cahill got together a briefing book that dealt with what they thought would be the probable questions and issues.[15] According to Dillon's private secretary, Marjorie Wellbrock, the preparations for the hearings involved many of the staff for almost a year before Dillon finally appeared at the hearings in the fall of 1933.[16] The intense preparation for the hearings probably contributed to the decline in Dillon Read's financing activity with little or no underwritings recorded in the three years from 1932 to 1934.[17]

When Dillon made his appearance as a witness at the hearings, it turned out that Pecora was much more interested in whatever would give publicity to his hearings than in the propriety of Dillon Read's past actions. None of the matters that Cahill and Nitze had worried about came up at the hearings at all. The questions that did come up were relatively unimportant, such as whether Dillon had made too much money on the Dodge Brothers deal.[18]

By the time Dillon appeared in October 1933, however, public interest in the hearings had dwindled and coverage of the hearings rarely made the front pages, being mostly relegated to the financial pages with only a handful of spectators on hand in the ornate Senate Caucus Room where the hearings were held. "All that emerged was a mass of dreary details," commented *Newsweek*. The press tended to blame Pecora for the drop in public interest, feeling that his questions often were "trivial" and designed to promote his own political ambitions. From Dillon's viewpoint, the drop off in public and press interest was an unexpected piece of good luck.[19]

Actually, Nitze does not think that Dillon fared poorly in the Pecora hearings, with two exceptions: the uncomfortable publicity relating to the incredible profits he made on his dealings in the 1920s (including the use of the closed-end trusts controlled by Dillon's firm) and Forrestal's utilization of a personal holding company to avoid paying taxes in 1928 and 1929 on his personal trading profits. The intricate control created over the investment trusts with a minimum investment by Dillon Read was not only legal but also conventional in that day and age, and had been fully disclosed in the offering circulars for the underwritings of these deals. The tax loopholes employed by Forrestal, however,—although legal—were far more embarrassing to Dillon, even though he personally did not utilize any of these tax devices. Actually, the press commented favorably on Dillon's testimony, noting that Pecora had seen fit to commend Dillon for his willingness to provide all of the considerable number of documents and data requested by counsel.[20]

Although Dillon did not have control over large amounts of customer deposits to use in financing his deals (as did many investment bankers) he had contrived an even better scheme. He was able to get control of the public's money by utilizing his control of the investment trusts, avoiding the inconvenient necessity of paying interest and having to pay back depositors' money on demand, as with conventional bank deposit accounts. Moreover, by purchasing a majority of the voting stock of the two Dillon-sponsored investment trusts with only a small fraction of the original capital subscribed, Dillon effectively controlled a liquid pool whose assets had grown to just under $140 million in the two trusts by late 1929 based on the firm's investment of only $5.1 million.

In one of Dillon's appearances at the hearings, he discussed at length the need to restore public confidence in the securities industry, saying this was crucial because so many refundings would be coming up in the years ahead. Senator Couzens brushed this aside with: "I just cannot conceive of public confidence being returned [to] investment houses after the disclosures . . . [of the mishandling of] . . . the investment trusts."

To which Dillon replied quietly, "I am sorry you feel that way, Senator Couzens."[21]

To Senator Couzens, the taking of the trust's assets "to further augment Dillon's own profits" seemed "rotten ethics and reprehensible" even though Dillon's practices were consistent with the rugged individualist *laissez-faire* philosophy of the era. Dillon's two investment trusts, however, incorporated many of the "inventions of the devil" that Otto Kahn later condemned. Unlike Kahn, who admitted that the banking ethics of the 1920s left much to be desired and acknowledged that reforms were necessary, Dillon saw nothing wrong in any of his firm's transactions.[22]

"May I ask you, Mr. Dillon, if you were to organize two investment trusts again, would you, in view of the disclosures, follow the same procedure?" Senator Couzens wanted to know.

"Yes," Dillon answered, "I do not think I should vary it. . . ." And a little later, when asked whether the public had been treated fairly, Dillon replied: "We could have taken 100 percent. We could have taken all that profit. We could have bought all the common stock for $5.1 million." Senator Alva B. Adams, a Colorado Democrat, ended the discussion by quoting Lord Clive's famous words: "When I consider my opportunities, I marvel at my moderation."[23]

At the end of his testimony, Dillon made a final statement regarding the record of his firm and the need for Congress to stimulate new capital formation and to revive the economy rather than embarking on senseless "witch hunts" to fix the blame for the 1929 Crash. In his statement, Dillon related that his firm "had raised over $3 billion in new financing during the prior decade and the overall default rate . . . of the firm's 368 bond issues . . . was only 7.7 percent . . . as of mid-1933."[24]

Dillon's stated default figures, however, were at sharp variance to a similar study contained in a *Harvard Business Review* study of bond underwritings and default rates covering the twelve years ended in 1932. In this study, Dillon Read's record ranked poorly in terms of bond defaults in contrast with the results for a group of sixteen major commercial bank security affiliates and private investment banking companies. According to the analysis, more than 20 percent of the dollar value of Dillon Read's bond issues had fallen into default, compared to only 2 percent for the House of Morgan and only 1 percent for Bonbright and Union Trust. Actually, only Lee, Higginson had a worse rate, with 23 percent of the dollar value of its bond issues in default.[25]

Following the Pecora hearings, a system of federal regulation of investment banking and securities dealings was enacted by Congress, administered by the newly-created Securities and Exchange Commission (SEC). In time, Wall Street grudgingly came to accept the SEC as an integral part of investment banking just as umpires are accepted in baseball.[26] As Dean Mathey commented, "Despite all the red tape and bother of the registration statements and rules governing trading, the SEC is Wall Street's best friend."[27] The new regulations constituted a revolution in the practices of the industry and marked the greatest turning point in American investment banking history. Previously, restraints had been almost entirely internal and the industry's elaborate self-imposed codes of conduct—the so-called gentleman's code—served as buffers against external controls. Now the industry had a cop instead of a code.[28]

But the bankers had not given up their independence and they fought back, launching a "bankers' strike" to force Roosevelt to amend or rescind the securities laws.[29] Although Dillon's financing activity declined precipitously in the early years of the Depression, they picked up in 1935 and reached pre-Crash levels under the leadership of Forrestal who became president of Dillon Read later in the 1930s. During this period, Dillon personally promoted a more conciliatory attitude on the part of the bankers towards securities reform.

Dillon worked behind the scenes for securities reform. For example, in late 1937, Dillon (insisting on secrecy) worked with SEC chairman William O. Douglas in drafting a new rule to curb "short selling" which had been manipulated by pool operators and others to drive down stock prices. Forrestal arranged the meeting between the two men providing it was kept secret and providing further that when the new rule was announced no one would divulge the name of the source or advisers. Douglas accepted these conditions and met with Dillon on a Sunday evening at Dillon's Park Avenue apartment.

After Dillon greeted him, Douglas gave him a typed sheet on which he had listed several possible versions of the rule. After studying the various proposals carefully for about five minutes, Dillon stood up and handed the paper back to Douglas, and, again swearing him to secrecy, said, "If you want to do an effective job, take the first one of these proposed rules." It was, in substance: "No one may sell short at less than one-eighth above the last sale price." Announced and promulgated soon thereafter, this regulation, known as the "short-sale rule," remains unchanged to this day.[30]

Aiding the Pecora investigation was the embezzlement conviction of Richard Whitney, president of the New York Stock Exchange and brother of Morgan senior partner, George Whitney. Prior to the denouement, Richard Whitney had been a paradigm of American society and scion of a prominent family whose earliest forefathers came to America in 1635. His fall from grace had all of the overtones of a classical Greek tragedy. His demise was regarded by the public as reflecting a collapse of character and morality on Wall Street and his fall hastened the regulations that the Pecora hearings sought.[31]

Prior to his troubles, the Whitneys and Dillons were friendly neighbors in Far Hills, New Jersey. When Richard Whitney was convicted of embezzlement and sent to jail in 1938, he was bankrupt and had lost the family home. Douglas Dillon later commented:

My father gave to [Whitney's] wife and children the use of a house on his property in Far Hills and they lived out the rest of their lives on my father's estate. After Whitney came out of prison in 1947, he joined his wife and family and also lived in this house provided by Dillon. This was a humanitarian gesture on [my father's] part because he felt . . . sorry for him and especially his very [loyal] wife. . . . My father felt compassion for her plight.[32]

Nitze commented, "I doubt that Dillon had a strong feeling and friendship for the Whitneys; it was his social ambition to know everyone in society around Dunwalke."[33]

More than any other development of the period, the Pecora hearings created the mood in the country that Wall Street's days of independence were over and that the presence of Washington would be felt there increasingly in the years to come. While Dillon and the rest of Wall Street essentially acted within the bounds of the ethical standards of the time, the bankers were found culpable in a striking wave of retroactive indignation. To complicate matters, new charges (although flimsy) were filed in October

1947 in an anti-trust case brought by the Justice Department against the entire investment banking industry. The trial lasted six long years and although the suit was dismissed by the Court, the litigation had a lasting impact on all concerned.

Although reform-minded himself, Dillon resented the imposition of outside controls on his own financing operations. Moreover, Dillon was still bitter about the treatment he had received at the Pecora hearings from Senator Couzens and the crude way he had been treated by the press. Above all, Clarence Dillon was fearful for his firm's very survival. One can only imagine the relief he felt when the long anti-trust trial finally came to an end and he was exonerated.

Embittered by the long hearings, Dillon developed a new direction in his life. Soon he would all but abandon active participation in Wall Street deal-making. His social aspirations came to dominate his life and he turned over the management of the firm to Forrestal and others. The tragedy of the 1930s is that men of the caliber of Dillon left the financial field; their valuable ability to stimulate economic development was lost in the mire of the developing Washington bureaucracy. The real enigma of Dillon's behavior is why he chose to leave the wars of Wall Street when the nation so desperately needed his creative brilliance to help wrest it from the deepest depression in our history.

Notes

1. Seligman, Joel, *The Transformation of Wall Street: A History of the Securities and Exchange Commission and Modern American Corporate Finance*, Boston, 1982, pp. 2-3.
2. Wigmore, Barrie A., *The Crash and its Aftermath*, Westport, Conn., p. 3.
3. The Pecora Hearings.
4. Chernow, Ron, *The House of Morgan*, p. 307 and Wigmore, Barrie A., *The Crash and its Aftermath*, p. 30.
5. Seligman, Joel, *The Transformation of Wall Street*, p. 17 and Brooks, John, *Once in a Golconda*, pp. 65-6, 78-9.
6. *Anne's Story.*
7. Paul H. Nitze interview, November 11, 1991.
8. Wigmore, Barrie A., *The Crash and its Aftermath*, p. 6.
9. Wigmore, Barrie A., *The Crash and its Aftermath*, pp. 6-7.
10. Wigmore, Barrie A., *The Crash and its Aftermath*, p. 7.
11. Wigmore, Barrie A., *The Crash and its Aftermath*, p. 535.
12. Chernow, Ron, *The House of Morgan*, p. 355.
13. Chernow, Ron, *The House of Morgan*, pp. 360-62.
14. Sobel, Robert, *The Life and Times of Dillon Read*, p. 179.
15. Paul H. Nitze interview, November 11, 1991.

16. Marjorie Wellbrock interview, October 30, 1991.
17. Author's survey of Dillon Read financings.
18. Paul H. Nitze interview, November 11, 1991.
19. Hoopes/Brinkley, *Driven Patriot*, p. 97.
20. Paul H. Nitze interview, November 11, 1991.
21. Sobel, Robert, *The Life and Times of Dillon Read*, p. 187.
22. Carosso, Vincent, *Investment Banking in America*, p. 346.
23. Carosso, Vincent, *Investment Banking in America*, p. 346.
24. The Pecora Hearings.
25. Moore, Terris, "Security Affiliates versus Private Investment Bankers—A Study in Security Originations," *Harvard Business Review*, XII, July 1934, pp. 478-84.
26. Brooks, John, *The Takeover Game*, pp. 56-57.
27. Mathey, Dean, *Fifty Years of Wall Street*, p. 27.
28. Brooks, John, *The Takeover Game*, pp. 56-57.
29. Seligman, Joel, *The Transformation of Wall Street*, pp. 114-15.
30. Douglas, William O., Go East, Young Man: The Early Years. The Autobiography of William O. Douglas," New York, 1974, p. 289.
31. "Richard Whitney," *National Cyclopaedia of American Biography*, Book 50, p. 167 and Brooks, John, *The Takeover Game*, pp. 333-35.
32. Douglas Dillon Interview, May 23, 1991.
33. Paul H. Nitze interview, November 11, 1991.

10

Dillon's Vacation Retreats and Hobbies

Even before the stock market crash in 1929, Clarence Dillon took long holidays to travel in Europe and elsewhere. The Crash and the ensuing depression seemed to spur his lust for travel and new adventures. Reflecting his family's French antecedents, Dillon's favorite foreign location was France, which became a sort of second home. In addition, Dillon developed vacation retreats in Maine as well as on the Caribbean island of Jamaica. His obsession for travel had begun in the early 1900s, when he and his bride Anne spent the better part of their two-year health-honeymoon trip in Paris and Geneva.

Although Dillon had an ongoing interest in France, he never learned French. By contrast, his son, Douglas, went on a crash course to learn the language to the point of fluency when he became Ambassador to France. Yet the father, who made a fetish of learning everything about things that were of interest to him, failed to master the French language. Nitze comments, "Dillon had a marvelous library of books in French but I guess he didn't think learning the language was all that important."[1]

Some time in the mid-1920s Dillon bought an apartment at 22 rue Barbet-de-Jouy on Paris's Left Bank. After the second world war, the Duchesse Joan de Mouchy, Dillon's granddaughter, lived there for a number of years. The apartment was ideally located not far from where the Invalides faces onto the extreme back end of the Rodin Musée.[2] There were no interior walls or configuration to each apartment in the building; those taking floors would arrange the space to suit themselves. Dillon finished his apartment with antique *boiseries* (wainscotting) and parquet flooring dating from the *Ancien Régime* to emulate a petit French chateau. Several of Dillon's close friends in Paris took up the other floors of the building, so that the apartments served as their own private residence compound. Dillon notes in his memoir: "The apartments at rue Barbet-de-Jouy [were] far more comfortable and pleasant than living at the Ritz." When Douglas Dillon was Ambassador to France, the apartment provided a convenient and practical place to have his children and friends for luncheons and dinners.[3]

The Dillons had many friends in Paris as well as elsewhere. Although the Rothschilds were mainly business contacts, Dillon gained social access from this relationship. His purely social relationships included Dean Jay and his wife Ann whom he had met originally in Milwaukee through friends there. Jay was the managing partner at that point for Morgan Harjes, the Paris branch of J. P. Morgan. Probably Dillon's closest friends in Paris were Henry Rogers and Alice Winthrop from Long Island, who had taken the apartment on the floor just above the Dillons at rue Barbet-de-Jouy.[4]

Dillon enjoyed the good life in France and was perfectly at ease as he wandered the streets of Paris searching for new adventures in this great capital of culture. On one of Dillon's trips to France in the mid-1930s he visited the Paris Rothschilds. When he expressed boredom with business conditions in New York, they recommended to Dillon that he consider buying a vineyard to give him something to do. The Rothschilds explained to Dillon that the wine business was in a slump at that point and several of the best vineyards were available at attractive prices. Another factor motivating Dillon was the desire of his widowed mother to pass her summers in France; she was looking for a property to replace a farm she had sold in Normandy. So Dillon took the Rothschilds' suggestion and went down to Bordeaux accompanied by his nephew, Seymour Weller, and Daniel Lawton, a leading wine expert whose family had been in the wine business in Bordeaux for several generations. They looked over several of the wine producing chateaux estates including Haut-Brion, Cheval Blanc and Margaux, all of which were then on the market.[5]

Dillon decided that he wanted to purchase Chateau Haut-Brion which with its vineyards represented one of the five so-called first growths of the Bordeaux section of France. Douglas Dillon notes, "I think my father liked the house [at Haut-Brion] better than the others. He felt that . . . Margaux was too pretentious, a later building . . . [built in 1815] . . . classic . . . but very big and heavy—a tremendous thing—whereas with Haut-Brion, one tower dated back to 1600 and the rest was added on later more or less just like a house. It wasn't fancy." He especially liked Haut-Brion's convenience. Located in the suburb of Pessac astride the ancient Bordeaux-Arcachon road, it took Dillon only 20 minutes to get to Haut-Brion from the Bordeaux railroad station. Douglas Dillon notes, "If you went to the Medoc wine country, it would [take] an hour or more on back roads way out in the country."[6]

The Bordeaux Wine Industry

The city of Bordeaux is at the center of an ancient and thriving wine region, the most important fine-wine producing area in the world. The vintners of Bordeaux export over twelve million gallons of wine a year principally to England, North America, Germany and the low countries. Bordeaux and its wines flourished as early as the Roman empire; it belonged to English kings for 300 years from 1154 to 1453, and the wines of the Graves district were known and appreciated in England as early as the thirteenth century.[7]

The Bordeaux wine industry benefits from its position near the sea and several major rivers, affording a moderate and stable climate—a virtual peninsula between the Atlantic Ocean and the Gironde river estuary. An old adage in the Bordeaux wine district avers: "To make good wine the vines must see the river." Forests on the ocean side protect it from strong salt winds and provide a buffer against violent ocean storms. The vineyards of Bordeaux are also blessed with a bedrock that is well-furnished with minerals and a sandy mixture of rocks, pebbles and gravel, the best *terroir* for growing grapevines. In the stony, gravelly ground that abounds in the area, the vine roots plunge fifty or more feet deep to tap the abundant underwater sources fed from Bordeaux's nearby Gironde river, which with its tributaries runs through the principal first-growth vineyards in the Medoc, Graves and St. Emilion.[8] The deeper the roots grow, the more stable the water environment, with the vines less subject to floods on the one hand or drought on the other. Moreover, the stones in the *terroir* of Bordeaux vineyards store heat on the surface and prevent rapid evaporation of moisture from under them, guaranteeing stable conditions of temperature and humidity that are critical to vine growth. Another plus for Bordeaux vintners is the region's stable temperatures during the critical summer growing season, contrasted to the wide temperature range experienced in other grape-growing areas.[9]

All Bordeaux wines are made from a mixture of three or four grape varieties, namely Cabernet Sauvignon, Merlot, Cabernet Franc and Petit Verdot. The proportions, or *assemblage*, depend on the taste of the proprietor and his estate's *terroir* with its varying content of minerals and water supply.[10] Overall, however, the composition of the land is primary in determining the *assemblage*, according to Jean-Bernard Delmas, Haut-Brion's long-time *directeur*. To cope with the diversity of subsoils, the vineyards of Haut-Brion are divided into twenty-seven discrete plots delineating different soil types. Of course, the skill and technology of the vintner along with weather have their place in fine wine making but it is the *terroir* that dominates the qualities of a wine.[11]

The Cabernet Sauvignon grape dominates the usual mixture in the

Medoc and Graves and makes for a heavier or "bigger" wine than those based on Merlot, which dominates the vineyards of St. Emilion, the other major wine district to the east of Bordeaux. All Bordeaux reds reach their peak from eight to twenty-three years after vintage and are long lasting—up to fifty years, sometimes more.[12] Each of these grapes also has a different amount of tannin, an important mineral which affects the structure and aging qualities of the wine.[13]

Beginning in the sixteenth century, some two hundred of the more than three thousand wine producing chateau estates of Bordeaux have been officially classified into different levels of perfection. Five chateaux have been classified as outstanding, the so-called *premier crus*: Chateau Haut-Brion in the Graves district and Chateau Lafite, Chateau Latour, Chateau Margaux and Chateau Mouton-Rothschild in the Medoc district, 25 miles north of Bordeaux. Most wine experts also include Chateau Cheval Blanc, Chateau Ausone and Chateau Petrus in St. Emilion, 25 miles east of Bordeaux, in this select group. Overall, sixty-one vineyards were designated as having superior wines and were classified into five levels of perfection. None of these vineyards has a very large acreage, between 100 and 150 acres, although Margaux's acreage is much larger with 650 acres in all.[14]

The differences among the wines of the great Bordeaux chateaux are all a matter of taste, according to Sasha Lichine, a noted Bordeaux vintner and son of Alexis Lichine, the late wine expert and author. Lichine notes, "It is difficult to pinpoint the differences. . . . It is like going to a museum . . . to look at some beautiful art. . . . The artists all use the same brushes and . . . paints but [each of them] paints differently; it is a matter of taste which one you like."[15] Paul Pontallier, the estate manager of Chateau Margaux, adds, "Comparing two Bordeaux wines is the same as comparing two different periods of music . . . the most important thing . . . is to enjoy the sensual pleasure of the music. . . . The same is true with great wines."[16]

Haut-Brion was Dillon's favorite French claret.[17] Very roughly, Haut-Brion could be described as having a very different "woody" flavor that distinguishes it from the wines of the other Bordeaux wine regions. The red wines of Chateau Haut-Brion tend to have more body and are more "earthy" than those of the Medoc and St. Emilion, which are more feminine and delicate. Haut-Brion has a "very bricky . . . earthy taste," Helen Fenouillet of Chateau Latour points out, "while Latour has a very strong taste of . . . fruit and oak—a big wine with . . . a very impressive taste . . . which . . . stays in your mouth for 10 minutes or more."[18] Moreover, the wines of Haut-Brion have a tendency to soften sooner and ripen more quickly.[19]

Following his tour of various chateaux available in the Bordeaux area, Dillon made up his mind to purchase Chateau Haut-Brion and its vineyards. In 1934, Dillon's Paris partner, W. Meade Lindsley Fiske, knowing of his partiality for Haut-Brion, heard that the chateau was immediately available and he cabled Dillon, stating:

"I think that we can buy Haut-Brion if we act fast."

Dillon replied: "Act fast."[20]

Chateau Haut-Brion

Before Dillon purchased it in 1934, Chateau Haut-Brion and its renowned vineyards had passed through the hands of at least fifteen different owners from its early beginnings in 1470, according to the records of the estate archivist, Alain Puginier. These included Napoleon's foreign minister, Talleyrand, who owned it briefly in the early 1800s. Talleyrand, known throughout Europe for his fabulous table, strived to keep the quality of his wine equal to that of his menus. However, he was unable to keep the property for more than a few years because his conflicting alliances kept him constantly on the move, forcing him into exile for a time in the United States.[21]

As it changed hands through the centuries, Haut-Brion varied in size, increasing or decreasing depending on the circumstances. With all of the splitups and reunions, six chateaux in the surrounding region have added Haut-Brion to their names. In 1983, Douglas Dillon bought one of them, Chateau La Mission-Haut-Brion. It lies across the Bordeaux-Arcachon road and was once a part of Haut-Brion, but there are no present plans to merge the two estates.[22]

The Larrieu family purchased Haut-Brion in 1836 and held it until 1920, the longest of all of its owners so far; at that point a bank foreclosed on its mortgage. Two years later it became the property of André Gibert, a retired Bordeaux banker. Gibert was a lone wolf and not very popular in the Bordeaux community. He infuriated the Bordeaux wine merchants by attempting to sell his wine directly to consumers, bypassing the merchants and brokers. After these efforts failed (and having no children of his own to run the estate), he decided to offer the chateau, vineyard and park as a gift to the City of Bordeaux if they would maintain it in perpetuity as a functioning vineyard. The Bordeaux city fathers thought "perpetuity" was a bit long to commit themselves. With this, Gibert lost his temper and broke off the discussions. Then, Fiske intervened and Gibert agreed to sell, not quibbling about price, and Dillon bought the property for about $250,000.[23]

At the time Dillon purchased the estate, Haut-Brion's wine distribution was in a state of disarray because of Gibert's prior futile attempts to bypass the traditional wholesale wine merchants. Dillon appointed his nephew, H. Seymour Weller, to oversee the estate's business, with particular emphasis on reestablishing the wine's traditional marketing alliances. As a first step, Dillon invited all the Bordeaux wine people to the chateau for a conference.

He told them: "I've just bought Haut-Brion and I know nothing about it and I want your help." The next day, the Bordeaux press rejoiced, exclaiming: "It's a miracle, Haut-Brion is once again part of us. Tradition has been restored."[24]

Then Dillon went to work spending considerable sums to restore and modernize the chateau, adding bathrooms and providing more adequate heat in all of the rooms while upgrading the electrical system. At the same time, Dillon put the vineyard in first-class order with all the equipment brought up to the highest standards. The private park and walks were spruced up, the fruit trees were pruned, and the vegetable garden was restored to its original state. The Dillons found copies of some old hand-loomed cloth to cover the furniture and they obtained a number of furnished pieces through Moss Harris of London.[25]

During the second world war, Dillon offered the chateau to the French government as a convalescent center and retreat for military officers. Actually it was never used as such; after the sudden collapse of France in mid-1940, the Germans seized Haut-Brion before the French even had a chance to use it. The Germans converted the chateau into their headquarters for flight officers of a squadron of Fokker Focke-Wulf FW 200 Condors, the big four-engine planes that flew out over the Atlantic to ambush Allied convoys; Merignac airport, just outside Bordeaux, was only ten minutes from the Chateau.[26]

Weller remained in charge of the Haut-Brion wine operation as his uncle's personal representative for over forty years until 1975 when Dillon's granddaughter, Joan, first took over responsibility.[27] Weller was born in Milwaukee, the son of Anne Douglass's sister, Virginia. As a youth he was sent to boarding school with his brothers in Switzerland. After the first world war began, he and his brothers left school and enlisted in the French army as ambulance drivers, transferring to the American Medical Corps after the United States entered the war. After the Armistice, Weller stayed in France and when Dillon opened an office in Paris in the early 1920s, he went to work for Dillon Read. Weller married a French girl, Therese Morin, and became a French citizen in the late 1930s.[28]

During the second world war Weller organized a dangerous undercover activity as part of the French resistance in which his unassuming outward appearance helped him maintain his coverup over his underground activities. Weller was always rather slow-spoken—his practice being not to look too bright. Using his guile skillfully, Weller established a radio connection with the Allied forces in England from his small home in the town of Neufles-St. Martin on the Normandy coast. In his basement, he hid downed Allied airmen and shipwrecked seamen until they could be evacuated on British ships sent to recover them. However, despite his efforts at secrecy, he got into some difficulty with the Germans, partially because of his underground activities but also because of his handling of the wine supplies at Chateau Haut-Brion.[29]

Hermann Goering sent for all the good wine at Chateau Haut-Brion and the Germans discovered there wasn't any, it having been hidden at Weller's orders before the German arrival. Actually, Weller had the workers carefully pile up all sorts of rubbish and other material from the fields on top of the cellar door, hiding it so successfully that although the Germans occupied the chateau for several years they never found the wine cellar. When the Dillons came back they found the wine cellars intact.[30]

In any event, the Germans came around to the view that Weller was doing something suspicious. Fortunately, Dr. Alexander Kreuter, a lawyer who was Dillon's prewar legal representative in Berlin and had become a civilian occupation officer in occupied Paris, found out from his sources that the Gestapo was after Weller. Kreuter warned Weller as an act of friendship. Weller rushed to his doctor and told him, "I need an operation and quick." So they operated on him and took out his appendix. A day or two later, the Gestapo arrived at the hospital demanding to see him and when they found him under medical treatment, they went away saying, "We'll be back in a week." By then, Paris fell and Weller was safe.[31]

After the war, Dillon retrieved the chateau and immediately set about to restore it. He had removed much of the family's silver and china before turning it over to the French, so that when the Germans arrived, the workmen simply shrugged their shoulders when the Germans questioned them; they were not the least intimidated by the Germans. In 1946, the French awarded Dillon a Certificate of Merit for his efforts on their behalf during the war.[32]

Haut-Brion has become the leading research-oriented vineyard in the Bordeaux area under the direction of the widely-acclaimed winemaker, Jean-Bernard Delmas; he and his father, George, have been in charge of Haut-Brion over the past seven decades. On-going research focuses on developing enhanced vines through a cloning program which Haut-Brion pioneered. In a major move to improve and control fermentation in the early 1960s, Haut-Brion was the first Bordeaux chateau to install stainless steel vats. In 1989, the chateau made a major new investment of $6 million in new stainless steel vats with automatic temperature controls, a key factor in wine fermentation.

According to Joan de Mouchy, Dillon's granddaughter, all of the profits from the chateau have been plowed back into further improvements under the stewardship of Clarence Dillon and his family. She stressed: "No part of the profits have ever left Haut-Brion. . . . Every *sou* that has been earned has been put back into the property."[33] Joan and her French husband, Duc Philippe de Mouchy, manage Chateau Haut-Brion, spending a few days there every two weeks—commuting from their home in the town of

Mouchy, 60 kilometers north of Paris. The Duc owns a large farm in Mouchy that has been in his family for over 400 years.[34] According to wine expert Robert Parker, Haut-Brion's wines have reached new heights of excellence since Joan de Mouchy took overall charge of the estate in 1975.[35]

In effect, Clarence Dillon looked upon Haut-Brion as his entree to the more genteel and cultured life that he sought after the precipitous fall of the stock market and the ensuing depression. While Dillon didn't visit Haut-Brion very often, the property was constantly on his mind; it clearly became a prime possession of his son, Douglas, who spends several weeks at Haut-Brion each fall sampling the latest vintages and helping organize the operations in conjunction with his daughter, Joan de Mouchy.

In the mid-1930s, when the Dillons bought Haut-Brion, vineyards were not good business propositions. They became profitable only some twenty-five years later. Douglas Dillon adds that it is difficult to get a fair estimate of a chateau's value—you have to rely on recent sales of comparable vineyards to extrapolate the *pro forma* value of Haut-Brion. "A useful extrapolation would be based on the mid-1989 sale of Latour (roughly comparable to Haut-Brion in size and prestige) which would give a projected value of around $100 million for Haut-Brion."[36] However, Giovanni Agnelli, the Italian billionaire owner of the Fiat automobile company, attempted to buy Perrier and Chateau Margaux in early 1992 and lost out to Nestle, SA, in a hotly contested multi-billion-dollar bidding action which seems to indicate a much higher value for Haut-Brion than Douglas Dillon's appraisal.[37]

On July 27, 1985, Chateau Haut-Brion celebrated the Fiftieth anniversary of its purchase by the Dillon family with a gala party at the chateau. Asked what his intentions are with respect to selling Haut-Brion, Douglas Dillon replied, "I don't know; there will be a lot of heirs and they may have different viewpoints—so you can't tell." At this point, it appears that Chateau Haut-Brion represents more of a so-called Dillon dynasty than the Dillon Read legacy. Douglas agrees, "Yes, it seems so."[38]

After his withdrawal from the day-to-day operations of Dillon Read and as part of his new lifestyle, Dillon would take up and pursue hobbies intensively but then drop them when he lost interest. For example, while in France in the summer of 1955, the Dillons went to a dog show and Anne particularly admired the poodles. They asked the woman who had been judging poodles if she would select a miniature poodle for them. She suggested that it would be best to select one in England, for at that time French moyens were more prevalent than miniatures. After much searching in England, they found a kennel from which they picked a miniature poodle and brought her back by steamer. Dillon then organized Dunwalke Kennels at his Far Hills estate and bred miniature-class poodles. One of their poodles, "Fontclair Festoon," was entered at the Westminister

Kennel Club show at Madison Square Garden and was judged "Best in Show Dog" for 1959.[39]

However, after this achievement, Dillon lost interest in breeding poodles and dropped the hobby. Restless for new challenges, Dillon seemed to move from one thing to another to satisfy his need for activity.[40] For example, earlier, he became an amateur photographer with a darkroom and a studio; he had many cameras and posed all sorts of people, doing his own developing in black and white and color. That hobby actually lasted for ten or twelve years but he had to drop it when he developed cataracts in his eyes. Needing a new challenge, Dillon set up a string of steeplechasers with four of his friends; the stable included seven chasers, four of them brought over from England and France along with about thirty other horses.[41]

In addition to traveling in France, the Dillons also went frequently to other European countries and England as well as Egypt and the Holy Land in North Africa. Their travel itinerary was leisurely, always by steamer; it was not until the early 1950s, when he built High Rock overlooking Montego Bay in Jamaica, that he began to use airplanes.[42] With Dillon's sister, Jeanie, they made a trip to South America in late 1941 aboard a banana boat. In Buenos Aires, the American ambassador gave a dinner for the Dillons at the Embassy. Later, at a men's luncheon with diplomats and bankers, Dillon was questioned about the war and he ventured the opinion that it would not be long before the United States would be drawn into the war in the Pacific. By the time they arrived home, Pearl Harbor had been attacked and Dillon was credited in Buenos Aires as the man with inside information on the actions of the Japanese.[43]

Dark Harbor, Maine

In the early 1920s Dillon developed a major summer residence for his family at Dark Harbor on secluded Islesboro, a millionaire's island enclave just three miles off Lincolnville on the Maine coast. Dark Harbor had become one of Maine's storied summer colonies where generations of families have been vacationing for nearly a century. There are country roads and winding lanes, hidden coves and magnificent vistas. It is a retreat similar to the rustic enclaves maintained by the Morgans and others at the turn of the century at Bar Harbor.

Yankee magazine describes Islesboro and Dark Harbor as:

a self-possessed little island, a place of private homes, chosen anonymity. . . . Beauty is natural, unself-conscious, and everywhere: still coves, rocky outcrops, brilliant wildflowers, the intense smell of sun-warmed pines and spruce, a curve in the road that suddenly reveals other green islands of Penobscot Bay floating in the distance. . . .

Most of the largest estates and fanciest old homes are concentrated near Dark Harbor in the summer colony started in the 1880s by a group of wealthy Philadelphians. . . . Every deed included a clause forbidding the erection of a "brewery, drinking saloon, slaughterhouse, bone-boiling establishment, sheds for the keeping of pigs," or other similar unsavory structures. . . .[44]

Charles Dana Gibson, a close friend of the Dillons, was a long-time promoter of Dark Harbor, declaring in 1907 that "one summer in Dark Harbor is worth a dozen summers abroad."[45] Gibson persuaded the Dillons to come up to Dark Harbor one summer in the early 1920s. They liked it and after vacationing in rented houses for two summers they decided to build a cottage of their own at Dark Harbor.[46]

Dillon then purchased five contiguous properties fronting on Gilkey Bay, containing about 22 acres in all with 1,100 feet of shore frontage.[47] The Dillon land purchases included the site of a local golf course and its clubhouse. Gilkey Harbor, across the island from Dark Harbor, is surrounded by about fifty huge mansions, most of them dating back to the turn of the century. Dillon's cottage was constructed in 1924; the house has a rural French provincial feel to it with a Normanesque tower in the center. It was designed by Mott B. Schmidt, the same architect who designed Dillon's Georgian townhouse in New York City.[48]

Various members of the Dillon family continue to own houses at Dark Harbor, creating a Dillon compound on the island. Douglas Dillon's house, which he bought for the bargain price of $25,000 shortly after the war, is built out on a promontory and features red awnings which have become a distinctive landmark for boatmen entering the harbor. In addition to Dark Harbor, Douglas Dillon maintains homes in Hobe Sound, Florida,[49] and at the family estate, Dunwalke, in Far Hills, New Jersey. Phyllis Dillon Collins, Douglas Dillon's older daughter, inherited her grandfather's cottage; Dorothy Dillon Eweson and her children also maintain cottages nearby.[50]

The Dillons generally went to Maine shortly before the Fourth of July, staying until after Labor Day. They always planned to stay longer but somehow never did. Although the weather is near perfect in Maine in September, they usually went abroad the latter part of September and liked to come home from Maine a couple of weeks before their departure. During the 1920s, the pressure of business forced Dillon to stay in New York during the summer while the family was in Maine. After his withdrawal, he was able to spend the entire summer in Maine. Among their neighbors in Dark Harbor were many of Dillon's lifelong friends. Besides the Gibsons, they included the Winthrop Aldriches, the Marshall Fields and a long list of prominent millionaires whose names read like "Who's Who."[51]

In his eighties, Dillon had a small oval pool built at Dark Harbor for his exercise. Fearing memory lapses, he kept a pile of polished small rocks at one end of the pool to help count the number of laps that he swam. After finishing each lap, he would keep count by moving a rock from one pile to the other.[52]

High Rock, Jamaica

Later, after his wife had suffered a major heart attack, Dillon developed another spectacular retreat, named "High Rock," facing on Montego Bay on the Caribbean island of Jamaica. High Rock came into existence to provide a comfortable place for Dillon and his wife to spend the winters. Anne's heart ailment effectively ended Dillon's annual trips to France and other distant places. While he would make periodic trips to Chateau Haut-Brion to check on its wine business, the long stays in France ended and Dillon gave up his apartment in Paris, transferring the antique *boiseries* and parquet floors to his daughter's new house built on the northeast corner of the Dunwalke estate in Far Hills.

Anne Dillon had periods of failing health at various times in her life. She was a healthy woman when young but in the last years of the first world war, and extending into the early 1920s, she was not well at all. Then Anne was in fine health for the next twenty years or so, but beginning in 1951 she began to fail again. After a heart attack in 1957, she was semi-invalided.[53] After Anne Dillon's health began to fail in the 1950s, Dillon hired a local doctor to take full time care of his wife. Although the doctor did not give up his private medical practice, he was on call to the Dillons twenty-four hours a day. The doctor also visited the Dillons in Jamaica and Maine. Dillon also had three nurses around the clock for his wife.[54]

Actually, Anne's cousin, Kingman Douglass and his wife, Adele Astaire, sister of the dancer, Fred Astaire, had discovered the Jamaica site while on holiday at their own cottage on Jamaica. Fred Brandi, then president of Dillon Read, also had a place in Jamaica.[55] When Kingman and Adele were with the Dillons for dinner one evening at Dunwalke, they talked enthusiastically about the marvelous site they had found for a cottage in Jamaica "with the blue of the sky, the soft air and the beautiful scenery set on a high bluff covered with woods and rocks overlooking the bay and descending steeply to its own beach." Suddenly Anne turned to her husband and said, "Why don't we buy it?"[56]

Dillon named the Jamaica cottage High Rock because it was built on top of a rock bluff about 300 feet above Montego Bay. It was built by Burrell Hoffman, a noted architect. All on one floor, the cottage was not a mansion but a comfortable house on about 7 to 10 acres of land with perhaps another

10 acres of land across the road.[57] A great covered porch ran along the whole length of the house on the bay side. Adjoining the cottage was a small swimming pool with beautiful gardens and a variety of fruit trees all around.[58]

The site was so rocky that Dillon had to bring in many tons of topsoil to landscape it. This proved to be a bonanza for the local people, who brought wagon loads of topsoil to the construction site for the landscaping. The Dillons carved about 14 acres of gardens into this rocky bluff, including a very primitive wood walking surface to cover the jagged rock underneath. These paths were constructed so as not to disturb the original virgin growth of the trees, many of which had orchids growing from their trunks. At the foot of the cliff they laid vegetable gardens with flower beds and a lawn. The cottage was finished January 1, 1956.[59]

Dillon continued to entertain actively at High Rock, inviting many socially prominent people as his guests for tea at his waterfront retreat. One highlight was the visit of John Foster Dulles, U.S. Secretary of State, an old friend of the family, in December 1958. Dulles flew to Jamaica in President Eisenhower's Super Constellation, "Columbine III," accompanied by Mrs. Dulles and five members of his staff. Dulles had not been well and the visit was for a rest. Dulles was a gourmet cook and spent a great deal of his holiday at his hobby.[60]

The Dillons celebrated their fiftieth wedding anniversary at High Rock in February 1958 with a complete orchestra flown in for the occasion from the States. Dillon loved his wife and owed her a great deal for enabling him to enter the world of society; the Dillons were listed in the Social Register primarily because Anne Dillon was descended from the Duns.[61] Dillon left the house to his daughter, Dorothy, but after a few years she sold it to Ralph Lauren, the sports clothes designer. She preferred to live in the north during the winter; High Rock didn't fit into her or her children's life styles.[62]

After Anne died in 1961, Dillon established a memorial to her at Dark Harbor. He had a granite stone carved in her memory with a touching epigraph composed by himself and set in the private garden that Anne had developed in 1924 in front of the cottage. The memorial reflects Dillon as a very private person who was dedicated to his wife. The epigraph was adapted by Dillon from the 137th Psalm which begins, "By the waters of Babylon. . . ."

Anne Douglass Dillon

On the shore of Gilkey's Harbor
In her garden by the sea
There amidst the flowers she loves
She comes again to me

She smiles to see my wonder
As she stands there at my side
And lays her precious hand in mine
There ever to abide.

(dated 1961 with the initials C overlaid on A)[63]

Notes

1. Paul H. Nitze interview, November 11, 1991.
2. Mrs. Dorothy Dillon Eweson interview, October 1 and 4, 1991.
3. *Anne's Story.*
4. Mrs. Dorothy Dillon Eweson interview, October 1 and 4, 1991.
5. *Haut-Brion,* a brochure published in 1989 by the vineyard, p. BE3 and Douglas Dillon interview, May 23, 1991 and letter to author from Douglas Dillon, November 19, 1992.
6. Douglas Dillon interview, May 23, 1991.
7. Outerbridge, David E., *Haut-Brion in New York,* a brochure published privately in 1992 by the vineyard, p. 2, hereinafter referred to as *Haut-Brion in New York.*
8. *Haut-Brion in New York,* p. 6.
9. Jean-Bernard Delmas interview, June 9, 1992.
10. Paul Pontailler interview, estate director, Chateau Margaux, June 10, 1992.
11. *Haut-Brion in New York,* pp. 6-7.
12. Hugh Johnson, *The World Atlas of Wine,* New York, 1971, pp. 74-5 and Alexis Lichine, *New Encyclopedia of Wine and Spirits,* New York, 1974, pp. 97-108, 123, 138, 283-8, 255-6, 308-14, 336-7, 427, 556-7.
13. Paul Pontallier interview, manager, Chateau Margaux, June 10, 1992.
14. From various interviews with estate managers and vintners in the Bordeaux area.
15. Sasha Lichine interview, owner, Chateau Prieure-Lichine, June 10, 1992.
16. Paul Pontallier interview, estate manager, Chateau Margaux, June 10, 1992.
17. *Anne's Story.*
18. Helen Fenouillet, guide, Chateau Latour, June 11, 1992.
19. Paul Pontallier, estate manager, Chateau Margaux, June 10, 1992.
20. *Anne's Story* and letter to author from Douglas Dillon, November 19, 1992.
21. *Haut-Brion in New York,* p. 8.
22. Prial, Frank J., "Haut-Brion: Quality has been a constant in its long history," *New York Times,* June 19, 1985.
23. *Anne's Story* and *Haut-Brion,* p. BE 3.
24. Duchesse Joan de Mouchy interview, June 8, 1992.
25. *Anne's Story.*
26. Douglas Dillon interview, May 23, 1991.
27. Letter to author from Douglas Dillon, November 18, 1992.

28. *Anne's Story* and written comments from Mrs. Dorothy Dillon Eweson received May 12, 1993.
29. Douglas Dillon interview, May 23, 1991.
30. Douglas Dillon interview, May 23, 1991.
31. Douglas Dillon interview, May 23, 1991.
32. *Anne's Story.*
33. Duchesse Joan de Mouchy interview, June 8, 1992.

While most of the research is directed at improving the quality of the wine, it has also resulted in significant improvements in winemaking equipment and the care of the grapevines, permitting sharp increases in wine output as well. Most of the grapevines in the region now are healthier than before and produce closer to their optimum. Previously some vines died from disease, but modern treatments for prevention have curbed the diseases. A look at the wine production statistics from the past twenty years tells the story. Vineyards used to produce 15-25 hectoliters of grapes per hectare but now with the new, more efficient equipment and improved farming methods, the Bordeaux vineyards now produce on average in good years 40 hectoliters per hectare, almost double the output twenty years ago. (Source: Helen Fenouillet interview, guide, Chateau Latour, June 11, 1992.

34. Mrs. Dorothy Dillon Eweson interview, October 1 and 4, 1991.
35. Parker, Robert M., Jr., *Bordeaux: A Comprehensive Guide to the Wines Produced from 1961-1990,* New York, 1991, p. 515.
36. Douglas Dillon interview, May 23, 1991.
37. James Stewart interview, guide, Chateau Mouton-Rothschild, June 11, 1992 and press reports appearing in the *New York Times.*
38. Douglas Dillon interview, May 23, 1991.
39. *Anne's Story.*
40. Douglas Dillon interview, May 23, 1991 and Secretary's Fiftieth Anniversary Report, *Harvard Class of 1905,* p. 143.
41. *Anne's Story.*
42. Joseph Haywood interview, October 28, 1991.
43. *Anne's Story.*
44. "This New England: The Doors of Islesboro," *Yankee,* April 1993, p. 134.
45. "This New England: The Doors of Islesboro," *Yankee,* p. 134.
46. Douglas Dillon interview, Dark Harbor, July 1, 1991.
47. Clarence Dillon estate papers.
48. *Anne's Story* and Douglas Dillon interview, Dark Harbor, July 1, 1991.
49. "A Dillon A Dollar," *Fortune,* February 1961, p. 93.
50. Douglas Dillon interview, Dark Harbor, July 1, 1991.
51. Other socially-prominent neighbors that were friends of the Dillons included: Herman and Ruth Draper, the Herman Kinnicutts, the Grayson M. P. Murphys, Frederick Kellogg, the Frank Polks, the Harold Pratts, Charlie Auchincloss, Charlie Leonard, Beatrice Iselin, Louise Iselin. From Boston: the Dudley Howes, the Frederick Tuckermans, Emory Hollingsworth and Ronald Lyman. From Philadelphia: the Drexel Pauls, the Jim Gowens, the George Wideners, Bill Elkins, Russell Sard and John Tuckerman. (Source: *Anne's Story.*)
52. Mrs. Phyllis Collins interview, July 1, 1991.

53. Mrs. Dorothy Dillon Eweson interview, October 1 and 4, 1991.

54. Mrs. Dorothy Dillon Eweson written comments received May 12, 1993 and Joseph Haywood interview, October 28, 1991.

55. Joseph Haywood interview, October 28, 1991.

56. *Anne's Story.*

57. Douglas Dillon interview, May 23, 1991.

58. Mrs. Dorothy Dillon Eweson interview, October 1 and 4, 1991.

59. *Anne's Story.*

60. Joseph Haywood interview, October 28, 1991.

61. Joseph Haywood interview, October 28, 1991.

62. Douglas Dillon interview, May 23, 1991 and Mrs. Dorothy Dillon Eweson interview, October 1 and 4, 1991.

63. *Anne's Story.*

11

Public Service and Social Elevation

The Depression environment haunted Dillon and in the 1930s he became concerned with the survival of the firm. Dillon avoided any activity which might invite further government investigation, traveled more to Europe, and began preparing the way for his son's accession to leadership. Philip Allen, one of Dillon's grandsons, notes: "Basically, my grandfather wanted to make space available for his son . . . to become head of Dillon Read. . . . But my grandfather was never that far away—[his office] was only a block away."[1] Frustrated by the economic malaise of the Great Depression, Dillon turned more of his attention to solving global problems as well as pursuing his new-found hobbies and, above all, enhancing the social position of the Dillon family.

Dillon was sensitive to the press's hounding him for his past. Douglas Dillon notes that his father never liked publicity, especially after the stock market crash and the Pecora hearings. There was such a revulsion at Dillon Read, that the partners destroyed most of the firm's records.[2] Dillon turned more and more to Forrestal to handle the firm's affairs, including the press. Forrestal had that rare quality needed for a public spokesman; he could empathize with the working press giving them useful information and newsworthy quotes. Janeway stated, "Dillon used Forrestal as his shield to deflect the press's attention from him. Forrestal kept Dillon out of the limelight and became the firm's spokesman."[3]

Douglas Dillon argues that his father never had "a guilt feeling" from the revelations of the Pecora hearings. His father acknowledged the need for reform in securities underwriting and supported the regulatory changes. Later, when the laws were changed, Douglas notes, "My father instilled in me the need for thorough `due diligence´ so that you wouldn't get sued."

Dillon pushed his staff to conform to those rules, putting a tough enforcer, Wilbur Dubois, in charge of the corporate finance effort to prevent any breakdown.[4]

A life-long Republican, Clarence Dillon believed in unfettered capitalism and was uncomfortable with the new regulatory set-up of the New Deal once he became familiar with its mind-boggling bureaucratic red tape. In speech after speech he railed out at the new regulatory morass, reminding his audiences that competition was the only effective safeguard for the economy. Entrepreneurs must serve the public or competitors will soon bring them down. Undoubtedly this was the message he delivered to FDR when he visited the President in the oval office in early 1936. Dillon, secretive as usual and shying away from publicity, described the visit as a "personal meeting between two old friends," with the conversation general in nature.[5]

After his election in 1932, Roosevelt asked Dillon if he would be "his eyes and ears on Wall Street." Dillon replied, "I can not do that as I am not in touch with what is going on [there]." Dillon added, "Nevertheless I am available . . . to help [serve my country] in any way [possible]."[6] Following this, Roosevelt again wrote Dillon in 1936 requesting his help:

Dear Clarence:

I wonder if you would be willing to write out for me during the next month your ideas or suggestions for changes in the tax laws. The joint committee of the Senate and the House will be meeting and will probably confer with me. I would not of course use your name but I would like to have some of your ideas for my personal assistance.

Always sincerely,

Franklin D. Roosevelt

Dillon accepted this assignment and Roosevelt showed his appreciation by inviting the Dillons to a special luncheon at the Capitol in connection with FDR's second inaugural.[7]

In excellent health and just fifty years of age, Dillon was not about to retire in the conventional sense of the term. Yet he was losing much of his taste for direct participation in the firm, now that it had been so diminished. As early as 1926 Dillon had rented separate offices in the Equitable Building at 120 Broadway; in 1930 he moved his private office and dining room there and, though he often went to the Nassau Street headquarters for conferences, he was away much of the time. Dillon also leased a suite at 40 Wall Street, across the street from Dillon Read, from which he ran US&FS.[8]

Dillon's long-time friend and business associate, William Phillips, also withdrew from Dillon Read in the mid-thirties for much the same reasons as Dillon; they both had become bored with the pace of business which offered few challenges and too much red tape with the new securities regulations.[9] Similarly, other top Dillon partners left the firm in the 1930s, either disillusioned with the outlook for the securities business and retiring or shifting to other firms. This was true of Bermingham, Mathey, Nitze and others. Eberstadt left in 1928; Forrestal left in 1940 to join Roosevelt's mobilization effort to prepare the country for war.

Although Dillon stressed the need for the financing of new enterprises to bring about economic revival, he inexplicably steered clear of backing new ventures in the 1930s. He refused to risk his capital even though the country desperately needed heroic leadership by men of Dillon's stamp to bring the nation out of the deep depression. Dillon restricted the firm's financing activities to "safe" fields such as the utilities and energy companies, believing creative new financings were too risky.

Dillon's avoidance of new financing ventures contradicted his statement at the 1933 Pecora hearings on the need for financing risky young start-up businesses. Moreover, he opposed the positive financings pushed by Forrestal, who took over active leadership of the firm in the late 1930s. Forrestal believed the system should encourage young people like himself to make it on their own as part of America's effort to pull itself out of the Great Depression. Forrestal was privately contemptuous of those who lived on inherited wealth rather than encouraging new risk-taking ventures to increase the nation's total wealth.[10]

There were opportunities in the market in the 1930s but Clarence Dillon missed out on them. For example, the smaller growth companies surged 142.9 percent in market value in 1933—nearly three times the market rise of the so-called safe larger blue chips. Later the smaller growth companies grew three times faster than the market in the years following the bear market lows of 1942.[11] Even the safe financing fields had political risks as he discovered when the federal regulators turned the glare of their investigation on the utility holding companies, by then Dillon's prime financing area. It was like a replay of the Pecora hearings. Janeway believes Dillon thought it was all over. "I don't think he thought it would ever come back in terms of his world," noted Janeway.[12]

Dillon had learned the secret of living a satisfying personal life; he was not so much retired as he was discovering new interests and reawakening old ones. He was deeply concerned with finance when the business was exciting and fast-moving; he was less interested when Wall Street fell into a torpor and largely under government regulation. Hugh Bullock, a Dillon associate in the 1920s, believes Dillon just got tired of the rat race after the 1930s. Bullock does not believe that he had given up on the American economy. He says Dillon was a born optimist.[13]

In any event, Clarence Dillon gave up active participation in the firm by the mid-1930s; Forrestal became president and ran the firm from January 1, 1938, until he left for government service in mid-1940. After Dillon transferred the leadership of the firm to Forrestal, he executed a new partnership agreement increasing the equity of the other partners. The new agreement, however, enabled Dillon to retain complete control while giving his partners increased incentive to produce more with less of their capital at risk.[14]

Behind his new life style was Dillon's desire to develop a social position for himself and his family. Charles Dana Gibson's wife, Irene Langhorne, introduced Dillon to a number of important people in England including her sister, Nancy Lady Astor and her husband, Viscount Waldorf Astor, a fourth generation descendant of John Jacob Astor. A stylish, pretty woman, with a sharp tongue and a zest for political roles, Lady Astor was the first woman to serve in Parliament where she loved to heckle, tease and argue with her long-time adversary, Winston Churchill.[15]

In a sense, Dillon collected well-placed friends pretty much the way he collected antique furniture and cattle—with loving care and dedication. For example, Lady Astor became an intimate friend of the Dillons. Although the Dillons always stayed at Claridges when in London, he and his family loved to visit the Astors at Cliveden, the Astors' country estate.[16] Douglas Dillon thought that Nancy Astor must have been in love with his father because she went on and on about his father to Douglas but there was no indication of any infidelity.[17] Nitze also thought Dillon may have had some extramarital relations, noting, "there were so many exciting women he met and socialized with; he was a great friend of Mrs. Alice Winthrop who with her husband had the apartment on the floor above the Dillon's at rue Barbet-de-Jouy . . . in Paris."[18]

Dillon's wife, Anne, made sure he was adequately chaperoned on his foreign trips in the 1930s. Paul Nitze accompanied Dillon on most of the trips as his personal assistant, and either Dillon's wife or his daughter, Dorothy, would also go along each time. Dillon's daughter notes, "my mother . . . didn't want him to go traipsing all around the place [and] she insisted that she or I go with him each time."[19]

Lady Astor introduced the Dillons to a number of her intimates including George Bernard Shaw and many other prominent personalities. Early in 1946, the Astors came to the United States and joined the Dillons on their yacht, *Nevada*, cruising about for several weeks, calling at Palm Beach, Hobe Sound, Boca Grande and other places; the next year, the Dillons and Astors returned for a longer visit to Boca Grande.[20] Another Langhorne sister married Sir Robert Brand, a prominent official in the British Treasury who had a lovely country estate, Eydon Hall, further north from Cliveden, which the Dillons also frequented. Another Dillon social acquaintance was the British ambassador to Washington during the second world war, Philip Kerr (Lord Lothian), who was also a good friend of Lady Astor.[21]

Dillon followed the foreign business of his firm closely and kept in close touch with clients while he was abroad. By the mid-1930s, he and his wife would leave for Paris in early April and remain in Europe returning to Dark Harbor in Maine for the summer months. The Dillons would then return to Europe for the fall months. While in Europe, Dillon maintained social contacts, transacted business, and attempted to gauge political developments; in this manner, he became one of the best-informed Americans on European affairs.[22] He regularly met with leading political figures in France, the United Kingdom, Italy, and Spain, who shared with him their thoughts on events in their countries. For example, Dillon recorded in his diary his 1939 conversations with Franco, Pétain, Laval, Reynaud, Daladier, Balfour and others.

Some of the leaders Dillon met did not impress him as indicated by this diary entry (February 24, 1939) of Dillon's meeting with the Duke and Duchess of Windsor:

> Wally said the English were [all] liars and hypocrites. The Royal family just didn't know what a war was all about. . . . The Duke believes he is the only one who saw things as they were but he still thought of England as a constitutional monarchy. . . . The Duke, when we were alone, talked like a child—asked Laval foolish questions—and has anti-Semitic Nazi leanings.[23]

Roosevelt continued to seek out Dillon's help for special assignments during this period. In September 1939, FDR asked Dillon to drop in at the White House for a discussion of world conditions. There, Dillon briefed the President on his conversations with world leaders during the previous summer and relayed other information he received from his foreign contacts. FDR requested Dillon to convey to Churchill the President's assurance that the American government would assist the British the best it could, despite the strong isolationist sentiment then prevalent in the United States. Roosevelt also asked Dillon to carry a confidential highly-secret personal message to Churchill not to heed Ambassador Kennedy, as he did not speak from the American point of view.[24] Kennedy had become the Ambassador to Britain in 1938. Like many Roosevelt appointments, this one infuriated Wall Street. It was clear that Roosevelt had appointed Kennedy because of his financial and other help in the 1936 election—a blatant political payoff.[25]

In early May 1940, Clarence Dillon analyzed the escalating European crisis in a discussion with Paul Nitze. Dillon had no doubt that the United States would enter the war. "The war will be fought with modern weapons," Nitze recalls Dillon having said. "So in a sense the balance will be decided between what the Ruhr produces and what Detroit can produce [and] Detroit will produce more." Nitze then asked if Dillon thought the British could prevent a cross-Channel invasion if France fell. Nitze's recollection of Dillon's thoughts was:

> Dillon was sure Britain would survive. They would control the Channel. The fleet would be the decisive force, so long as the French fleet was kept out of German hands. [Thus,] it was essential that the French fleet be destroyed. In my presence he telephoned his old friend, [Lord] Beaverbrook, [the influential publisher of the London *Daily Express* and one of Churchill's closest advisers] in London, to urge him to bring his influence to bear immediately inside the British Government toward a decision that the French fleet be attacked and sunk before the Germans could seize control of it. The survival of a nation is at stake, Dillon said, the higher needs of preserving a civilization overcome scruples.[26]

On July 3, Churchill issued an ultimatum to the French to surrender their fleet anchored at Oran or face attack by the British fleet blocking the entrance to the harbor. The French refused and the British fleet opened fire. It lasted just nine minutes. Three French battleships and numerous support vessels sunk or blew up; 1,250 French sailors died that day. While the French battleships, the *Strasbourg* and the *Richelieu*, escaped, they subsequently anchored in ports outside Hitler's control. Altogether, the battle was a major military and political success for Churchill[27] and proved the wisdom of Clarence Dillon.

By then, Roosevelt's mobilization effort had swung into full action. In a complete reversal of his "New Deal" castigation of Wall Street, Roosevelt reached out to these same financiers for their help in organizing the effort to make America the "Arsenal of Democracy." Roosevelt told Paul Shields that he thought the time had come to build a bridge between Washington and Wall Street. As a result, the securities business became one of the prime sources for government talent searches and provided a disproportionate share of problem solvers and trouble shooters including Forrestal who headed up the nation's program to rebuild the Navy.

With their broad-based training, it is no wonder that investment bankers from Dillon Read and other Wall Street firms went on to become prominent figures in government, both in the war and in the peace thereafter. As Dillon's son, Douglas, recollected in an oral history recorded at Columbia University years later:

> Public service was a good deal closer to the traditional activities of an investment banker than those of businessmen generally. The investment banker's job is to get things done . . . to make do with whatever the problems are. [Traditional] investment bankers are not like businessmen who . . . can

lay down edicts that have to be followed. Investment bankers are much more flexible . . . and are willing to compromise . . . their opinions in order to [arrive at a] solution.[28]

As many of Dillon Read's key men became involved in wartime activities, it was necessary for Clarence Dillon to reassert his direct leadership of the firm during the 1940s. Since there was relatively little activity in the investment banking business during the war years, Dillon soon became active in the war effort, himself, organizing the Navy Relief Program. In early 1942, Admiral King, undoubtedly at Forrestal's suggestion, asked Dillon to head up a national campaign to raise $10 million (well over $100 million in today's dollars) for the Navy Relief Society.

Dillon organized an all-out one year campaign and actually exceeded that funding goal by a wide margin. The Navy Relief Fund was used to help widows and families of naval officers killed in the war or so seriously disabled as not to be able to work again. This filled an important need and boosted morale markedly for the Navy during the early years of the war.[29] Dillon also worked actively in similar British and French relief programs.[30] Dillon had other assignments in wartime Washington, one of which took him to England and France with Forrestal.[31]

As the war came to an end, Clarence Dillon looked confidently to the return of his son, Douglas, to become the leader of the family business, Dillon Read & Co., and to drive it forward in the postwar years to its former eminence. But Douglas had gotten the bug of government service and he was determined to pursue his own interests. First, however, at his father's insistence, he consented to make one more try to develop a career as an investment banker.

Notes

1. Philip D. Allen interview, April 9, 1992.
2. Douglas Dillon interview, May 23, 1991.
3. Eliot Janeway interview, April 4, 1991.
4. Douglas Dillon interview, May 23, 1991.
5. *New York Herald-Tribune*, January 24, 1936.
6. *Anne's Story*.
7. Clarence Dillon private papers.
8. Marjorie Wellbrock interview, October 30, 1991.
9. Douglas Dillon interview, Dark Harbor, July 1, 1991.
10. Hoopes/Brinkley, *Driven Patriot*, p. 81.
11. "Small-Stock Party Still Has Room For Latecomers if History is a Guide," *Wall Street Journal*, January 20, 1992.

12. Eliot Janeway interview, April 4, 1991.

13. Hugh Bullock telephone interview, April 11, 1991.

14. "The Upheaval at Dillon, Read," *Euromoney*, September 1982, p. 258.

15. Once while visiting him at Blenheim, Lady Astor said: "If I were married to you, I would put poison in your coffee." Churchill replied: "And if I were married to you, I would drink it." (Sources: Chernow, Ron, *The House of Morgan*, pp. 435-6 and Cowles, Virginia, *The Astors: The Story of a Transatlantic Family*, London, 1979, p. 202.)

16. Mrs. Dorothy Dillon Eweson interview, October 1 and 4, 1991.

17. Douglas Dillon interview, Dark Harbor, July 1, 1991.

18. Paul H. Nitze interview, November 11, 1991.

19. Mrs. Dorothy Dillon Eweson interview, October 1 and 4, 1991.

20. *Anne's Story.*

21. Mrs. Dorothy Dillon Eweson interview, October 1 and 4, 1991.

22. *Anne's Story.*

23. Sobel, Robert, *The Life and Times of Dillon Read*, p. 209.

24. *Anne's Story.*

25. Chernow, Ron, *The House of Morgan*, p. 439.

26. Nitze, *From Hiroshima to Glasnost*, p. 5.

27. Lukacs, John, *The Duel: Ten May to Thirty-One July: The Eighty-Day Struggle Between Churchill and Hitler on which the Fate of the World Depended*, New York, 1991, pp. 160-2.

28. "Oral History of Douglas Dillon," conducted by John Luter, *Columbia University Oral History Department*, 1973.

29. C. Douglas Dillon letter, December 7, 1992; also "Clarence Dillon, National Citizens Committee Chairman, Gives Check and Reports More Gifts Planned" (photo caption), *New York Times*, July 11, 1942.

30. *Anne's Story.*

31. Secretary's Fiftieth Anniversary Report, *Harvard Class of 1905*, p. 143.

12

The Second Generation:
Douglas and Dorothy Dillon

Clarence Dillon hoped that his son, Douglas, would carry the Dillon Read firm to new heights in its second generation under the Dillon family control. Born in Switzerland in 1909 while his parents were on an extended tour of Europe, Douglas Dillon came to the United States at the age of six months. Dignified, modest, tall but somewhat gangling, blue-eyed, strong-chinned and good looking, with a high forehead and an air of deliberation, Douglas is a cosmopolite. Both a man of the world and a conservative by birth and training, Douglas has aged gracefully in his role as the far-reaching patriarch of the Dillon family. He knows Europe, particularly France, almost like a native.[1]

Douglas and his sister, Dorothy, spent a secluded, affluent childhood in a series of suburban homes around New York City, the grandest being the baronial Dunwalke mansion that his father created in the fox-hunting estate section of Far Hills, New Jersey.[2] Douglas was a gifted child; he could read swiftly and understandably at the age of four[3] but he was a hellion as a schoolboy. On one occasion, he threw all of his teacher's books out of a school window onto the trolley tracks in the street, and the Dillons were asked not to send him back. When Douglas was eight years of age, a frightening accident occurred in the garage of the Rye, New York, house the Dillons were renting. Someone had left gasoline in a pail and Douglas, an inquisitive youngster, decided to find out what would happen if he dropped a lighted match into it. His face and hands were badly burned, especially his hands.[4] Even after more than seventy-five years the palms of his hands are still rough from the scars.

To curb his rambunctious tendencies, Douglas was sent to strict private schools, the most challenging being the smallish Pine Lodge School in Lakewood, New Jersey. Its tough, no-nonsense headmaster insisted that

131

each of his students learn the art of speed reading among other disciplines; as a result, Dillon can riffle through even technical papers at 400 words a minute.[5] While at Pine Lodge, Douglas met and became close friends of two of the Rockefeller brothers—Laurance and John III.[6] He later also came to know and become an intimate of Nelson Rockefeller.[7]

After Pine Lodge, Douglas went on to Groton, graduating second in his class and entering Harvard in 1927. Unlike his father, Douglas was serious about his studies but still managed to be quite active on campus. Too lean to play football, he managed the freshman and varsity teams and played squash and tennis. Douglas's major academic interest was American history and literature. He had little interest in fiscal theory, boasting that "I never took a course in economics in my life."[8]

Clarence Dillon was intent that the firm be headed by a Dillon and he drilled that into his son. Douglas graduated from Harvard *magna cum laude* in 1931 and later became a member of Harvard's Board of Overseers, serving as its president for four years. In March of his senior year, he married pretty, buoyant Phyllis Chess Ellsworth from Boston's Back Bay. "I had finished my thesis, so I had time to get married," he said.[9] While cruising around the world in 1934 with his wife on a post-honeymoon trip, Douglas showed some of his father's gambling talents, winning big at the table in Monte Carlo utilizing a special playing formula that he had devised to break the bank; he cashed in and used part of his winnings to buy a set of Napoleon-era china which is still in the family. Much like his father, he dropped his new-found hobby of "beating the bank" because it had become "too boring" for him.[10]

Douglas had quietly begun to turn against the idea of following in his father's footsteps, even though he agreed to join the firm after completing his studies. At first, his main activity consisted in acting as a liaison officer between his father at 40 Wall and Forrestal and Phillips at 28 Nassau Street. Every morning he would first discuss business matters with his father at 40 Wall; then he would walk over to the firm's offices at 28 Nassau to learn from Phillips and Forrestal what was happening there, returning in the afternoon to 40 Wall to report his findings to his father. After serving his apprenticeship with his father, he decided to leave the firm to buy a seat on the Stock Exchange to become a floor broker, the seat purchase financed by a gift of $185,000 from his ever-present father.[11]

After five years, Douglas sold the seat and returned to Dillon Read to work with his father for the balance of the 1930s.[12] This time he joined US&FS and took an active interest in managing the fund's portfolio, with excellent results. He became a director of US&FS in 1938, and, after his return from the Navy, he became president in 1946, a post he held until he went to Paris as Ambassador to France in 1953. He became chairman of US&FS in 1967 and he subsequently presided over the dissolution of the fund in 1984.[13]

Prior to 1955, US&FS was highly leveraged, which caused its common stock asset value to fluctuate widely. Some years it doubled in value only to drop precipitously in ensuing bear markets; in the early 1930s, US&FS's net asset value per share was actually negative. Despite the volatility, the long-term investment performance was outstanding. During Douglas Dillon's thirty-two year stewardship, US&FS's annual investment return (based on net asset values with distributions added back) averaged 19.1 percent a year, far ahead of the 10.1 percent average annual return of the *Standard & Poor's* 500 stock index.[14]

Toward the end of the 1930s Douglas developed his investment banking skills. His most impressive deal was reorganizing American Viscose Corporation as an independent business (previously, it had been a subsidiary of the British firm of Courtaulds Ltd.). After France fell in 1940, Britain stood alone in the war with Nazi Germany. British resources were soon exhausted and Churchill turned to Roosevelt for help. But the isolationists in the United States opposed aid to Britain in strict conformity to American neutrality and the widely-held desire of the American public to avoid involvement in European wars. There was also a public perception that Britain had not fully utilized the vast resources of the British empire.[15]

Roosevelt and Treasury Secretary Morgenthau conceived a dramatic plan to refute these charges. They asked for an act of self sacrifice on the part of the British—the sale of a major British industrial holding in the United States to demonstrate that Britain had exhausted all of its liquid resources before pleading for aid. On the eve of Congressional action on Lend-Lease, the Roosevelt Administration targeted Britain's single most valuable industrial possession in the United States—the American Viscose Company, the world's largest rayon producer—and imposed a draconian seventy-two hour deadline for announcing the sale. Dillon Read and Morgan Stanley were designated as joint-managers of what constituted a giant initial public offering of a privately-held company.[16]

However, in the unsettled wartime markets, textile shares had been fluctuating widely; the Dillon-Morgan price paid for the American Viscose shares reflected this risk. While Britain received $54 million, the seventeen firm Dillon-Morgan syndicate resold the shares publicly for $62 million, pocketing an $8 million underwriting fee, a healthy 15 percent premium. Churchill was furious, accusing the underwriters of fleecing the British at a time when they could not back out of the deal. Viscose's British parent, Courtaulds, Ltd., bitterly claimed the sale understated its subsidiary's true tangible assets by a substantial amount. In postwar litigation, Courtaulds finally received additional compensation from the British government.[17] Throughout the rancorous negotiations, Douglas demonstrated his banking flair and his innate qualities of diplomacy, systematically overcoming the objections of the British.[18] These qualities would serve him well in his later public career.

When Forrestal became Navy Undersecretary in 1940, Douglas Dillon and August Belmont joined him in Washington, preparing a special report for Forrestal on the status of Navy Department procurement. In the late fall of 1940, Douglas was commissioned as an Ensign in the Naval Reserve and went on active duty in May 1941, a few weeks after he had completed the American Viscose deal; his initial Navy assignment was as a decoding officer in New York City. A short time later, Douglas was transferred to Washington to assist Colonel William J. Donovan in organizing the Office of Strategic Services (OSS) which later became the CIA. Immediately after Pearl Harbor, Dillon asked for and received permission from Donovan to go on active sea duty with the Navy. After completing his aviation training at Quonset in January 1942 (where he finished at the top of his class), Dillon saw action with the fast carrier task forces during the invasion of Guam and Saipan.[19]

Later he served as Assistant Operations Officer of Aircraft with the Seventh Fleet in the southwest Pacific theatre of operations, flying along the Indochina coast and elsewhere in Black Cat bombers on dangerous reconnaissance missions. "We were shot at a little," he recalls modestly. "I know what tracers look like [and] there were some close misses," Douglas says, "but never any that would make good [newspaper] copy."[20] For his military service, during which he advanced to the rank of Lieutenant Commander, Douglas Dillon was awarded the Air Medal, the Navy Commendation Ribbon and the Legion of Merit with Combat Device.[21]

During the immediate postwar period, he returned to the family business to work at Dillon Read and US&FS until February 1953, when he went into government service again. Over the next twelve years, he was successively Ambassador to France, Undersecretary of State for Economic Affairs, Undersecretary of State and Secretary of the Treasury. Government service is something of a tradition for Dillon Read partners, with William Draper, Paul Nitze, James Forrestal and Peter Flanagan serving in high posts at one time or another. "But Forrestal and I were the only ones to get to Cabinet level," Douglas Dillon says.[22] (Nicholas Brady became the third Dillon partner to serve in the Cabinet, as George Bush's Treasury Secretary.)

Douglas Dillon's desire for a public career dates back to the early 1930s when, as he puts it: "I got the bug pretty soon after I went to work," but it was a bizarre twist of fate that actually got his government career started. In the late 1930s, he had been active in local Republican party politics in Somerset county, New Jersey, when the county chairman (a house painter) fell off a ladder, broke his leg and was incapacitated. Douglas Dillon was drafted to run the fall campaign and he learned his politics in a crash course.[23]

Later when he returned from war service, Douglas picked up where he left off and soon became vice chairman of the Republican State Committee. He entered the inner circle of the Republican foreign policy experts when he helped the Dulles brothers, Christian Herter and McGeorge Bundy write speeches for Governor Thomas E. Dewey's unsuccessful presidential campaign against Truman in 1948. Later, he organized the New Jersey for Eisenhower campaign and went to the 1952 Republican Convention as a member of the New Jersey delegation pledged to Eisenhower. Douglas's faction succeeded in persuading the New Jersey delegation to pledge its votes to Eisenhower in opposition to an uncommitted slate proposed by the governor, who favored the nomination of Robert Taft. That paid Douglas's political entrance fee and soon he was asked by Secretary of State-designate, John Foster Dulles, an old friend of the family, to go to France as the U. S. Ambassador.[24]

Douglas Dillon took very seriously the new assignment as Ambassador to France. First, to make way for his public career, Douglas deeded over his reserve secondary life estate as a gift to the Dillon Fund, a New York Charitable Corporation.[25] He then went on a crash course and increased his knowledge of French to fluency. He spoke only schoolbook French, but he and his wife Phyllis met the challenge by spending an hour daily with a French tutor. Within weeks Dillon was visiting the Quai d'Orsay without an interpreter.[26] Phyllis also became very involved in French affairs and with her husband contributed to a number of French cultural institutions. Reflecting these efforts, the French government awarded Phyllis Dillon the Legion of Honor in 1957; she was the only wife of a U. S. ambassador to be so honored up to that time.[27]

Eisenhower wanted Dillon to be an activist ambassador promoting Ike's plan for a closely integrated, well-armed Europe, prepared to rise to its own defense against any Russian attack.[28] As Ambassador to France and later in the State Department itself, Dillon exhibited a natural gift for quiet diplomacy coupled with a firm initiative. In his various State Department posts, he gained control over the multitude of agencies involved in foreign economic policy. He crossed swords more than once in demanding and usually getting the bureaucracy and the Congress to provide additional funds for foreign aid; the aid program was bigger by virtue of his sponsorship.[29]

Dillon combined an international outlook with the cultured and urbane manner of the classic diplomat. His poise and polished charm could be misleading, suggesting diffidence rather than dedication. According to one foreign diplomat, "Dillon reminds me of some English aristocrat who likes others to think of him as a dilettante but once you get down to the question at hand, you find he knows more about it than you do."[30]

Although Dillon was very disappointed that his son had chosen a public career after returning from the war rather than following him in the investment banking business, he was thrilled when Douglas was appointed Ambassador to France. However, he opposed Douglas's decision to come back to work in government first as the Undersecretary of State and later as Secretary of the Treasury in the Kennedy administration.

According to Douglas:

> My father wanted me to pick up the reins and run [the family investment business]; that was his wish from the 1920s on. . . . He made this clear to me on a number of occasions during my years in Washington. He considered work in the Washington bureaucracy to be of far less importance than what he often referred to as "real work" in private business where you could create something worthwhile.[31]

Douglas's greatest achievement was the Organization for Economic Cooperation and Development (OECD), sometimes called the Dillon Plan. A successor to the Marshall Plan, it was designed to enable free nations with hard and convertible currencies to meet the Soviet threat to competitive coexistence. Dillon argued that the most important economic question facing the United States and the rest of the free world was "what economic system the less developed nations would ultimately choose in their struggle against poverty." Acting for the United States, Douglas formally signed the OECD charter in December 1960, only a few days before Kennedy asked him to become Secretary of the Treasury.[32]

Despite Dillon's support of the Republican presidential candidate in 1960, President Kennedy chose him for Secretary of the Treasury. Kennedy picked Dillon because he desperately wanted to forestall criticism of the New Frontier programs by placing a sound money man in the sensitive Treasury job. Dillon, with his banking and diplomatic experience, was obviously an excellent choice for Kennedy's purpose. The two had first met in 1956 at Harvard, when Dillon was grand marshal at the twenty-fifth reunion of his class and Senator Kennedy the recipient of an honorary degree. After the ceremony they dropped by the select Spee Club (both were members) to chat, later becoming friends and occasional golfing companions. Like Kennedy, Douglas Dillon was not born with a silver spoon in his mouth but a most solid gold spoon. He was probably the wealthiest Secretary of the Treasury since Andrew Mellon in 1928.[33]

When Kennedy offered him the job, however, Douglas Dillon had plenty of doubts and got only lukewarm encouragement from Nixon and Eisenhower. However, Ike told him, "You can hardly refuse if the President of the United States says he needs you." After a week of soul searching, Dillon took the post. Upon taking up his post in the Treasury's classic, multi-tiered, temple-facaded building next door to the White House, Dillon called for every document since 1789 that provided a job description of the Secretary's position, then set out to make over the department on his own terms. Despite Eisenhower's doubt that Dillon would be able to work for sound fiscal policy under Kennedy, from the outset Douglas told the world that fiscal stability was essential to national security and that the strength of the free world was tied to the strength of the dollar; backing him up, Kennedy himself uttered similar sentiments.[34]

Unlike his predecessors, Douglas took advantage of his free hand to build a Treasury staff that professionals rated as probably the best since the days of Alexander Hamilton.[35] Accustomed to running his own show, Douglas surrounded himself with a staff of bright young men to handle the detail work. This was the nucleus on which his policy was built.[36] Dillon says, "I was really on the firing line. . . ." Douglas then returned to private life, noting "eight years in Washington is enough. . . ."[37]

Although he returned to US&FS, he determined to continue to pursue interests outside of Wall Street and distanced himself from the family's investment banking business because, as he put it, "I didn't want to go back to that sort of work." Pressed on why he did not want to follow in his father's footsteps, Douglas responded:

> I got into [Wall Street in the 1930s] after the glory days were over. There was very little work to be done and most of the business became more and more a question of whom you knew, played golf with, or took to dinner or to the theatre. It was not because you had some brilliant idea. . . . The opportunity to do different things, that existed in the twenties, was gone, and, by my nature, I'm not good at trying to get business by socializing.[38]

Douglas Dillon also took an active interest in cultural affairs in New York City, becoming a major contributor and patron of the Metropolitan Museum of Art. The Museum appointed him as a regular trustee upon his return (he had been an honorary trustee while in Paris as the U.S. Ambassador) and in 1970 the Museum elected him president. Upon his election, Douglas told *The New Yorker*:

> I've been interested in the Museum since I became a trustee, in 1951. I think I was the youngest on the board. I'd always liked beautiful things . . . but you couldn't say that I was a collector then, though my wife was interested in [antique] furniture. [When] I went to Paris as ambassador . . . we bought some pictures and French furniture for the Embassy, visited Versailles and . . . got to know the director of the Louvre, Georges Salles . . . and arranged . . . a show . . . at the Orangerie. We brought back . . . a dozen Impressionist paintings, some of which I think are quite good, and quite a bit of porcelain. My wife likes porcelain. She's a trustee of the Museum of Modern Art. She is a conservative modern.[39]

Douglas Dillon's interest in the Museum has been a lifetime avocation. There is a Dillon Gallery devoted to Chinese paintings and sculpture in the Metropolitan Museum of Art, endowed by the family. The galleries came into existence in the early 1980s. Initially, the Dillons gave $2.5 million to renovate the galleries to exhibit the Chinese paintings. They have given overall about $10 million to the museum in various gifts over the years. The big gifts started after Clarence Dillon's death in 1979 and relate to a trust fund that had been set up previously.[40] The Met held a special silver anniversary celebration in 1984 for Douglas Dillon upon his retirement from his museum posts.[41]

Although his son chose to pursue a non-financial career, Clarence Dillon must have been pleased with the social development of Douglas's family. After a failed earlier marriage,[42] Douglas's younger daughter, Joan, married Prince Charles of Luxembourg, the dashing fun-loving brother of the reigning grand duke and a Bourbon descendant of Henry IV. This marriage produced two children, Princesse Charlotte de Luxembourg and Prince Robert de Luxembourg. Joan's husband died of a heart attack ten years later in Florence, Italy.[43] After Prince Charles's death, Joan married Duc Philippe de Mouchy in 1978 and together they manage Chateau Haut-Brion.

Although Douglas wanted to distance himself from his father and pursue his own interests far from Wall Street, the similarities between them are striking. For example, the two men had life-long interests in agriculture, with Douglas overseeing the family's far-flung agricultural and cattle-breeding activities at Dunwalke and elsewhere before and after his father's death. Douglas also shares his father's love for France; he has taken a deep personal interest in the 120-acre family-owned Chateau Haut-Brion with its vineyards that produce the most subtle and exhilarating wines of the Bordeaux district. Douglas visits Haut-Brion each fall during the *Vendanges* reserving a select share of its annual output for his own use. He takes a connoisseur's quiet pride in his knowledge of wines. "I can tell the year of a given Bordeaux or the district that it came from," he says, "but I can't get both the year and the vineyard, as some profess to do."[44]

Also like his father, Douglas has an incredible sense of investment value and timing as evidenced by his outstanding performance in managing the US&FS investment portfolio.[45] His approach to decision-making bears an unmistakable resemblance to that of his father. Like his father, Douglas is a problem solver with an ability to concentrate, absorb, and differentiate. He can pace himself so effectively that he can spend twelve hours a day effortlessly acquiring the information he needs to make judgments. "He has a fantastic memory for figures, and catches one of us up every so often," said one of his aides, "yet he can cut to the heart of a mass of details." Once Douglas has stocked up on all the relevant information, he makes up his mind as decisively as his father did.

Despite all the similarities, philosophically Douglas would like to be more than just his father's son, and in many ways he is quite different from his father. Douglas is far more patient and diplomatic than his father was in dealing with his aides. In addition, Douglas backed up his love of France by making a commitment to become fluent in the language to further his effort to assimilate the French culture. Finally, the overriding difference between the two men is that Douglas chose to make his mark in government and public service rather than in Wall Street.

Clarence Dillon's daughter, Dorothy, was also prepared for entry into society. After her graduation from Foxcroft in 1930, she was introduced at a debutante party given by Dillon and his wife at the Ritz Carlton in New York City.[46] She then attended Barnard College but left school in 1933, marrying Philip Elsworth Allen in 1934. Her son, Philip Allen, believes his grandfather played a major role in persuading her to marry his father. Philip notes, "my father was at that point [a young investment banker] . . . and my grandfather thought he was bright and attractive and would make a good husband." Allen Senior later joined Dillon Read at Clarence Dillon's invitation.[47] Allen's marriage to Dorothy produced three children, two boys, Philip and Douglas, and a girl, Anne Christine.

Later, Dorothy decided to return to Barnard to complete her studies, majoring in mathematics and graduating in 1950.[48] By then, her marriage to Philip Allen had ended in divorce. Nitze recalled sadly that he was the one who introduced Philip Allen to Dorothy, adding: "I regret to say it because he was a lemon. . . . He had an infinite capability of making a simple problem complex."[49] During the 1950s, after her divorce from Allen, Dorothy became quite active in Barnard affairs. In 1956, she joined her father and brother in making a major contribution to the Wollman Library and Lehman Hall at Barnard. Later that year, she was named an alumnae trustee of Barnard and in 1965 she became a trustee.[50]

In 1956, Dorothy married Sidney Shepherd Spivack whom she had met in the early 1930s, again through Nitze.[51] According to her son, Philip Allen:

> I honestly believe that some of the best years my mother ever had were with Sidney Spivack. They did a lot of travelling and enjoyed the same things together. . . . Spivack was very outgoing and liked to meet people. . . . It was a terrific thing for her.[52]

This marriage ended when Spivack died of cancer in 1969.[53] Seven years later, Dorothy tried again, marrying Eric Eweson in 1976 but her hard luck continued; Eweson died of a heart attack in 1988 leaving her a widow for the second time.

Thus, the Dillon family pursued social and public service interests outside of Wall Street in its second generation. With few exceptions, none of Dillon's grandchildren has become involved with Dillon Read or the field of investment banking. Dillon's five grandchildren have involved themselves mainly in agriculture and wine producing, although Philip Allen manages investments for his mother and uncle and for ten years was employed in various capacities at Dillon Read and other securities firms.[54] Mark Collins, Clarence Dillon's great-grandson, was a First Boston vice president before becoming involved in the Treasury Department and as an Alternate Executive Director of the World Bank in 1991.[55]

Notes

1. "Business Abroad: He [Douglas Dillon] Has the Say on Trade, Aid," *Business Week*, December 7, 1957, p. 131 and "A Dillon, a Dollar," *Fortune*, p. 95.

2. "The Talk of the Town: C. Douglas Dillon," *The New Yorker*, April 4, 1970, p. 36 and "The Economy: Man With the Purse," *Time*, August 18, 1961, p. 13.

3. "The Economy: Man with the Purse," *Time*, p. 13.

4. *Anne's Story*.

5. "The Economy: Man With the Purse," *Time*, p. 13.

6. *Anne's Story* and "The Economy: Man with the Purse," *Time*, p. 13.

7. Letter to author from C. Douglas Dillon, November 18, 1992.

8. "The Economy: Man With the Purse," *Time*, p. 13.

9. "Talk of the Town, C. Douglas Dillon," *The New Yorker*, p. 36.

10. "The Economy: Man With the Purse," *Time*, p. 13.

11. "The Economy: Man with the Purse," *Time*, p. 13.

12. Secretary's 50th Reunion Report, *Harvard Class of 1905*, p. 142.

13. Written comments by C. Douglas Dillon, February 24, 1993.

14. Based on data from US&FS annual report for the year ending December 31, 1983 and *Moody's Banks and Finance Manual*, selected editions.

15. Chernow, Ron, *The House of Morgan*, p. 462.

16. Chernow, Ron, *The House of Morgan*, p. 462.

17. Chernow, Ron, *The House of Morgan*, p. 463.

18. "The Economy: Man with the Purse," *Time*, p. 14.

19. "The Economy: Man With the Purse," *Time*, p. 14 and written comments from C. Douglas Dillon, February 24, 1993.

20. "A Dillon, a Dollar," *Fortune*, p. 215 and written comments by C. Douglas Dillon, February 24, 1993.

21. "Talk of the Town: C. Douglas Dillon," *The New Yorker*, p. 36.

22. "Dillon Read Refuses to Play the Game," by Julie Connelly, *Institutional Investor*, January 1979, p. 41.

23. Douglas Dillon interview, May 23, 1991.

24. Douglas Dillon interview, May 23, 1991 and "Oral History of C. Douglas Dillon," conducted by John Luter, *Columbia University Oral History Department*, 1973.

25. Douglas Dillon interview, October 29, 1991.

26. "The Economy: Man with the Purse," *Time*, p. 14.

27. "C. Douglas Dillon Wife, Phyllis, dies at age 71," *New York Times*, June 21, 1982.

28. *Current Biography*, 1953, p. 162.

29. "Dillon to Bring Two Deficits Under Control," *Business Week*, March 4, 1961, p. 31.

30. "Dillon to Bring Two Deficits Under Control," *Business Week*, p. 31.

31. Douglas Dillon interview, May 23, 1991 and letter to the author from C. Douglas Dillon, November 18, 1992.

32. "A Dillon, A Dollar" by Gilbert Burck, *Fortune*, p. 215.

33. "Fact and Comment: What Manner of Man is C. Douglas Dillon?" by Malcolm Forbes, *Forbes*, p. 10.

34. "A Dillon, A Dollar," *Fortune*, p. 93.

35. "The Economy: Man With the Purse," *Time*, p. 15.

36. "Dillon to Bring Two Deficits Under Control," *Business Week*, p. 31.

37. "Talk of the Town, C. Douglas Dillon," *The New Yorker*, p. 36.

38. Douglas Dillon interview, May 23, 1991.

39. "Talk of the Town, C. Douglas Dillon," *The New Yorker*, pp. 35-6.

40. Douglas Dillon recalled, "My father gave me a considerable amount of money in the form of securities as a wedding present in 1931. In December of that year, I put most of these securities in a trust fund so that the income would go to my father and after that return to me after he died." Later, Douglas gave his life interest in the trust to the Dillon Fund. While the trust was small in the thirties, it has grown greatly since and the trustees of the Dillon Fund decided to give the income received every year to non-profit institutions such as the Metropolitan Museum of Art." (Sources: C. Douglas Dillon interview, October 29, 1991 and letter to author from C. Douglas Dillon, November 18, 1992.)

41. "New York art world celebrates 75th anniversary of American Federation of Arts and C. Douglas Dillon, recently retired Chairman and longtime benefactor of Metropolitan Museum of Art" (photo caption), *New York Times*, October 16, 1984.

42. *Anne's Story* and letter to author from C. Douglas Dillon, November 18, 1992.

43. "Family With No History Has Remarkable Story," *San Angelo Standard-Times*.

44. "The Economy: Man with the Purse," *Time*, p. 14 and "A Dillon, a Dollar," *Fortune*, p. 94.

45. "Dillon to Bring Two Deficits Under Control," *Business Week*, p. 31.

46. Clarence Dillon private papers.

47. Philip D. Allen interview, April 9, 1992.

48. Philip D. Allen interview, April 9, 1992 and Barnard College's Registrar Office.

49. Paul H. Nitze interview, November 11, 1991.

50. Various accounts in the *New York Times*, April 27, 1958, June 6, 1958 and June 15, 1965.

51. Nitze, Paul H., *From Hiroshima to Glasnost*, p. xix.

52. Philip D. Allen interview, April 9, 1992.

53. Joseph Haywood interview, October 28, 1991.

54. Mrs. Dorothy Dillon Eweson written comments received May 12, 1993.

55. C. Douglas Dillon written comments, February 24, 1993.

13

Retrospective

Few and fortunate are the people who appear when their particular talents are needed most—who are in the right place at the right time. Churchill and Napoleon are obvious examples of leaders who were in tune with their times. Many others go unappreciated when the times and circumstances are not suited to their talents. Clarence Dillon was fortunate in this respect. His character, personality and abilities were ideally suited to the Wall Street of the 1920s where he achieved his astounding success in the investment banking industry.

The enigma of Clarence Dillon, the acknowledged "Baron" of Wall Street, still remains. Why did this spectacular risk-taking entrepreneur decide to withdraw from the challenging world of Wall Street—from the game Dillon himself had earlier described to a Harvard classmate as "more fascinating than a game of no-limit stud poker." Many of the Wall Street stars of the 1920s survived the Crash. Some retired as Dillon did but many more remained to succeed again in the securities business.

Why didn't Dillon come back for another hand?

The saga of his former partner, Ferdinand Eberstadt—who started up a new investment banking firm in the teeth of the Depression in 1931 and achieved outstanding success providing financing for his "little blue chips" —reinforces the judgement that Dillon had become too conservative and cautious to keep on surpassing his competitors in deal making. He no longer had the motivation necessary to succeed in that endeavor.

As Nitze put it:

Clarence Dillon was no longer driven to emulate David by defeating the Goliaths of the world by his superior wit and brilliance. He was more interested in preserving his wealth, enjoying and helping his family, developing his position in "high society" and exercising influence in world affairs.[1]

The question remains however: Why didn't Dillon reenter the business after the recovery began in the 1930s? This was the same banker-entrepreneur who had miraculously saved Goodyear with a risky $90.5 million bailout in the 1921 depression, snatched Dodge out of the maws of J. P. Morgan with a spectacular $146 million cash buyout in 1925, launched the investment trust industry with a bold $90 million dual offering in 1924 and 1928, rebuilt and revitalized the German economy with $340 million in new capital in the last half of the 1920s, and stubbornly pursued the auto merger of the century—Chrysler's $236 million acquisition of Dodge in 1928. Had Dillon suddenly lost his nerve?

Although his exact motives will always remain a mystery, there are several plausible theories as to why he curtailed his financing activities. One hypothesis has it that after 1933, Dillon was a bitter "wounded" wolf, turned off investment banking by the adverse publicity produced by the Pecora and other Congressional hearings on the Wall Street scandals. After the Crash, Dillon was called to Washington many times to testify before hostile Senate committees looking for convenient scapegoats to blame. The widening Wall Street witch hunt was further exacerbated in the late 1930s by the damaging Congressional investigations of public utility holding companies and investment trust abuses, which led to further regulation and bureaucracy.

While Dillon was personally untouched by the scandals, Pecora suggested that Dillon had made too much money at the public's expense— not that he had ever done anything illegal. Dillon's use of the public's money in his two investment trusts—to engineer deals and to "bail out" unsold securities underwritings rather than putting his own capital at risk— made him particularly vulnerable. Dillon's trusts had placed 8 percent of their portfolios in Dillon underwritings, some representing offerings that Dillon had trouble selling to the public. In fact, however, some of these deals became very profitable investments thereafter.

For example, the two trusts bought 150,000 shares of Louisiana Land & Exploration from Dillon's unsold syndicate holdings for $300,000 in 1928; this investment multiplied many fold over the years, augmented by numerous stock splits as Louisiana Land developed its prolific oil and gas properties. The trusts eventually sold their holdings in Louisiana Land taking estimated profits of about $30 million—more than 100 times their original cost.[2] Whatever his feelings about the future of Wall Street and the economy, Dillon's management of the trusts was stellar, far outperforming the market and other investment trusts.

One of Dillon's major life goals was to become accepted in society; after the Crash, he put much of his energy into achieving this goal while preserving his capital. This shift in life style contrasts sharply with the picture of Dillon as the defender of risk-taking and entrepreneurship, a position he espoused at the Pecora hearings as follows:

> Those [bankers] who deal in the more seasoned securities are apt to be a little smug. . . . I am sure that the courageous financier who raises money for [new] industries where there are real risks, is rendering a greater service to his country [than] the smug conservative banker. . . .

A leader in Dillon's position had an obligation to innovate and finance small emerging growth companies in order to energize the economy and create new jobs in the early and mid-1930s. In the earlier part of the century, for example, Rockefeller and Carnegie had demonstrated creative leadership by using their wealth and financial leverage to drive the economy forward. In the 1930s, Forrestal had strived to push Dillon's firm into innovative financings that would keep the system open so that other people like himself could make it on their own.[3] By aborting Forrestal's efforts, Dillon failed to provide critical leadership when his country and his firm needed it most.

A second theory has it that Dillon really thought the Crash signalled not only a prolonged economic slump but the secular decline of capitalism and Wall Street as the center of world power. The spectacular large-scale deals of the 1920s were gone and the whole market was paralyzed. Wall Street was a ghost town of shattered dreams and empty boardrooms, and the prestige of the investment bankers was at an all-time low.[4] From a 1929 peak of over $9 billion, domestic underwritings fell to only $644 million three years later, 93 percent below the 1929 record.[5] Dillon's underwritings, which reached a peak of $522 million in 1925, declined steadily thereafter to an insignificant amount in 1932, and the firm had no underwritings at all in 1933 and 1934.

Nitze notes that after the Crash Dillon told him that Wall Street financiers would no longer control their own destiny because critical economic and financial decisions would be made in Washington, not in New York. Actually, Dillon never gave up on the U.S. economy. Hugh Bullock notes, "Dillon was `a born optimist.'" But despite his inbred optimism, Dillon changed his goals to developing the social position of his family rather than concentrating his efforts on deal making in Wall Street.

A final theory denies that Dillon ever left the wars of Wall Street. Gruff and demanding, he kept abreast of the firm's affairs and continued to be in complete command wherever he was situated. Nitze recollects being at Dillon's Jamaica estate in the Caribbean in the 1950s: "Promptly at 10 o'clock every morning, Dillon would get on the telephone and call New York and talk to Fred Brandi, who was then president of the firm, . . . demanding explanations of every transaction and conducting the business from afar."[6] Some staffers quipped that Dillon probably would continue to run the firm from his grave. Absentee owners, however, rarely succeed at running enterprises as complex and risk-oriented as investment banking firms. Such businesses need the direction that only a "hands-on" approach can provide.

Even though Dillon Read drifted after Dillon left the day-to-day management of the firm, its staying power was fantastic. During the late 1930s, it managed to maintain its premier position as a lead underwriter by concentrating on utility financing. One of Dillon's major clients in the 1920s and 1930s and into the 1940s was Harrison Williams's North American utilities complex. Dillon's firm raised $917.1 million in new capital for North American or its affiliated companies in fifty-four offerings. During the Depression these deals helped Dillon Read sustain its position as a major originating firm accounting for about 7 percent of total U.S. underwritings.[7]

Dillon had first met Williams on the War Industries Board during the first world war. Now, he used this contact as his major financing source. But even this asset deteriorated when Harrison Williams insisted on pyramiding North American's holdings unsoundly through the Blue Ridge and Shenandoah trusts. As a result, Dillon refused to finance any further North American offerings after 1931 although he continued to finance North American's operating subsidiaries which were sound. Later, in 1938 and 1939, Dillon launched five offerings for the reorganized North American Company, totalling $114.2 million.

The impact of Dillon's physical absence from the day-to-day operations of the firm, however, eventually took its toll. The incredible momentum and staff built up by Dillon, which had carried the firm to the top level of the investment banking pyramid, was eventually dispersed and the firm slowed down in the fiercely competitive postwar banking business. No longer a bulge bracket firm, Dillon Read developed into a smaller Wall Street boutique relying on its elite client list to produce business. Dillon's stubborn reluctance to commit the firm's money stifled Dillon Read's growth long after Wall Street had recovered. Companies that Dillon had rescued or financed now deserted the firm to go with other more innovative investment bankers. "Most of them, as things got more competitive, went, one by one," says Douglas Dillon. Dillon's imaginative financings were imitated, not at the firm he built, but by others.[8]

Historically, the function of investment banks was to raise capital for companies on the basis of long associations and old friendships. It had little to do with the distribution and trading of securities—that was left to the brokers and other retail firms which were in a different world. However, in the postwar markets the giant institutional investors became strongly oriented to trading, and the securities markets became extremely volatile.

Trading had now become the biggest single source of revenue to investment banks. Whereas the old underwriting business was based on experience and prestige, now block trading and venture investing called for huge commitments of a banking firm's own money.[9] Pierpont Morgan would have turned over in his grave if he knew that trading and commissions produced well over half the revenue of his old firm in the 1980s.[10]

In the 1920s, Clarence Dillon operated on "shoestring" capital to finance his high-risk, high-profit deals, relying on his dealer syndicate, US&FS and bank loans to fund them. The Wall Street community has never been large when measured by the size of its firms. "A cottage industry," Wall Streeters affectionately say.[11] After the Investment Company Act was passed banning investment bankers from financing their deals with captive accounts such as US&FS, Dillon Read could no longer compete as a major originating firm. Its limited capital was clearly incapable of competing with firms with billions of dollars in capital. Staying small and profitable became increasingly difficult.

The increasingly conservative hand of Clarence Dillon, whose earlier aggressive style had given the firm much of its tone, now held it back. Douglas Dillon, however, told *Institutional Investor* that the firm had always been risk averse, noting that "to some extent that has been true since my father's day. We've always had a weather eye out for undue risk."[12] In the early 1920s, Dillon's syndicate took huge positions in promising enterprises based on his thoroughgoing and conservative "due diligence" analysis and investigation.

After the firm declined drastically in activity in the 1970s, Douglas Dillon reasserted his authority and turned to Nick Brady to head up Dillon Read.[13] Brady breathed new life into the grand old firm and Dillon Read soon became more competitive and profitable. Despite Brady's efforts, however, Dillon Read could not recapture its special bulge bracket underwriting status largely due to its spartan capital base. After the death of his father in 1979, therefore, Douglas Dillon was determined to sell out and in an extraordinarily generous gesture he agreed to sell the family interest to his Dillon Read partners at book value[14] which was less than one-half its true market value.

Later, after an internal task force formed by Brady concluded that Dillon Read would need to greatly expand its capital base and diversify to become competitive again,[15] Brady decided that the firm could not slug it out alone and after several failed merger efforts, Travelers Insurance Company purchased Dillon Read in 1986 for $157.5 million. After completing the merger, Brady left the firm in 1988 to become Secretary of the Treasury in the Bush administration.

However, following the collapse of junk bonds and the real estate market in the late 1980s, Travelers incurred major financial losses and was forced to sell the investment banking subsidiary back to Dillon Read for $122 million, taking a loss of $36 million on its five year ownership.[16] A deal was then worked out with Baring Brothers, Britain's oldest and most illustrious merchant bank, whereby Dillon Read's management reacquired 60 percent of the firm from Travelers and control, with Baring acquiring the balance of the firm.[17]

In a complete reversal of the roaring 1980s, the Barings-Dillon deal may confirm the ultimate soundness of the conservative business strategy of Clarence Dillon. The early years of the 1990s witnessed the emergence of a more conservative securities business, intent on unwinding much of the leverage built up in the industry during the heady 1980s. In this calmer, less frenetic field, smaller firms such as Dillon Read may have more staying power. In a classic case of irony, it may be that Clarence Dillon's conservatism was the critical factor that saved Dillon Read. From his grave, old man Dillon may have had his way after all.

Final Evaluation

Clarence Dillon played at least two major roles in his long life. One role was that of the swashbuckling buccaneer roaming the seas of Wall Street for profitable ventures and bounty. This phase could be called the "Wealth Acquisition" phase. After Dillon had amassed his fortune in the late 1920s, he correctly forecast the Crash and Depression and curtailed his firm's exposure. At this point, he turned his attention aggressively to his second life role—"Social Acceptability"—to develop his personal cultural life while preserving his wealth and influencing international events.

These two major roles overlapped each other throughout his long life with one or the other taking the lead from time to time. During Dillon's early career, from 1914 to 1929, "Wealth Accumulation" dominated his activities and "Social Acceptability" was a secondary pursuit. Slamming together mega-deals in Wall Street during the roaring twenties did not leave much time to enjoy the social atmosphere at Dark Harbor in Maine or in the Far Hills, New Jersey, estate area. But Dillon kept a presence in the social milieu as much as the exciting and demanding world of Wall Street permitted.

After the 1929 Crash, Dillon reduced "Wealth Accumulation" and escalated the "Social Acceptability" phase of his life developing luxurious homes in Europe, America and the Caribbean to cater to his growing list of social contacts. He basked in the glory of seeing his son become Ambassador to France and relished his new-found social prestige when his granddaughter, Joan, married into European nobility. During this latter phase of his life, he cut back on his involvement in the day-to-day operations of his firm and restricted his presence to irregular visits. He never quite gave up control, however, running the business in absentia by long-distance telephone from wherever he happened to be in the world.

The long economic depression and his growing involvement in social pursuits caused him to become more conservative and unwilling to take risks. He had already made his fortune and was one of the richest men in the world. Why should he jeopardize his wealth and his social position by taking undue investment risks? Accordingly, Dillon Read which had been one of the most aggressive firms in Wall Street during the 1920s became ultra-conservative in the 1930s and 1940s and missed out on some of the great new investment opportunities of the post-1930s arena. Dillon's ultra-conservatism ultimately caused his firm to drop out of the top brackets in Wall Street's hotly competitive market.

In this sense, Dillon failed in his own calling. The 1930s were crying out for investment in exciting new industries such as electronics, aircraft, pharmaceuticals, chemicals and other new fields. Dillon systematically refused to finance these emerging industries, although his former partners such as Mathey and Eberstadt made fortunes on their own in these profitable new venture fields. In Dillon's later life he denied himself the heroic role of helping to rescue America from a devastating economic collapse just as he had rescued Goodyear and other recession-battered companies in the early 1920s.

Dillon amassed one of the great fortunes in America. In 1957, *Fortune* magazine ran an article listing Clarence Dillon among the fifty richest people in the country, with between $100 million and $200 million in assets. Using a conservative growth factor of 8 percent, this fortune should have grown to over $1.5 billion by the time of Dillon's death in 1979. Dillon emulated Carnegie, however, in that he tried with some success to give away most of his wealth during his lifetime. Philip Allen, his grandson, states that he gave most of it to his family, with some going to Harvard and other institutions—but the bulk of it went to the family in the form of trusts that continue for the grandchildren.[18] While the Dillon family is no longer at the top of the most wealthy in the country, the 1992 *Forbes* survey estimated their total net worth at $450 million and possibly much more, depending on what Haut-Brion is really worth plus the true value of the forty-one separate trusts Dillon established for his family during his lifetime.[19]

Unlike Carnegie, Dillon had a family with many grandchildren, and much of his wealth was given to his progeny. As a result, the recipients of his largesse became super rich in their lifetimes. This largesse enabled Dillon to reduce the impact of death taxes on his estate. At the time of his death, the probated value of his estate subject to state and federal tax was just a little over $8 million; the estate tax actually paid amounted to only $3 million.[20]

Dillon and his family have been active contributors to a wide range of charities and other non-profit institutions. Respecting Dillon's wishes, the estate gave to Princeton 125 acres and the main house, Dunwalke, as an "academic retreat and conference center."[21] Other beneficiaries of Dillon's and/or the estate's generosity include: Harvard University for professorships and the Dillon Field House; New York's Lincoln Center for the Performing Arts; the Metropolitan Museum of Art; Princeton for a library to house the Dulles papers; a public library in Bedminister, New Jersey; Heidelberg University; contributions to help restore the Parthenon on the Acropolis in Athens; a major contribution to the Roosevelt library at Hyde Park to house the late president's papers; New York Hospital for their Fund for Medical Progress; a memorial chapel to St. Luke's Episcopal Church in Bedminister, New Jersey; the Patriot Memorial Chapel in the south transept of Washington Cathedral; and the Conference Hall and Tapestry for the Assembly Hall of the World Council of Churches in Geneva, Switzerland (the last three dedicated to the memory of his wife, Anne Douglass Dillon).[22]

Clarence Dillon lived in remarkably good health well into his nineties, except for cataracts which had developed in both of his eyes in the late 1940s. In 1949, Dillon had the first of two painful eye operations to remove the cataracts. Afterwards he wore thick eye glasses for the rest of his life.[23]

A painful accident in the late 1970s slowed him down considerably but by then Dillon was ninety-five years of age. According to Haywood, Dillon suffered a fall in 1978 and thereafter was semi-invalided. Even this setback failed to take away Dillon's zest for life. According to his daughter Dorothy, Dillon continued seeing his family every day and taking short outdoor walks whenever the weather and his physical condition permitted. To aid him, Dillon had one long-time practical nurse constantly with him; she lived in the house. Dillon also kept up with his mail, spending time with his secretary every day keeping abreast of current developments.[24]

After his accident, however, Dillon slowly deteriorated and finally died about a year later in April 1979. The immediate cause of death was uremia due to renal (kidney) insufficiency and arterial nephrosclerosis (various kidney disorders). Another significant contributing medical factor was arteriosclerosis (hardening of the arteries).[25]

It is difficult to summarize the achievements of a man such as Clarence Dillon whose life spanned almost a century. He exploited opportunities in the 1920s through his creative and daring financings as well as the many mergers he conceived to enable business organizations to thrive under more competitive conditions. The unsolved enigma of his life was why he chose not to risk his wealth when the country desperately needed his financing ingenuity to speed the recovery of America from the deepest depression in its history. Despite this failing, this truly remarkable and complex man developed a core of highly-motivated investment bankers who set up their own investment firms or joined government to make major impacts on the world including Dean Mathey, Douglas Dillon, Nicholas Brady, James Forrestal, Ferdinand Eberstadt and Paul Nitze. Moreover, Clarence Dillon built up the independent firm of Dillon Read & Co. that has survived a wide variety of calamities over its 160-year history and continues to prosper as the financial world prepares for the unknown challenges and opportunities of the twenty-first century.

This was the mark of the man they called "Baron."

Notes

1. Paul H. Nitze, written comments, March 31, 1993.
2. Author's estimates based on data from *Poor's Industrials*, 1929 edition, p. 2635; *Moody's Industrial Manual*, 1960 edition, p. 532; 1970 edition, pp. 1802-3; and 1981 edition, pp. 3817-21.
3. Hoopes/Brinkley, *Driven Patriot*, p. 81.
4. Hoopes/Brinkley, *Driven Patriot*, p. 106.
5. Carosso, Vincent, *Investment Banking in America*, p. 307.
6. Paul H. Nitze interview, November 11, 1991.
7. Author's survey of Dillon Read financings.
8. Jereski, Laura, "Clarence Dillon: Using Other People's Money," *Forbes*, p. 274.
9. Brooks, John, *The Takeover Game*, pp. 13-14.
10. Ferris, Paul, *The Master Bankers*, New York, 1984, pp. 93-94.
11. Ferris, Paul, *The Master Bankers*, p. 94.
12. Connelly, Julie, "Dillon Read Refuses to Play the Game," *Institutional Investor*, January 1979, p. 41.
13. Connelly, Julie, "Dillon Read Refuses to Play the Game," *Institutional Investor*, pp. 41-42 and Reddish, Jeannette M., "People of the Financial World," *Financial World*, May 15, 1978.
14. Sobel, Robert, *The Life and Times of Dillon Read*, p. 315.
15. "The Upheaval at Dillon, Read," *Euromoney*, p. 272.
16. "Travelers Corp. Said to be Winding Up Sale of Dillon Read," *Wall Street Journal*, November 12, 1991.
17. Eichenwald, Kurt, "Travelers is Selling Dillon Firm; Management Joins Barings as Buyers," November 13, 1991.
18. Philip D. Allen interview, April 9, 1992.
19. "The Forbes Four Hundred: Family Fortunes," *Forbes*, October 19, 1992, p. 224.
20. Clarence Dillon estate papers.
21. Douglas Dillon interview, May 23, 1991.
22. Various sources including Dillon's private files, estate papers and his memoirs.
23. Douglas Dillon interview, May 23, 1991 and Secretary's Fiftieth Anniversary Report, *Harvard Class of 1905*, p. 143.

24. Dorothy Dillon Eweson written comments received May 12, 1993.
25. Joseph Haywood interview, October 28, 1991 and Clarence Dillon estate papers.

Bibliography

Personal Interviews and Correspondence

Philip D. Allen, interview, April 9, 1992.

Edward J. Bermingham, Jr., letter, August 15, 1984.

Nicholas F. Brady, Dillon, Read & Co., Inc., letter, May 30, 1984.

Hugh Bullock, interview, April 18, 1984, April 11, 1991, telephone.

Suzanne Campbell, telephone, January 7, 1992 and various letters.

Phyllis Dillon Collins, Dark Harbor visit and interview, July 1, 1991.

Clarence Dillon private papers in possession of Mrs. Dorothy Dillon Eweson at Dunwalke estate, Far Hills, New Jersey.

C. Douglas Dillon, interview, May 3, 1984, May 23, 1991, Dark Harbor visit and interview, July 1, 1991, interview, October 29, 1991 and letters to author, November 18, 1992, December 7, 1992, October 12, 1994, October 15, 1994, October 20, 1994 and written comments received by author February 24, 1993.

C. Douglas Dillon, oral history conducted by John Luter, *Columbia University Oral History Department*, May and June 1972 (published in 1973).

Ferdinand Eberstadt, interview, July 17 and 18, 1969 (conducted by Calvin Lee Christman).

Ferdinand Eberstadt private papers, *Seeley G. Mudd Manuscript Library*, Princeton University.

Frederick Eberstadt, interview, September 9, 1987, telephone, April 14, 1991, letter, September 26, 1991.

Mrs. Dorothy Dillon Eweson, interview, October 1, 1991, October 4, 1991, visits to review private papers, October 1, 4, 8, and 11, 1991, letter, October 22, 1991 and written comments received May 12, 1993.

Joseph Haywood, interview, October 28, 1991 and written comment.

Eliot Janeway, interview, April 3, 1984, April 4, 1991.

Dr. John Lattimore, telephone, April 15, 1991.
Walter Lubanko, interview, April 16, 1984.
Charles J. V. Murphy, letters, October 7, 1982 (to Edward F. Willett), May 26, 1984, January 22, 1985, and March 3, 1985; interview with Robert Lovett, no date.
Paul H. Nitze, telephone, April 15, 1991, interview, November 11, 1991, written comments received in January 1993 and April 1993.
Alexander Schwartz (son of A. Charles Schwartz), telephone interview, May 1, 1984.
Peter L. Wastrom, interview, March 29, 1984.
Marjorie Wellbrock, interview, October 30, 1991.
Robert G. Zeller, interview, May 1, 1984.

Interviews in the Bordeaux (France) Wine District

Jean-Claude Berrouet, Oenologist, Chateau Petrus, Pomerol, June 12, 1992.
Pascal Delbeck, Estate Manager, Chateau Ausone, Saint-Emilion, June 12, 1992.
Frederic Delmas, Wine Negociant, Alfred Schyler & Cie., Bordeaux, June 12, 1992.
Jean-Bernard Delmas, Directeur, Chateau Haut-Brion, Pessac, June 9 and 12, 1992.
Mme. Germaine Darracq, Public Relations, Chateau Haut-Brion, Pessac, June 9, 1992.
Helen Fenouillet, guide, Chateau Latour, Pauillac, June 11, 1992.
Sasha Lachine, Owner, Chateau Prieure Lichine, Cantenac, June 10, 1992.
Kess Van Leeuwen, Vineyard Manager, Chateau Cheval Blanc, Saint-Emilion, June 12, 1992.
Jean-Phillipe Masclef, Research Analyst, Chateau Haut-Brion, Pessac, June 9, 1992.
Duchesse Joan de Mouchy, President, Chateau Haut-Brion, Pessac, June 8, 1992.
Alain Puginier, Archivist, Chateau Haut-Brion, Pessac, June 9, 1992.
Paul Pontallier, Estate Manager, Chateau Margaux, Margaux, June 10, 1992.
Robert H. Revelle, Maitre de Chais, Chateau Lafite Rothschild, Pauillac, June 11, 1992.
Gilbert Rovam, Vineyard Manager, Chateau Lafite Rothschild, Pauillac, June 11, 1992.
James Stewart, guide, Chateau Mouton Rothschild, Pauillac, June 11, 1992.

Books

Allen, Frederick Lewis. *Only Yesterday.* New York. 931.
Allen, Hugh. *The House of Goodyear.* Akron. 1936.
Allyn, Stanley C. *My Half Century with NCR.* New York. 1967
Auerbach, Joseph, and Hayes, Samuel L. III. *Investment Banking and Diligence.* Boston. 1986.
Auletta, Ken. *Greed and Glory on Wall Street: The Fall of the House of Lehman.* New York. 1986.

Barnard, Harry. *Independent Man, the Life of Senator James Couzens.* New York. 1958.

Baruch, Bernard. *Baruch: The Public Years—My Own Story.* New York. 1960.

Birmingham, Stephen. *Our Crowd.* New York. 1967.

Beasley, Norman. *Men Working: The Story of Goodyear Tire & Rubber.* New York. 1931.

Brandeis, Louis. *Other People's Money, and How the Bankers Use It.* New York. 1932.

Brooks, John. *Once in a Golconda: A True Drama of Wall Street, 1920-1938.* New York. 1969.

_____. *The Takeover Game.* New York. 1987.

Bullock, Hugh. *The Story of Investment Companies.* New York. 1959.

Burroughs, Bryan, and Helyar, John. *Barbarians at the Gate: The Fall of RJR Nabisco.* New York. 1990.

Callahan, David. *Dangerous Capabilities: Paul Nitze and the Cold War.* New York. 1990.

Carosso, Vincent. *Investment Banking in America.* Cambridge, Mass. 1970.

Carrington, Tim. *The Year They Sold Wall Street.* New York. 1985.

Chandler, Alfred D. Jr. *Pierre Dupont and the Making of the Modern Corporation.* New York. 1971.

Chernow, Ron. *The House of Morgan: An American Banking Dynasty and The Rise of Modern Finance.* New York. 1990.

Christman, Calvin. *Ferdinand Eberstadt and Economic Mobilization for War.* Ph.D. dissertation, n.p., Ohio State University. 1971.

Chrysler, Walter, in collaboration with Boyden Sparkes. *Life of an American Workman.* New York. 1937.

Clemens, Gus. *The Concho County.* San Antonio, Texas. 1981.

Cleveland, Harold van B., and Huerta, Thomas F. *Citibank, 1812-1970.* New York. 1985.

Coit, Margaret. *Mr. Baruch.* Boston. 1957.

Cowles, Virginia. *The Astors: The Story of A Transatlantic Family.* London. 1979.

Crabb, Richard. *Birth of A Giant: The Men and Incidents that Gave America the Motorcar.* Philadelphia. 1970.

Cray, Ed. *Chrome Colossus: General Motors and Its Times.* New York. 1980.

Dawes, Charles G. *A Journal of Reparations.* London. 1939.

Dillon, Clarence. *Anne's Story.* n.p. Far Hills, N.J. 1965.

Dorwart, Jeffrey. *Eberstadt and Forrestal, a National Security Partnership, 1909-1949.* College Station, Texas. 1991.

Douglas, William O. *Go East, Young Man: The Early Years. The Autobiography of William O. Douglas.* New York. 1974.

Duff, Katharyn and Seibt, Betty Kay. *Catclaw Creek, an Informal History of Abilene in West Texas.* Burnet, Texas. 1980.

Dunn, Robert W. *American Foreign Investments.* New York. 1926.

Ferris, Paul. *The Master Bankers.* New York. 1984.

Galbraith, John Kenneth. *The Great Crash.* Cambridge, Mass. 1961.

Grant, James. *Bernard M. Baruch, the Adventures of a Wall Street Legend.* New York. 1983.

Grayson, Theodore J. *Investment Trusts: Their Origin, Development, and Operation.* New York. 1928.

Hirsch, Felix (Berlin Verlag in collaboration with Inter Nationes). *Gustav Stresemann, 1878/1978*. Bonn, West Germany. 1978.

Hoopes, Townsend with Douglas Brinkley. *Driven Patriot: The Life and Times of James Forrestal*. New York. 1992.

Isaacson, Walter with Evan Thomas. *The Wise Men: Six Friends and the World They Made*. New York. 1986.

Janeway, Eliot. *The Struggle for Survival*. 2d. ed. rev. New York. 1968.

_____. *The Economics of Crisis: War, Politics, and the Dollar*. New York. 1968.

Jensen, Michael C. *The Financier*. New York. 1976.

Johnson, Hugh. *The World Atlas of Wine*. New York. 1971.

Johnston, Moira. *Takeover: The New Wall Street Warriors: The Men, the Money, the Impact*. New York. 1986.

Krock, Arthur. *Memoirs: Sixty Years on the Firing Line*. New York. 1968.

Kuczynski, Robert R. *Banker Profits from German Loans*. Washington, D. C. 1932.

Lichine, Alexis. *New Encyclopedia of Wine and Spirits*. New York. 1974.

Litchfield, Paul. *Industrial Voyage: My Life as an Industrial Lieutenant*. New York. 1954.

Lukacs, John. *The Duel; Ten May to Thirty-One July: The Eighty-Day Struggle Between Churchill and Hitler on Which the Fate of the World Depended*. New York. 1991.

Marichal, Carlos. *A Century of Debt Crises in Latin America*. Princeton. 1989.

Mathey, Dean. *Fifty Years of Wall Street with Anecdotiana*. Princeton. 1966.

Matz, Mary Jane. *The Many Lives of Otto Kahn*. New York. 1963.

May, George S. *A Most Unique Machine: The Michigan Origins of the American Automobile Industry*. Detroit. 1979.

McNeil, William C. *American Money and the Weimar Republic*. New York. 1986.

Newman, Harry Wright. *A Branch of the Douglass Family with its Maryland and Virginia Connections*. Garden City, N.Y. 1967.

Nitze, Paul H. with Ann M. Smith and Steve L. Rearden. *From Hiroshima to Glasnost: At the Center of Decision—A Memoir*. New York. 1989.

O'Reilly, Maurice. *The Goodyear Story*. Elmsford, N.Y. 1983.

Parker, Robert M., Jr. *Bordeaux: A Comprehensive Guide to the Wines Produced from 1961-1990*. New York. 1991.

Pecora, Ferdinand. *Wall Street Under Oath: The Story of Modern Money Changers*. New York. 1939.

Perez, Robert C. *Inside Investment Banking*. Westport, Conn. 1985.

_____. *Inside Venture Capital*. Westport, Conn. 1986.

_____. with Edward F. Willett. *The Will to Win: A Biography of Ferdinand Eberstadt*. Westport, Conn. 1989.

Phalon, Richard. *The Takeover Barons of Wall Street*. New York. 1981.

Redlich, Fritz. *The Molding of American Banking: Men and Ideas*. 2 vols. New York. 1947-1951.

Reich, Cary. *Financier: the Biography of Andre' Meyer*. New York. 1983.

Rogow, Arnold A. *James Forrestal: A Study of Personality, Politics, and Policy*. New York. 1963.

Schwartz, Jordan A. *The Speculator: Bernard M. Baruch in Washington. 1917-1965*. Chapel Hill, N.C. 1981.

Seligman, Joel. *The Transformation of Wall Street: A History of the Securities and Exchange Commission and Modern American Corporate Finance.* Boston. 1982.

Seltzer, Laurence. *A Financial History of the American Automobile Industry.* Boston. 1928.

Sobel, Robert. *The Life and Times of Dillon Read.* New York. 1991.

Stresemann, Gustav. *Essays and Speeches on Various Subjects.* Reprint edition. Freeport, N.Y. 1968.

Sutton, Eric, editor and translator. *Gustav Stresemann, His Diaries, Letters and Papers.* 3 vols. London. 1935-1940.

Swaine, Robert T. *The Cravath Firm and Its Predecessors, 1819-1947.* 2 vols. New York. 1946.

Train, John. *The New Money Masters.* New York. 1989.

Wechsberg, Joseph. *The Merchant Bankers.* Boston. 1966.

Wigmore, Barrie A. *The Crash and its Aftermath.* Westport, Conn. 1985.

Business, Financial and Other Publications

"Again, Dillon." *Time.* January 11, 1926.

"The Amended Securities Act" (analysis of legislation by Arthur H. Dean of Sullivan and Cromwell). *Fortune.* July 1934.

"American Underwriting Houses and Their Issues." *National Statistical Service.* Vols I & II. New York. 1925-29.

Anderson, T. and S. Bronte. "The Upheaval at DR." *Euromoney.* September 1982.

"Baruch." *Fortune.* October 1933.

"Nicholas F. Brady: The New Deal-Maker at the Old Guard Firm." *Business Week.* July 12, 1976.

Bruch, Connie. "The World of Business: The Old Boys and the New Boys." *The New Yorker.* May 8, 1989.

"Chrysler." *Fortune.* August 1935.

Connelly, Julie. "Dillon Read Refuses to Play the Game." *Institutional Investor.* January 1979.

Corporate Financing Directories. *Investment Dealers' Digest.* New York. Annual issues, 1935-1990 (including ten-year summaries for 1950-1960, 1960-1970 and 1970-1980).

Costigliola, Frank. "The United States and the Reconstruction of Germany in the 1920s." *Business History Review, 50.* Winter 1976.

Current Biography. Biographies for C. Douglas Dillon, Ferdinand Eberstadt, James Forrestal and Paul H. Nitze.

"Clarence Dillon: Portrait." *Newsweek.* October 14, 1933.

"C. Douglas Dillon." *Newsweek,* January 26, 1953.

"Dillon to Bring Two Deficits under Control." *Business Week.* March 4, 1961.

"Dillon's Ambassadorship Brings Responsibility for Ike's Plan." *United States News.* January 30, 1953.

"A Dillon A Dollar: What Will New Secretary of Treasury Do?" *Fortune.* February

1961.

"C. Douglas Dillon Has the Say on Trade, Aid." *Business Week*. December 7, 1957.

"Dillon Read, Ltd. Paribas Ex-Boss (P. Moussa) Starts Over Again." *Fortune*. October 1, 1984.

"The Dodge Deal." *Literary Digest* 85. April 25, 1925.

Eberstadt, Ferdinand, editor. "The Dawes Plan." Brochure published privately by Dillon, Read & Co., Inc. in New York. 1925.

"Ferdinand Eberstadt." *Fortune*. April 1939.

"The Economy: Man With the Purse." *Time*. August 18, 1961.

Forbes, Bruce C. "Clarence Dillon, The Man Who Bought Dodge." *Forbes*. May 15, 1925.

Harvard Class of 1905 Secretary Reports. *First Report, 1906; Second Report, June 1911, Fourth Report, June 1920, Sixth Report, June 1930; Fiftieth Anniversary Report, Norwood and Cambridge, Mass. 1955.*

"Haut-Brion." Brochure published privately in France by Chateau Haut-Brion. 1989.

Hayes, Samuel L. III. "Investment Banking: Power Structure in Flux." *Harvard Business Review*. March-April 1971.

_____. "The Transformation of Investment Banking." *Harvard Business Review*. January-February 1979.

"In the New Wall Street." *Fortune*. October 1935.

"Investment Banking." *Fortune*. September 1939.

Janeway, Eliot. "Mobilizing the Economy: Old Errors in a New Crisis." *The Yale Review* 40, No. 2 (Winter 1951). December 1950.

Jereski, Laura. "Clarence Dillon: Using Other People's Money." *Forbes*. July 13, 1987.

"Jews in America." *Fortune*. February 1936.

Knowlton, C. "How the Richest Colleges Handle their Billions," by C. Knowlton. *Fortune*. October 26, 1987.

Merwin, John. "J.P. Morgan: The Agglomerator." *Forbes*. July 13, 1971.

"Mr. Dillon. He Thinks Only in Millions." *Liberty*. March 6, 1926.

Moore, Terris. "Security Affiliate Versus Private Investment Banker—A Study in Security Originations." *Harvard Business Review* XII. July 1934.

Narbonne Archives (Bulletin de la Commission Archéologie de Narbonne), Années 1964 et 1965, June 28, Narbonne, France.

National Cyclopaedia of American Biography. Biographies for Nancy Astor, E. J. Bermingham, August Belmont IV, Clarence Dillon, C. Douglas Dillon, Abner Kingman Douglass, Ferdinand Eberstadt, W. Meade Lindsley Fiske, J. V. Forrestal, S. Parker Gilbert, Charles Dana Gibson, Henry Walke, George Whitney.

"This New England: The Doors of Islesboro." *Yankee*. April 1993.

"The New York Stock Exchange." *Fortune*. January 1934.

Outerbridge, David E. "Haut-Brion in New York." Brochure published privately in France by Chateau Haut-Brion. 1992.

Phalon, Richard. "Oh Death, Where is Thy Sting?" *Forbes*. December 5, 1983.

Probated Estates:

Anne Douglass Dillon, November 1961.

Clarence Dillon, April 25, 1979.

Boleslaw Lapowski, 1949.

Gerome Baum Lapowski, October 16, 1948.

Bertha Dillon, January 20, 1953.

"The Quiet Crusader: Nick Brady's Plan to Curb Fast-Buck Management and Deal Mania." *Business Week.* September 18, 1989.

"Record of Addresses to General Sales Meeting Held January 6-7, 1928." Dillon, Read & Co., Inc.

Reddish, Jennette M. "People of the Financial World." *Financial World.* May 15, 1978.

"The Rothschilds." *Fortune.* February 1930.

"Secretary Dillon Answers Important Questions." *Banking.* March 1961.

"The Securities Act of 1933 (enacted May 27, 1933) Analysis by Arthur H. Dean of Sullivan and Cromwell." *Fortune.* August 1933.

"Securities and Exchange Commission." *Fortune.* June 1940.

Seigfried, André. "The Passing of England's Economic Hegemony." *Foreign Affairs. July 1928.*

"Senate Inquiry into Stock Exchange Practices." *Commercial and Financial Chronicle.* October 1, 14 and 21, 1933.

Smith, Richard Austin. "The Fifty-Million-Dollar Man." *Fortune.* November 1957.

"Talk of the Town, C. Douglas Dillon." *The New Yorker.* April 4, 1970.

"A Third Motor Car Colossus, The Chrysler-Dodge Merger." *Literary Digest* 97. June 16, 1928.

"Wall Street Itself: A Simple Tour of the Canyon in 1937 Suggests That Economic Profundities Are Neither Welcome Nor Apropos." *Fortune.* June 1937.

"What Manner of Man is C. Douglas Dillon?" *Forbes.* July 15, 1962.

"Will Dillon Read Become the Prototypical Merchant Bank?" *Institutional Investor.* June 1984.

Willett, Edward F. "Coal, Iron and Steel in Europe." Brochure privately published by Dillon, Read & Co., Inc. in Paris. 1928.

Williams, Frank J. "A New Leader in Finance: Clarence Dillon." *American Review of Reviews.* February 1926.

Winkler, John. "Profiles: A Billion Dollar Banker." *The New Yorker.* October 20, 1928.

"Owen D. Young." *Fortune.* January 1931, February 1931, March 1931.

Government Publications

United States. 72nd Congress, 1st sess. Senate. Committee on Finance. Hearings. *Sales of Foreign Bonds or Securities in the United States.* Washington, D.C. 1932.

_____. 73rd Congress, 1st sess. Senate. Committee on Banking and Currency. *Stock Exchange Practices.* pt. 4, Dillon, Read & Co., Inc. October 3-13, 1933. Washington, D.C. 1934.

_____. 73rd Congress, 2nd sess. Senate. Report No. 1455. *Stock Exchange Practices Report.* Washington, D.C. 1934.

_____. 76th Congress, 2nd sess. Hearings Before the Temporary National Economic Committee, Pursuant to Public Resolution No. 113. *Investigation of the*

Concentration of Economic Power. Washington, D.C. 1940.
United States Department of Commerce. *Historical Statistics of the United States, 1789-1945*. Washington, D.C. 1949.
United States District Court, New York (Southern District). *Corrected Opinion of Harold R. Medina, United States Circuit Judge, in United States of America v. Henry S. Morgan, Harold Stanley, et al. doing business as Morgan Stanley & Co. et al.* New York. 1954 ed.

Newspapers

Abilene Reporter-News
Akron Times-Press
Barron's Weekly
Commercial & Financial Chronicle
Daily Princetonian
El Paso Times
Los Angeles Examiner
New York Evening Post
New York Journal
New York Herald-Tribune
New York Times
San Angelo Standard-Times
New York Sun
Wall Street Journal
Worcester Academy Weekly

Index

161

About the Authors

Robert C. Perez, Ph.D., received his bachelor's degree from Yale in 1950 and his MBA and Ph.D. from New York University Graduate School of Business Administration. His doctoral dissertation analyzed the mutual fund field and its distribution system; his research spurred a number of doctoral research efforts in the emerging field of marketing financial services. Dr. Perez spent his entire business career with Ferdinand Eberstadt becoming a partner in his firm in 1973. Dr. Perez left Wall Street in the early 1980s to become a finance professor, initially at Fordham and later at Iona College Hagan School of Business. Dr. Perez has done extensive research aimed at increasing the investment returns of the Social Security Trust Funds through improved asset allocation. The results of his research have been published extensively in the scholarly and financial press. He has also participated in scholarly forums dedicated to improving social security's investment performance. Dr. Perez has authored five other books on financial subjects, the most recent being a biography of Ferdinand Eberstadt.

Edward F. Willett, Ph.D., received his AB degree in economics from Princeton in 1924, where he stood first in his class academically. Dr. Willett worked five years for the investment banking firm of Dillon, Read & Co., Inc. in the 1920s developing particularly close relationships with Ferdinand Eberstadt and James Forrestal. In 1929 he left Dillon Read with Eberstadt, and in 1931 he helped found F. Eberstadt & Co. He then left that firm three years later to earn his doctorate in economics at Princeton and to pursue a teaching career at Princeton and at Smith College. In 1945-46, during his sabbatical year, he became Research Assistant to Secretary of the Navy James Forrestal. One of Dr. Willett's reports to Forrestal became the basis for the American postwar foreign policy towards the Soviet Union. For this and other research work, Dr. Willett received the Navy Distinguished Civilian Service Award, the Navy Department's highest civilian award. Dr. Willett has also written a number of books, articles and reports on a wide range of subjects.